Movement Genesis

Movement Genesis

Social Movement Theory and the 1980s West German Peace Movement

Steve Breyman

WestviewPress

A Division of HarperCollins*Publishers*

for Sheryl

Copyright © 1998 by Westview Press, A Division of HarperCollins Publishers, Inc.

Published in 1998 in the United States of America by Westview Press, 5500 Central Avenue, Boulder, Colorado 80301-2877, and in the United Kingdom by Westview Press, 12 Hid's Copse Road, Cumnor Hill, Oxford OX2 9JJ

A CIP catalog record for this book is available from the Library of Congress.
ISBN 0-8133-8811-2

The paper used in this publication meets the requirements of the American National Standard for Permanence of Paper for Printed Library Materials Z39.48-1984.

10   9   8   7   6   5   4   3   2   1

Contents

Tables and Figures

Abbreviations and Acronyms

AC	Action Conference
AGDF	Service for Peace Action Group (Aktionsgemeinschaft Dienst für den Frieden)
APO	Extraparliamentary Opposition
ASF	Reconciliation Action/Peace Service (Aktion Sühnezeichen/Friedensdienst)
AsF	Social Democratic Women's Working Group (Arbeitsgemeinschaft sozialdemokratischer Frauen)
BAF	Federal Congress of Autonomous Peace Initiatives (Bundeskongress autonomer Friedensinitiativen)
BBU	Federal Association of Environmental Protection Citizen Initiatives (Bundesverband Bürgerinitiativen Umweltschutz)
BUF	Federal Conference of Independent Peace Groups (Bundeskonferenz unabhängiger Friedensgruppen)
BUKO	Federal Congress of Development Action Groups (Bundeskongress entwicklungspolitischer Aktionsgruppen)
C^3I	Command, control, communications, and intelligence
CC	Coordinating Committee
CDU/CSU	Christian Democratic Party/Christian Social Union of Bavaria (Christlich-Demokratische Union Deutschlands/Christlich-Soziale Union Bayerns)
CND	Campaign for Nuclear Disarmament (UK)
DFG-VK	German Peace Society-United War Resisters (Deutsche Friedensgesellschaft-Vereinigte Kriegsgegner)
DGB-Jugend	German Trade Union Federation-Youth (Deutscher Gewerkschaftsbund-Jugend)
DFU	German Peace Union (Deutsche Friedens-Union)
DKP	German Communist Party (Deutsche Kommunistishe Partei)
DS	Democratic Socialists (Demokratische Sozialisten)
EKD	Protestant Church of Germany (Evangelishe Kirche in Deutschland)
ERW	Enhanced radiation weapon (neutron bomb)
ESG	Protestant Student Associations (Evangelishe Studentengemeinden)

FBN	Women in the armed forces? We say No! (Frauen in die Bundeswehr?—Wir sagen Nein!)
FDP	Free Democratic Party or Liberals (Freie Demokratische Partei)
FfdF	Women for Peace (Frauen für den Frieden)
FÖGA	Federation of Nonviolent Action Groups (Föderation gewaltfreier Aktionsgruppe)
FRG	Federal Republic of Germany (West)
GDR	German Democratic Republic (East)
GHI	Gustav Heinemann-Initiative
GLCM	Ground-launched cruise missile
IFIAS	Initiative for Peace, International Exchange and Security (Initiative für Frieden, internationalen Ausgleich und Sicherheit)
IKV	Interchurch Peace Council (the Netherlands)
IKVU	Church from Below Initiative (Initiative Kirche von Unten)
INF	Intermediate-range nuclear forces
IPPNW	International Physicians for the Prevention of Nuclear War
Judos	Young Democrats (Jungdemokraten)
Jusos	Young Socialists (Jungsozialisten)
KOFAZ	Committee for Peace, Disarmament and Cooperation (Komitee für Frieden, Abrüstung und Zusammenarbeit)
KPD	Communist Party of Germany (Kommunistische Partei Deutschlands)
LD	Liberal Democrats (Liberale Demokraten)
MdB	Member of Parliament (Mitglied der Bundestag; FRG)
MIRV	Multiple, independently targetable reentry vehicles
MP	Member of Parliament (UK)
MSB	Marxist Student League Spartacus (Marxistischer Studentenbund Spartakus)
NATO	North Atlantic Treaty Organization
NBC	Nuclear, biological and chemical (weapons)
NFU	No-first-use (of nuclear weapons)
NFZ	Nuclear-free-zone
NIMBY	Not In My Backyard
NGO	Nongovernmental organization
NPD	National Democratic Party (Nationaldemokratische Partei)
NOPE	Not On Planet Earth
NSM	New social movement
NWC	New Working Class

PC	Pax Christi
PMO	Peace movement organization
POS	Political opportunity structure
PSR	Physicians for Social Responsibility
RMT	Resource mobilization theory
SANE	Committee for a Sane Nuclear Policy
SDAJ	Socialist German Worker Youth (Sozialistische Deutsche Arbeiterjugend)
SDI	Strategic Defense Initiative (Star Wars)
SJD	Socialist German Youth—The Falcons (Sozialistische Jugend Deutschlands—Die Falken)
SMI	Social movement industry
SMO	Social movement organization
SMS	Social movement sector
SPD	Social Democratic Party (Sozialdemokratische Partei Deutschlands)
STS	Science and Technology Studies (or Science, Technology and Society)
VDS	United German Student Associations (Vereinigte Deutsche Studentenschaften)
VVN/BdA	Union of Nazi Regime Survivors/Association of Anti-fascists (Vereinigung der Verfolgten des Naziregimes/Bund der Antifaschisten)
WCC	World Council of Churches
WILPF	Women's International League for Peace and Freedom

Acknowledgments

They shall beat their swords into ploughshares, and their spears into pruning hooks; nation shall not lift up sword against nation, neither shall they learn war anymore. But they shall sit every man under his vine and under his fig tree; and none shall make them afraid.

—Isaiah 2:4

The relationship between this work, originally my doctoral dissertation, and my "nuclear" family life is rather complex. Suffice it to say that, try as I may, I never quite persuaded Sheryl and our children, Karl, Natasha, and Vanessa, that their function was to help me write a book. My parents, Patricia and James Breyman, have been supportive, loving and proud throughout the long slog. During the research phase, my brother Mike helped keep me sane by sharing his wealth of knowledge about the finer points of halibut, calico, white sea bass, and surf perch fishing. I have warm memories of many a serene outing from Carpinteria to Haskell's, from Goleta Beach to the Biltmore, and from the oil rigs to the Islands.

I incurred sufficient intellectual and practical debts during this project to rival those of my student loans. First and foremost, I am grateful for the unflagging support and confidence Peter Merkl, chairman of my dissertation committee, patient sailing instructor, support letter writer, and dear friend, has shown all my work. I am thankful too for the consideration shown me by Wolfram Hanrieder, Michael Gordon, and Dick Flacks, members all of my dissertation committee. Michael can take credit for whatever clarity might characterize my prose. His tough criticism of a year's worth of graduate political economy seminar papers moved me to rein in my tendency toward obfuscation and purple prose. Dick is responsible for my initial interest in the study of social movements. His course on the topic, which I took as a junior, convinced me the study of protest and mobilization was what somebody like myself ought to be doing. But he really deserves praise for providing a model of the critical intellectual, the scholar-activist, of how to make both life and

xv

history. Cedric Robinson's course on Marxism taught me, again while still an undergraduate, the importance of critical thinking and of speaking truth to power. He, too, has found that tenuous mix of action and reflection, of the life in balance. My friends, especially, John Peterson, Mary McKenzie, Wayne Cohan, Nitish Dutt, Elizabeth Bomberg, Jack Miller, Greg Freeland, Marisela Marquez, Sonia Garcia, Richard Clucas, Joe Martorana, and Richard McKinney, are due thanks for companionship and love.

Librarians at the University of California, Santa Barbara, the Hoover Institution, Marquette University, and Rensselaer Polytechnic Institute were (mostly) uncomplaining about my never-ending requests. A faculty seminar at Pomona College in 1990 provided useful feedback on major arguments. My friends and colleagues connected to the UC Institute on Global Conflict and Cooperation (IGCC) made numerous helpful suggestions about the project. Art Fricke is due thanks for preparation of the index and final manuscript.

Finally, let me express my gratitude to those institutions providing funding over the years: the UC Regents for a Fellowship during my Masters program; the UCSB Department of Political Science for TAships during the research phase; Peter Merkl for an RAship for work on the Greens and social movement theory; the UCSB Graduate Division for a Social Science Research Grant; the UCSB General Affiliates for a Dissertation Fellowship; the IGCC for a Summer Seminar Fellowship, an International Fellowship, and a Dissertation Fellowship; the Friedrich-Ebert-Stiftung for an International Fellowship; the Marquette University Department of Political Science for providing a research assistant (Guo Sujian) to help with library work and the bibliography; and the McNair Postbaccalaureate Achievement Program for providing a research assistant (Stefanie Pollock) during revisions.

1

Background and Overview

The groundwork for the great social movements of the past was laid through many years of searching, intellectual interchange, social experimentation, collective action, organization, and struggle. The same will be true of the coming stages of social change.

—Noam Chomsky

To make sense of the rise and fall, origins and nature, of the 1980s West German peace movement requires work that is part political sociology and part social movement theory building. An analysis of the peace movement's organizations, leadership, strategy, goals, tactics, and mobilization comprises the political sociology part of this study. To understand the origins of the West German peace movement, one must take into account the movement's structure and its constituent organizations. The theory-building part brings together social movement theory with the political context within which the movement arose and developed, and with the movement itself, in some sense as alive and vital as the people who built it. The study centers on the years 1979-1983, the period of movement mass mobilization. I explain where the movement came from and why it arose when it did. My main aim is to interrogate, criticize and extend the theoretical literature on the etiology of social movements.

I introduce the socioeconomic context of the book, and briefly outline my approach to its research questions in the next section. I follow the book's outline with a discussion of the methods and sources of the study.

I conclude with some thoughts about the purpose and justification for this study.

The Sociopolitical Context of the Movement

Postindustrialism

In a rare example of intellectual convergence, most observers concurred by the late seventies that the Atlantic community had passed from one historical moment to another; they agreed we had witnessed the dawn of "postindustrial society." To say that postindustrial society has replaced industrial society is an exaggeration; rather, the new forces and relations of production overlie those of the previous epoch in the manner of industrialism's missionary coupling with agrarian society. Or, to switch metaphors, the relationship of postindustrialism to industrialism is like that of layers of sediment in a river bed that have been disturbed, and thus mixed up, by the wader-clad feet of the angler.

Western societies and economies experienced dizzying changes in the past three decades. Perhaps most important among the changes was the shift from economies based on manufacturing to economies based on services.[1] The heavy manufacturing and mining sectors such as steel and coal—the very soul of industrial capitalism—which once belched smoke across skies from Pittsburgh to Düsseldorf, and from Manchester to Turin, were reduced by the 1970s and 1980s to rump industries. Unionized work forces shrank significantly, especially in the United States, and comparative advantage in crude manufactures shifted from the West to newly industrializing countries like Brazil and South Korea.

The origins of industrial malaise and decline are varied, controversial and complex, but an odd if imperfect consensus arose—ranging from neoclassical economists to neo-Marxist social theorists—about two main roots. The first is disruptions in the energy supply caused by the 1970s oil shocks. The second is the paradoxically harmful effects on economic growth of the modern welfare state, originally designed to sustain effective consumer demand during business downturns. Outside the consensus, Piore and Sabel located contemporary advanced capitalism's difficulties in "the limits of the model of industrial development that is founded on mass production: the use of special-purpose (product specific) machines and of semiskilled workers to produce standardized goods."[2] Complementing these sometimes contradictory economic explanations were political and sociological analyses that blamed welfare bureaucrats and political entrepreneurs for exacerbating the crisis. The former put the state at the service of politically powerful constituencies; the larger the transfer payment program, and the greater the number of beneficiaries, the easier it was to coerce the state into further expansions. The latter subverted the state from without; huckstering candidates successfully bought votes with pledges of benefits that cost more to make good on than the state could afford given its primary mission of facilitating capital accumulation.[3]

Sociological analyses led to conclusions about "ungovernability" and the "crisis of democracy."[4] Some liberals lost faith in broad political participation, state regulation of the economy, and redistributive policies; they consequently transformed themselves into neoliberals, or more commonly, neoconservatives. Capitalism and democracy need each other, according to those formerly in favor of both equity and efficiency, yet are incompatible. The neoconservative solution: democracy for the elite and welfare for the destitute. Neo-Marxists saw the welfare state as a stalemate between labor and capital.[5] Workers were unable to bring about socialism, and capital proved unable to fully defend the market. The imposition of proto-socialist forms of exchange on capitalist economies, at the behest of subordinate classes, led to "stagflation" (recession plus inflation). Once again, democracy was a threat to capitalism. The schools naturally diverged on remedies for the predicament; the disintegration of capitalism will (hopefully) clear the way for socialism for the one, the collapse of pseudo-socialist experiments will pave the road to a less fettered capitalism for the other.

Rising, albeit unevenly, from the ruins of once mighty factories, are the fruit of the "third industrial revolution," "high technology" and new and old services of various stripes. Services as economic phenomena are, of course, not new to contemporary Western economies. The preindustrial household and domestic class was the largest in England until the latter third of the nineteenth century. The industrial service sector— transportation, utilities, finance, insurance, real estate, and personal services—remains large and crucial for the production of goods. What is new about postindustrial services is their character: they are directed at both ordinary citizens (health, education, and welfare), and experts (professionals and technicians in research and development, evaluation, computers, and systems analysis). Rather than contribute to equitable and productive growth, these new services act as a drag on the economy, fuel speculation, and contribute mightily to inflation.

Paralleling the change in the economic base of advanced capitalism, was a shift in the class structure of Western societies. Displaced from the center of economic life by the decline of manufacturing sectors, the traditional working class was overshadowed by a new middle class of college-educated service professionals.[6] This knowledge class is still primarily populated by baby boomers, children sired by veterans returning from World War II, and includes those born as late as the early sixties. These are people who work neither against nature as in preindustrial society, nor against fabricated nature as in industrial society, but *with* other *people.* A portion of this generation—distinctive politically, economically and culturally—constitutes the bulk of new social movement members.[7] These people, socialized during the relative peace and prosperity of the postwar period, have the requisite political skills, leisure time, and values to be movement activists.

The intense levels of political participation characteristic of the affluent and educated part of the postwar generation posed a challenge to the representative institutions—political parties and parliaments—of Western democracies.[8] Alienated and stymied by impersonal and ever larger governmental and corporate bureaucracies, significant sectors of the first postwar generation called for participatory democracy and engaged in the "new politics."[9] While no single definition of the new politics emerged, most analysts agreed that the new politics rejects the materialist agenda and seeks to replace it with a postmaterialist set of political, economic and social priorities; uses new vehicles of interest aggregation and representation such as citizen initiatives and single-issue movements; poses a radical challenge to the status quo of conventional politics; and is rooted in the postmaterialist new middle class.[10] Peace movement activists of the 1980s were quintessential practitioners of the new politics.[11]

The political cultures of Western democracies have undergone a "silent revolution" in the past several decades.[12] This incomplete revolution—marked by demographic, value, and lifestyle changes—affected primarily college-educated baby boomers and culminated in a new value system: postmaterialism. Postmaterialist priorities include intellectual and social freedom and a deep concern for aesthetics and the quality of life. Postmaterialists are in conflict with materialists, of the same and other generations, who prize economic stability, are hawkish on defense, and are worried about law and order.[13] Postmaterialists were more numerous and the new politics more prevalent in West Germany than elsewhere.[14]

The Missile Controversy

As these social and political-economic changes deepened and spread, the foreign ministers of the North Atlantic Treaty Organization (NATO) decided in December 1979 that the alliance needed new missiles to counter a Soviet build-up. Since the mid-seventies, the Soviet Union had deployed a new, mobile, three-warhead intermediate-range nuclear missile aimed at Western Europe for which NATO had no comparable system. There was no "good" military justification for the Soviet deployment; the USSR had ample strategic nuclear forces to cover the targets assigned to the new missiles, known in NATO parlance as SS-20s. And NATO, Great Britain, France, and the United States had sufficient strategic nuclear weaponry to counter the threat posed by the SS-20. Nevertheless, and for a variety of political and military reasons, alliance leaders agreed to the "double-track decision." The first part of the decision was for a deployment track: 464 intermediate range ground-launched nuclear Cruise missiles (GLCMs or Tomahawks), and 108 mobile, intermediate-range Pershing II ballistic nuclear missiles. Collectively, these 572 weapons became known as intermediate-range nuclear forces (INF) or Euromissiles. Ninety-six of the Cruise missiles and all of the Pershings were slated for deployment in the Federal Republic at the end of 1983, following the development and testing of the weapons. Other NATO member-states agreed to take the balance of the Tomahawks.

The second part of the decision, the arms control track, offered to negotiate the fate of the missiles with the Soviet Union. This was an unprecedented offer. Prior to this point, both East and West had generally deployed new weapons first, and worried about their consequences for strategic stability and arms control following deployment, if ever. The arms control track ensured that the NATO decision would remain in the forefront of Western European public consciousness for four years. It opened NATO decisionmakers, and the U.S.-USSR INF negotiations in Geneva, to unparalleled public intervention and interference from foes of nuclear deterrence, the arms race, and the Cold War. Angry and frightened West European citizens opposed to new (and old) nuclear weapons mobilized mass movements against the NATO decision. The West German branch of this extraordinary transnational anti-nuclear weapons movement provides the focus for this study.

Movement Novelty, Origins, and Theory

The theories of postindustrialism, postmaterialism and the new politics contribute to our understanding of recent political change, including the rise of new social movements (NSM). Chapter 2 takes off from this point. It wrestles first with the overgrown jungle that is the terminology of social movement definitions. After several slashes with the conceptual machete, we can see clear to a meaning of use throughout this study.

Whether contemporary movements are "new" or not is a question that has spurred stimulating theoretical debates for two decades. Several leading European social theorists made contributions to the debate, including Jürgen Habermas, Claus Offe, and Alain Touraine. A real tug of war over theoretical approaches erupted, and numerous journals devoted special issues to the subject. I examine the various perspectives with an eye both to their applicability to the West German peace movement case, and to what they might add to an understanding of peace movement origins. The review is organized around three main claims regarding NSMs: that they act in new spheres of conflict; that they display new forms of identity and consciousness; and that they employ new group types and new action forms. I return to the question of peace movement novelty in Chapter 9, where following the political sociology of the movement, it is possible to draw conclusions about whether the German anti-missile movement was an NSM.

The 1980s peace movements are fascinating for those interested in social and political theory. Bert Klandermans wondered,

> Why did this mass movement develop only in the late 1970s? Nuclear armament started in the 1940s. Why, then, did it take so long before this massive movement against nuclear armament developed? Moreover, on the eve of what turned out to be the largest movement of the last three decades, those people who had been studying earlier phases of the peace movement—such as the Ban-the-Bomb movement or the anti-Vietnam War protest—were convinced the movement was moribund. . . This sudden resurgence, which nobody had predicted, took them by surprise.[15]

I am interested in what social and political theory can tell us about the origins, character, and action of peace movements. The sort of theory that interests me might be called "macro" rather than "micro;" my current concern is with why movements come to be and what happens when they do, rather than with why individuals choose to participate in them. I begin the etiological examination of the West German peace movement in Chapter 3. The theories that can help us make sense of these concerns are several. Certain political approaches stress the breakdown of societal consensus and examine the evolution of the international political economy and the enlarged role of the state in everyday affairs.[16] It is the Leviathan of the all-encompassing state with which the new social movements do battle.[17] The important notion of "party failure" and an extended concept of electoral dealignment have sprung from these analyses.[18] Party failure theory locates the attractiveness of social movements and the rise of movement-parties like the Greens in the inability of established parties to solve pressing problems on the political agenda: unemployment, degraded environment, declining social services, and rising dissent.[19] Public opinion polls of the late 1970s revealed that more West Germans were involved in various movements and citizen initiatives than were members of all political parties combined.[20]

Five other theoretical approaches are plumbed in Chapter 3 for what they can tell us about the roots of the German peace movement: "fear of war" (Kriegsangst), collective behavior, resource mobilization theory, the political process:model, and new social movement theory. There are several types of war fears that bear on the genesis of peace movements. A fear of war—based upon a sober analysis of the world situation—appeared justified during the period of peak movement mobilization. Collective behavior theories were once leaders in the study of social protest. Their eclipse by more recent theorizing does not completely eliminate their usefulness. The several variations of collective behavior theory explain the origins of movements by focusing on (1) social structural breakdown that spurs noninstitutionalized attempts at social change; (2) the psychology of movement adherents; and (3) the role of beliefs in movement action.

Social movements are the sport utility vehicles of the new politics; as new truck models are released, so are new owners' manuals. So it is that since the late 1960s, social movement scholars have moved away from structural functionalist and collective behavior theories towards dynamic models informed by innovative advances in sociology, political science, economics and psychology. Although a heterogeneous field, three main schools have emerged: resource mobilization theory, the political process approach, and the new social movement approach. Resource mobilization approaches concentrate on the availability of personal and group resources (time, money, people, experience), and the role of political entrepreneurs and organizations to explain the origin and development of social movements.[21] The political process approach considers social movements primarily political rather than psychological phenomena. The central contention of the political process model is that politics matters more for the rise and mobilization of social movements than does social structural or cultural change.[22] The new social movement approach is situated in the tradition of Marxian and functionalist macro-sociological analysis and relates the emergence of the movements to the unfolding of postindustrial society.[23] I assess the extent to which the six theories satisfactorily explain movement origins, and propose a synthetic model of movement roots, in Chapter 9.

Organization, Constituencies, and Spectrums

Chapter 4 compares the characteristics of "old" social movement organizations (SMOs) to those of "new" SMOs in order to determine the movement's structure and leadership; it describes the importance of organizations and the operation of leadership in the movement; and it begins the examination of movement constituencies. There is more to a movement than its organizations. But organizations are sources of movement action. And it is movement action that allows for movement political impact and policy influence. Groups organized along occupational lines played a significant and visible role in the movement. The most important were peace researchers, but numerous doctors, lawyers, teachers, and others could be found in the front ranks of the movement. Many of the professionals were typical new social movement members initiated into extraparliamentary politics by the anti-missile movement in the early eighties—young, highly educated, left-libertarian and affluent. Others were older veterans of previous peace, civil rights, environmental, or student campaigns. The aim of Chapter 4 is to begin to clarify "who" and "what" was the West German peace movement in the 1980s.

The concept of organizational "spectrums" helps distinguish among the political and ideological tendencies of movement constituencies, and is the subject of Chapter 5. An understanding of the diversity and internal politics of the the leading organizations of the movement is advanced through such categorization. There were five spectrums in the 1980s West German peace movement: Christian, Independent, KOFAZ (Communist), Social Democratic/Young Socialist, and Green. Groups not easily placed in a spectrum come in for analysis too. The aim of Chapter 5 is a clear understanding of the leading groups and tendencies of the movement; it completes our analysis of movement identity and constituencies begun in Chapter 4.

Strategy, Goals, Tactics, and Mobilization

Movement strategy consists of the communication, planning, and interaction connected to objectives. I approach the analysis of movement goals by examining what movement theorists themselves said they were and by digging below the surface to uncover the determinants of objectives. The numerous controversies that arose over strategic issues provide a theme underlying the discussion of strategy and goals in Chapter 6. Tactics are the means used to realize ends, and the subject of Chapter 7. I examine the determinants of tactical choice; analyze the "action repertoire" concept and repertoire change; discuss the nature of the relationship between movement action and its audiences; survey the variety of action forms in theory and practice; raise the question of tactical nonviolence; and close with a brief analysis of affinity groups as employed by the movement in its struggle against the NATO decision.

Through mobilization, the topic of Chapter 8, movement organizations gather and invest resources—guided by strategy and acting tactically—for the pursuit of goals. Resources include all persons, entities and relationships which can help a movement negotiate dilemmas, solve problems and attain goals. Mobilization can be subdivided into two components: the creation of commitment and the activation of commitment. Commitment must be created before it can be activated. The activation of commitment involves two interdependent processes: the mobilization of commitment, and the recruitment of activists and generation of other resources. I analyze the criteria and context for propelling adherents into action before presenting a model of anti-nuclear weapons movement mobilization. As mobilization proceeds in phases, I close the chapter with a discussion of the particular cycles experienced by the Federal German peace movement of the 1980s.

Method and Sources

My own evolving philosophy of social science—away from positivism, towards critical theory and social constructivism—parallels developments in the social sciences. Philosopher Paul Feyerabend began his "escape from positivism" by distinguishing between two thought traditions: the abstract and the historical.[24] The abstract thought tradition formulates rule-bound statements affected by events only in accordance with the rules. Such an approach,

> it is said, guarantees the "objectivity" of the information conveyed by the statements, or of the "knowledge" they contain. It is possible to understand, criticize, or improve the statements without having met a single one of the objects described (examples: elementary particle physics; behavioral psychology; molecular biology which can be run by people who never in their life saw a dog, or a prostitute).[25]

Historical traditions also use statements but of a very different sort. Objects are assumed to have a language of their own and it is the task of the investigator to learn these languages. Learning takes place not on the basis of rules but by immersion in the world of the object. The objects' languages are learned as they are, rather than as they appear after manipulation by experiment or quantification. Objectivity, argued Feyerabend, "cannot describe a process of this kind which depends on the idiosyncrasies of both objects and observers (it makes no sense to speak of the 'objective existence' of a smile which, depending on context, can be seen as a kind smile, a cruel smile, or a bored smile)."[26] The story of

Western thought is one of conflict between abstract and historical traditions. Feyerabend suggested "that *good sciences are arts, or humanities, not sciences in the textbook sense*" (his italics).[27] This study is neither "objective" nor "science" "in the textbook sense;" nor I do think it possible to make sense of peace movements without having "met" one. I employ humanistic interpretation and social scientific analysis that rests squarely in the historical tradition.

The research here is "exploratory." The complexity of social movement reality requires qualitative rather than "rigorous" methods. I interpret and compare the primary and secondary sources that are the material for this study. The comparison comes in, for example, when confronting general theories with specific information about the movement, and accounts of the movement with general theories. I try to avoid the fate Somerset Maugham said awaited the incautious social scientist: "She plunged into a sea of platitudes, and with the powerful breast stroke of a channel swimmer made her confident way toward the white cliffs of the obvious." A qualitative comparative approach that emerges from the historical tradition may provide both lifeboat and lighthouse.

I draw on both primary and secondary sources for this study. Included in the primary sources is the literature (publications, memos, appeals, etc.) of the peace movement itself. Secondary sources include a wide array of descriptive and theoretical accounts—scholarly and journalistic—of the peace movement, social movement theory, comparative politics and international relations theory, and other relevant subjects.

Conclusion

The choice of the 1980s West German peace movement as the focus of my study is justified in humanistic terms as it was a movement that involved millions of more or less ordinary citizens in one of the most important efforts of our time: the prevention of nuclear war and the creation of a peaceful and just world order. It embroiled much of West German society in a historic debate over the meaning of security in the nuclear age and over the meaning of German identity decades after the end of the Second World War. The study is justified in theoretical terms as it follows logically from the body of research cited in this chapter: it appeared in a postindustrial society, it is a manifestation of new politics, and postmaterialism, and there are several theories which attempt to explain its rise and action.

The book should be of interest to comparativists in political science and sociology because the study examines a cross-national phenomenon that transcended the classical cleavages of class, race, gender, region, party affiliation, and religion. Social psychologists may find the discussion of value change and fear or war pertinent to their concerns. Anthropologists may share my interest in cultural change—in the ways people perceive the world, and the ways they act on their perceptions. Historians might compare the peace movement sociology here to that of social movements from other times and places. Students of science and technology studies should find of interest the discussions of defense policy expertise, and the politics, social construction and sociology of peace movement knowledge, and the analysis of popular intervention in a controversy over the most hazardous technology of all time.

Notes

1. Zbigniew Brzezinski, *Between Two Ages: America's Role in the Technotronic Age* (New York: Viking Press, 1970).
2. Michael J. Piore and Charles F. Sabel, *The Second Industrial Divide: Possibilities for Prosperity* (New York: Basic Books, 1984), p. 4.
3. Lester C. Thurow, *The Zero-Sum Society: Distribution and the Possibilities for Economic Change* (New York: Basic, 1980).
4. For the best known of such works, see Samuel P. Huntington, Michel Crozier, and Joji Watanuki, *The Crisis of Democracy: Report on the Governability of Democracies to the Trilateral Commission* (New York: New York University Press, 1975). A wry look at the difficulties of governance in postindustrial West Germany can be found in Hans Magnus Enzensberger's "Ungovernability: Notes From the Chancellor's Office," in his *Political Crumbs* (London: Verso, 1990).
5. Claus Offe, "Competitive Party Democracy and the Keynesian Welfare State: Factors of Stability and Disorganization," in Thomas Ferguson and Joel Rogers, eds., *The Political Economy* (Armonk, NY: M.E. Sharpe, 1984).
6. Daniel J. Bell, *The Coming of Post-Industrial Society: A Venture in Social Forecasting* (New York: Basic Books, 1973); and Ralf Dahrendorf, *Class and Class Conflict in Industrial Society* (Stanford: Stanford University Press, 1959).
7. Alain Touraine, *The May Movement: Revolt and Reform* (New York: Random House, 1971); and Alain Touraine *The Post-Industrial Society* (New York: Random House, 1972).
8. Jürgen Habermas, *Legitimation Crisis* (Boston: Beacon Press, 1975); and James O'Connor, *The Fiscal Crisis of the State* (New York: St. Martin's Press, 1973).
9. Russell J. Dalton, *Citizen Politics in Western Democracies: Public Opinion and Political Parties in the United States, Great Britain, West Germany, and France* (Chatham, NJ: Chatham House Publishers, 1988).
10. See Samuel H. Barnes, Max Kaase, et al., *Political Action: Mass Participation in Five Western Democracies* (Beverly Hills: Sage Publications, 1979). On the new politics and the German party system, see Kai Hildebrandt and

Russell J. Dalton, "The New Politics: Political Change or Sunshine Politics," in Max Kaase and Klaus von Beyme, eds., *German Political Studies*, vol. 3 (1978).

11. Boris Frankel, *The Post-Industrial Utopians* (Madison: University of Wisconsin Press, 1987), chapter 3.

12. Ronald Inglehart, *The Silent Revolution: Political Styles Among Western Publics* (Princeton: Princeton University Press, 1977).

13. Andrew J. Pierre, ed., *A Widening Atlantic? Domestic Change & Foreign Policy* (New York: Council on Foreign Relations, 1986).

14. Kendall Baker, Russell J. Dalton and Kai Hildebrandt, *Germany Transformed: Political Culture and the New Politics* (Cambridge: Harvard University Press, 1981); and Russell J. Dalton, Scott Flanagan and Paul A. Beck, eds., *Electoral Change in Advanced Industrial Democracies* (Princeton: Princeton University Press, 1984).

15. Bert Klandermans, "The Peace Movement and Social Movement Theory,"*International Social Movement Research*, vol. 3 (1991), p. 2.

16. Three such political analyses include, Suzanne Berger, "Politics and Antipolitics in Western Europe in the Seventies," *Daedalus*, vol. 108, no. 1 (1979); Volkmar Lauber, "From Growth Consensus to Fragmentation in Western Europe—Political Polarization over Redistribution and Ecology," *Comparative Politics*, vol. 15, no. 3 (1983); and Thomas R. Rochon, "Political Change in Ordered Societies—The Rise of Citizens' Movements," *Comparative Politics*, vol. 15, no. 3 (1983).

17. J. Craig Jenkins, "Social Movements, Political Representation, and the State: An Agenda and Comparative Framework," in J. Craig Jenkins and Bert Klandermans, eds., *The Politics of Social Protest: Comparative Perspectives on States and Social Movements* (Minneapolis: University of Minnesota Press, 1995).

18. Kay Lawson and Peter H. Merkl, eds., *When Parties Fail: Emerging Alternative Organizations* (Princeton: Princeton University Press, 1988).

19. Michael Wallace and J. Craig Jenkins, "The New Class, Postindustrialism, and Neocorporatism: Three Images of Social Protest in the Western Democracies," in Jenkins and Klandermans, eds., *The Politics of Social Protest*.

20. Jutta Helm, "Citizen Lobbies in West Germany," in Peter H. Merkl, ed., *West European Party Systems* (New York: The Free Press, 1979), p. 576.

21. Well-known resource mobilization works include Anthony Oberschall, *Social Conflict and Social Movements* (Englewood Cliffs, NJ: Prentice-Hall, 1973); John D. McCarthy and Mayer N. Zald, "Resource Mobilization and Social Movements: A Partial Theory," *American Journal of Sociology*, vol. 82 (1977); and J. Craig Jenkins, "Resource Mobilization Theory and the Study of Social Movements," *Annual Review of Sociology*, vol. 9 (1983).

22. Doug McAdam, *Political Process and the Development of Black Insurgency* (Chicago: University of Chicago Press, 1982).

23. Examples of new social movement theorizing include Karl-Werner Brand, *Neue Soziale Bewegungen: Entstehung, Funktion und Perspektive neuer Protestpotentiale—Eine Zwischenbilanz* (Opladen: Westdeutscher, 1982); Claus Offe, "New Social Movements: Changing Boundaries of the Political," *Social*

Research, vol. 52 (1985); and Alberto Melucci, "The New Social Movements: A Theoretical Approach," *Social Science Information*, vol. 19 (1980).

24. Paul Feyerabend, *Philosophical Papers* (New York: Cambridge University Press, 1981), chapter 1; and Paul Feyerabend, *Wissenschaft als Kunst* (Frankfurt: Suhrkamp, 1981).

25. Paul Feyerabend, *Farewell to Reason* (London: Verso, 1987), p. 294.

26. Feyerabend, *Farewell to Reason*, p. 295.

27. Feyerabend, *Farewell to Reason*, p. 295.

2

Movement Definitions and Novelty

Intuitions without concepts are blind, concepts without intuition are empty.

—Kant

My main intention in this chapter is to present the case for the newness of new social movements. This aim addresses a question of central importance to the study of contemporary social movements. Was the 1980s West German peace movement an NSM? Before presenting the case for NSM novelty and the theoretical review, I first provide a brief discussion of several definitions of social movements, examine the controversy over the place of organizations in these definitions, and present the definition upon which the rest of the study builds. I return in Chapter 9 to the question whether the West German anti-nuclear weapons movement was a new social movement.

What is a Social Movement?

At the outset we find ourselves enveloped by a thicket of disciplinary language and conceptual confusion. Sociologists employ the terms social movements, social movement organizations (SMOs), and challenging groups. Political scientists speak of collective action, citizens' movements, pressure or interest groups, and nongovernmental organizations

(NGOs). Anthropologists refer to movements of change, cultural movements, and adaptive movements. While it is not at all clear that these various disciplines are talking about precisely the same phenomena, it is abundantly clear that the study of popular movements (yet another term!) is both wonderfully interdisciplinary and hopelessly mired in a terminological swamp. Like many social science subfields, the study of social movements resists attempts at linguistic rescue. For reasons stemming from the philosophy of social science and the reward structure of the academy, the sometime Maoist policy of letting a hundred flowers bloom or the Smithian tendency toward laissez faire will remain the norm. There are, however, real problems lurking in the swamp which require at least exploratory scrutiny. As a term of art (or science), "social movement" has been much abused. But my intentions are modest; I want only to find a path out of the marsh, on which to proceed further, rather than play U.S. Army Corps of Engineers and drain conceptual bogs.

The term social movement is sometimes used in distinction from religious or political movements, and from movements among particular groups such as gay liberation or the student movement. As all movements have political implications as well as effects on the social order, the terms social movement and political movement overlap to a considerable extent; I do not distinguish between them. When the term social movement entered vocabularies, early in the nineteenth century, it had a quite specific meaning: *the* social movement meant the movement of the new industrial proletariat.[1] By the 1920s, the rise of peasant and farmer movements, of fascism and National Socialism, and of independence movements in colonial countries, mandated a broadening of the term.

Luther Gerlach and Virginia Hine define a movement as "a group of people who are organized for, ideologically motivated by, and committed to a purpose which implements some form of personal or social change; who are actively engaged in the recruitment of others; and whose influence is spreading in opposition to the established order within which it originated."[2] William Bruce Cameron adds "fairly large" to Gerlach and Hine's "people."[3] Possible additional modifications include substituting "attempts" for "implements," to allow for movement failure, and "spreads" for "is spreading" to stress the problematic that is movement influence. Gerlach and Hines do not elaborate on what constitutes a "group," on what is "influence," or on how the spread of influence is assessed.

For John Wilson, a social movement is "a conscious, collective, organized attempt to bring about or resist large-scale change in the social order by noninstitutionalized means."[4] I would modify Wilson's definition to allow for more conventional—"institutionalized"—action in order to account for the potential "aging" or professionalization of a movement. Professionalization may or may not signify devolution into interest groups.[5] Theodore Lowi writes of interest groups and social movements as largely overlapping.[6] While such overlap can and does exist, interest groups need not have once been movement groups; surely in many instances they were not. And not all movement organizations need become, in an advanced career stage, interest groups. The loosening of the coupling of organization and action, manifested in the tendency of interest groups to glibly label themselves movements, makes it important to be clear about what is and is not a movement. The scale of change a movement attempts to bring about or resist can vary over time. Generally, the scale of change is always open to question. The fluidity of social conflict makes a priori designations of "large" versus small-scale change, such as Wilson's, too restrictive. Working for or against large-scale change is a long-term process, in any society. In the short-run, incrementalism and the smallest-scale change is frequently the object of movement actions.

Joseph Gusfield considers social movements "socially shared activities and beliefs directed toward the demand for change in some aspect of the social order. . . . What characterizes a movement as a particular kind of change agent is its quality as an articulated and organized group."[7] Roberta Ash Garner defines a social movement as "a set of actions of a group of people. These actions have the following characteristics: they are self-consciously directed toward changing the social structure and/or ideology of a society, and they either are carried on outside of ideologically legitimated channels of change or use these channels in innovative ways."[8]

The definitions above share an emphasis on groups. More recent attempts at clarifying an analytically useful definition of social movement take issue with this group focus. Before discussing this literature, it is appropriate first to be clear about what is meant by the term SMO. Social movement organizations can be distinguished from the larger social movement out of which they emerge and by which they are sustained. Roberta Ash defined SMOs as "formally constituted and internally organized groups that frequently are the acting components of the movement."[9] These action networks vary as to their formality, structure, leadership, ideology, tactics, and goals. Various SMOs in a particular movement may both compete and cooperate, while divisions of labor may spring up among them. Some analysts contend that the emphasis on organizations in the study of social movements risks overlooking significant forms of political activity. For instance, Frances Fox Piven and Richard Cloward argued that:

The effect of equating movements with movement organizations—and thus requiring that protests have a leader, a constitution, a legislative program, or at least a banner before they are recognized as such—is to divert attention from many forms of political unrest and to consign them by definition to the more shadowy realms of social problems and deviant behavior.[10]

I share their concern that less organized discontent is frequently ignored or not considered movement phenomena. At the same time, it is groups and organizations with articulated agendas, or at least minimum goals, that are the hardest for authorities to ignore, and thus have the greatest impact. Precisely because inchoate protest can be written off as deviance, the creation of more or less formal groups is important for the pursuit of movement ends. The "shadowy realms" of movement activity, however well-organized, are discussed in the section on collective behavior theory below.

Charles Tilly's uneasiness with the emphasis on groups provided the basis for his definition:

A social movement is a sustained series of interactions between power holders and persons successfully claiming to speak on behalf of a constituency lacking formal representation, in the course of which those persons make publicly visible demands for changes in the distribution or exercise of power, and back those demands with public demonstrations of support.[11]

He was aware of the choices confronting such a definition—deciding how little formal representation is a lack of it, setting thresholds for the visibility of demands, and so on. But his main aim was to refocus attention from groups to interactions between challengers and authorities. First, to the problems with his definition. Tilly likened the relationship of groups to movements as that between armies and wars or parties and political campaigns. This is too loose use of the term "group." Tilly sometimes appears to mean class or socio-economic segment or status group (like wine growers), and at other times he appears to mean organization (like the General Federation of Winegrowers). This problem is not successfully resolved. Another problem with Tilly's definition is the phrase ". . . a constituency lacking formal representation. . . ." For the peace movement, the problem is not lack of formal representation; citizens of postindustrial democracies are formally represented at several levels. Instead, it is, among other factors, the actual or perceived inadequacies of representation by parties, trade unions, legislatures, and executives, that draw the participant to the peace movement. These formal organs of representation fail to represent all the interests of constituents, and if the unrepresented interest is a stake of high value, such as peace, expressions of discontent emerge.

Troublesome too is Tilly's contention that the "group image is a mystification." He likens "real social movements," as opposed to mere groups, to "the mounting of demonstrations:" "involvement ebbs and flows, coalitions form and dissolve, fictitious organizations loom up and fade away, would-be leaders compete for recognition as the representatives of unorganized constituencies, leaders make deals with police and politicians."[12] This is a more or less accurate picture of the nature of a social movement but it does not displace groups or organizations from their premier place in the constellation of social movements. What are these leaders, self-appointed or not, besides leaders of groups? What are coalitions but tentative and temporary groupings of groups? What is "fictitious" about organizations? Even though umbrella organizations are constructed for demonstrations, this makes them no more fictitious than is the enterprise behind a fictitious business name. They may be short-lived, as are most new businesses, but they are purposive and focused. They are puppets, sure, but with strings; they are dummies with a mission, like those of ventriloquists. Taken to an extreme, this line of reasoning might ask: Is not what we call a movement little more, in policy terms at least, than a conglomeration of SMOs? The *work* (organizing, planning, propagandizing) is done by SMOs (and frequently by a handful of individuals organized into collectives or committees within any given SMO). In this light, the whole (movement) is less than the sum of its parts (SMOs).

For Tilly, a group is "durably organized around a well-defined interest." Again, the problems of microdefinition arise. What is "durable"? What is a "well-defined interest"? In the course of a social movement, the durability of its organizations may vary, as will the extent to which its interest(s) are well-defined. The case of the anti-Euromissile movement is illustrative. Opposition to the deployment of Cruise and Pershing missiles is about as well-defined an interest as can be found in any movement. And the movement's life spanned that of the controversy over deployment of the missiles. The anti-missile movement proper began shortly after the December 1979 double-track decision and lasted through (and to some extent, though in diminished form and energy, beyond) the onset of actual emplacement. The massive mobilizations died down after the autumn of 1983, leveling off to a comparatively low level of activity by much smaller numbers of activists, many of whom were connected to long-lived organizations. Observing groups—while at the same time watching for interactions between the powerful and the less so—allows the analyst to explain the movement's career. Tilly's definition, nevertheless, has merit. His admonishment that "we mistakenly think of a social movement as a coherent group rather than as a political product, as a solo performance rather than as an interaction" is well taken.[13] Surely social movements are not "solo performances," and just as certainly, SMOs are not all there is to social movement study. The notion of "sustained interaction" is an important insight, for this is what organizations are constructed to do.

By way of capping this examination of other social movement definitions, I offer my own:

> *People mobilizing themselves and other resources to change other people, social structures, and social relations using means which may be unconventional for ends which may include the radical.*

This is an ecological definition that points to the interactions between a movement and its environment; it is a definition that emphasizes the connections between movement constituencies and the objects of movement action. It also ventures a claim about the character of movement tactics, strategy and goals (perhaps best fit for mass movements). "Resources" are broadly defined to include all persons, entities and relationships which can aid a movement or movement organization in negotiating dilemmas, solving problems and attaining goals. "Mobilization" refers to the processes by which movement organizations gather and invest resources for the pursuit of goals. The vehicles for resource mobilization are typically organizations consciously constructed for that purpose. To change people is to alter personal values, attitudes, and ideology; such change is reflected in both public and private behavior. This people-changing can be reactionary or progressive. To change social structures is to change institutions, both public and private, and thus, ultimately to change culture and the social and political order. Social relations are the links between people and structures. This definition underlies the examination of the peace movement throughout the study.

From Locomotive of History to Nomads of the Present

Questions as to what is new, if anything, about new social movements have exercised theorists for years. There is as yet no consensus as to whether the alleged novelty of these "contemporary movements" (Jean Cohen's term) is genuine or not.[14] David Plotke provided an important insight—much NSM theory is the conscious product of radical scholars' attempts to overcome orthodox Marxism as sociological analysis and political project. Plotke thought that this opposition, while fruitful, led numerous theorists sympathetic to NSMs to hold untenable positions regarding the movements' novelty.[15] By the late eighties, Thomas Rochon detected a waning of theoretical claims on behalf of the novelty of NSM. He suggested that the first wave of studies trumpeting the freshness of these movements was muted by a second wave that found substantial overlap between the behavior of new and old movements.[16] The breadth and diversity of NSM theory poses difficult choices for the analyst who reviews it for insight into the novelty and origins of the German anti-Euromissile movement. Indeed, Richard Stöss went so far as to claim that due to the lack of conceptual clarity, NSMs are but a "myth," invented by social scientists.[17] The difficult choices were eased by Barbara Epstein's fine treatment of NSM theory to which this section owes much.[18]

The work of Antonio Gramsci serves as an implicit starting point for many NSM theorists. Even NSM theorists like Alberto Melucci who explicitly reject Marxism as a framework for understanding the roots and action of NSM, owe much to Gramsci's account of the changes in capitalism and class conflict stemming from the completion of the industrial project and the consequent rise in the importance of the production and consumption of consumer goods. Gramsci called this stage of capitalism "Fordism" for two reasons. It refers to Henry Ford's role in the development of assembly line production and Taylorist scientific regulation of work and to his perhaps equally important realization that mass produced goods required mass markets populated by consumers with sufficient income to purchase those goods. Brute force was no longer appropriate for the control of laborers who were at the same time consumers of mass produced durable goods. Late capitalism increasingly required a work force that identified and cooperated with the system. Social control efforts shifted to the realms of education, culture and consciousness.

Gramsci also set the stage for broader definitions of the working class. Still the vanguard of the revolution, for Gramsci, the working class would now act in conjunction with other social forces. The hostility of much of the traditional working class in the U.S. to the anti-war and counter-cultural movements of the sixties caused New Left thinkers to formulate "new working class" (NWC) theory. Paralleled in some sense by the similar sociological accounts of neoconservatives like Zbigniew Brzezinski, Samuel Huntington, and Daniel Bell, NWC theory argued that portions of the middle class were being drawn into the working class by the expansion of corporate control into new economic sectors. The university was touted by both schools as the training ground for the new middle or working class which would emerge to serve corporation and state.[19] NWC theorists saw student radicalism as a response to the process of proletarianization and the cold, bureaucratic nature of what Clark

Kerr called the "multiversity." Similar attempts to explain the U.S. civil rights movement and the resurgence of feminism in Marxist categories were less successful. Redefining students, civil rights activists, and women as workers did not help explain how revolution was to come about without the traditional working class. Stretching the working class to include the ecologists and pacifists of the 1970s and 1980s was, for many analysts, even less satisfactory. Marxist theory, despite its renaissance during this period, appeared unable to adequately address questions of generation, race, gender and culture.

The Marxist search for a revolutionary class was carried on by the French structuralists of the "Regulation School" and by radical American political economists emphasizing the "social structure of accumulation."[20] The Regulation School assigned each stage of capitalism its own "regime of accumulation," a specific strategy of economic developmeı.ṭ, and "mode of regulation," a particular package of policies and class relations that smoothed the function of the regime of accumulation. The Fordist stage of capitalism was accompanied, in this view, by Keynesian policies and a capital-labor peace treaty. Although Fordist economic growth peaked in the U.S. during the mid-sixties, the ensuing decline was camouflaged by spending for the Great Society and the Vietnam War, and thus not appreciable until the mid-seventies. Sharing their French colleagues assessment of the requirements for the fluid functioning of capitalism, the American political economists stressed the role of class struggle rather than the internal dynamics of the economic system in their explanation of the changing strategies of capital accumulation. It was, they argued, labor movement success in the thirties that explains the origins of the welfare state and the social peace, and not any inherent features of capitalism. The breakdown of Fordism in the 1960s was due not to its bankruptcy as a strategy of accumulation but to working class dissatisfaction with the labor-capital accord. Capital was consequently forced to search for new forms of control. Movements of the thirties, in this view, can be seen as part of Fordism's construction crew, and movements of the sixties as part of the wrecking crew.

Enter European NSM theorists, mostly Italians and Germans, who connected (post)Fordist political economy to a critical analysis of state, culture, ideology, and collective identity. It is their emphasis on culture as a battleground of equal if not greater importance than politics and the economy in contemporary societies, and their rejection of historical materialist political strategies and conceptions of history, that distinguishes them from the French and American Marxist political economists. Assumptions of working class interest in socialism and the labor movement's historical mission are replaced by a focus on peace, ecology and feminist movements as the leading agents of social change. Most German theorizing on NSM posits an ambivalent connection between NSM and modernization processes.[21] The communicative compression of society through urbanization, rapid transport, instant communications, and well-educated citizens is a prerequisite for the rise of mass NSMs.[22] Civil rights and liberties are necessary to provide the political space for movement mobilization. And "discourse rationality" is a precondition for building consensus that change can be brought about by a movement. The future is contingent, open to human intervention in ways thought impossible by socialist workers' movements.[23] NSM are seen as reactions to deep social contradictions or unsolved problems. Social sectors especially sensitive to the impact of these problems are strengthened through modernization processes.[24] Movements arise to promote the blocked change or solve the difficult problem. Their life-history is controlled in some real way by the structural problem; they will not disappear until their problem is solved.[25]

The fact that the field of NSM studies is still unsettled does not minimize the value of reviewing some of the contributions. My concern here is less with the general nature of recently emergent movements, and more with what the theoretical perspectives might add to an understanding of the specific case of peace movement origins. To that end, three propositions about NSMs come in for scrutiny: (1) they act in new arenas of conflict; (2) they display new forms of identity and consciousness; and (3) they employ new types of organization and action. My discussion of the three propositions owes much to Alberto Melucci's *Nomads of the Present* and its fine introductory essay by John Keane and Paul Mier, as well as to Melucci's more recent work.[26]

New Arenas of Conflict

NSM theorists argue that new movements operate in new arenas of conflict. Whereas nineteenth century movements were embroiled in struggles over the production and distribution of material goods and resources, some sectors of contemporary social movements challenge the administrative logic of complex social and political systems primarily on symbolic grounds. Today's movements are said to operate as "signs," and are more concerned than past movements with the ways in which complex societies generate information and communicate meanings to their members. Part of the novelty of these new arenas of conflict stems from the ongoing shift in "complex societies" (Melucci's term) from the management of economic resources to the production of social relations, including symbols, identities and needs. In this context, Michel Foucault considered new movements, an opposition to the effects of power which are linked with knowledge, competence, and qualification: struggles against the privileges of knowledge. But they are also an opposition against secrecy, deformation and mystifying representations imposed on people. . . . What is questioned is the way in which knowledge circulates and functions, its relations to power. In short, the regime du savoir.[27]

New conflicts thus revolve around the skill of individuals and groups to control the conditions of their own action. Postindustrial societies depend upon relatively autonomous constituent units—without the acquisition of capacities for learning and action, individuals and groups could not self-regulate (and society could not reproduce); they would be unable to generate, gather, decode and exchange information. For Zsuzsa Hegedus, this new society is "characterised by its *'auto-creativity'*: by its genuinely new capacity to *invent and realise*, and therefore to *choose*, its own *futures* in an *autonomous manner* " [her emphasis].[28] Simultaneously, the extraordinary differentiation of complex societies makes necessary increased integration and intensification of control. It is now the code rather than the content of social life, argue NSM theorists, the preconditions of action more than behavior, that are central to contemporary societies. This is not to say that "old" conflicts such as those over class or political rights have faded completely, but that the new movements contain a plurality of levels of interest and action.

The emphasis on the central role of information extends, in practice, from relatively narrow demands for the right of citizens' access to practical facts (such as the location of missile deployment sites or the extent of ecological damage caused by toxic waste dumps) to broader debates over symbolic resources, such as the challenge of the women's movement to the exploitation of women in pornography or advertising. New movements publicize grievances and anxieties about everyday life, and uncover the hidden power relationships that come together in its shared customs and routines. These are arenas of conflict that transcend space, gender and caste; support is thus drawn from across class, sexual and national boundaries. These new arenas are, coincidentally, partly the product of the increased reach of society. Areas once exempt from direct control and regulation—self-definition, affective ties, sexuality, biological needs—are now open to postindustrial society's capacity to intervene in the production of meaning. This extension, argue NSM theorists, and the concurrent demand from citizens for control over their "personal lives," combine to create new areas of conflict.

New Collective Identities

New movements are engaged, according to our second proposition about the novelty of NSMs, in the creation of new collective identities, new forms of consciousness.[29] Melucci defines collective identity as "a shared definition of the field of opportunities and constraints offered to collective action."[30] The "common cognitive frameworks" that are collective identities enable movement activists to "calculate the costs and benefits of their action."[31] For Verta Taylor and Nancy Whittier, collective identity is "the shared definition of a group that derives from members' common interests, experiences, and solidarity."[32] Bert Klandermans makes clear that rather than fixed or stable, collective identities are "transient phenomena," shifting due to evolution in movement membership.[33] For Foucault, the formation of collective identities is situated in,

> struggles which question the status of the individual: on the one hand, they assert the right to be different and they underline everything which makes individuals truly individual. On the other hand, they attack everything which separates the individual, breaks his links with others, splits up community life, forces the individual back on himself and ties him to his own identity in a constraining way . . . they are struggles against the "government of individualization."[34]

For Jean Cohen, new collective identities take the form of a "self-understanding that abandons revolutionary dreams in favor of the idea of structural reform, along with a defense of civil society that does not seek to abolish the autonomous functioning of political and economic systems—in a phrase, self-limiting radicalism."[35] One product of the formation of new identities, for Melucci, is that today's movements have moved beyond instrumental thinking to consider participation a goal in itself. This is possible because actors consciously practice in the present the future social changes they preach. The focus on the present makes movement goals temporary and fungible. Gone are universal plans of history, all-encompassing visions of a future utopia; collective actors are, in Melucci's phrase, "nomads who dwell within the present." Melucci sees NSMs as profoundly circumspect about politics. They raise "metapolitical" issues that cannot be arbitrated by parties, and thus advertise the shortcomings of mainstream politics. There is a developing crisis of political representation in complex societies. NSMs are, thinks Melucci, "homeless" in this sense; their concerns cannot be represented readily by established parties, legislatures or other political mediators.

New movement adherents make plain the global character of life in postindustrial societies. Nationalism and other "ethnolocalisms" are surmounted, for many, by a new identity as planetary citizens, as members of an interdependent species dependent upon the carrying capacity of the Earth.[36] Peace and ecology movements are vocal witnesses to humanity's capability to devastate its natural environment. A green movement motto, "think globally, act locally," reflects a consciousness infused with an awareness of the need for folk action and the centrality of universal ecological principles: all things are connected, life is a seamless web. Ronald Inglehart calls this new consciousness "postmaterialist."[37] Overlapping to a remarkable degree with NSM activists, postmaterialists have been able, as a result of the prolonged postwar period of affluence and prosperity, to largely jettison materialist values and authoritarian orientations—economic growth, job and physical security, conformity to societal norms, discipline and order. The postmaterialist replacements include concern for the environment, diminished emphasis on economic rewards, libertarianism, demands for participatory democracy, openness to unconventional political participation, and experimentation with new life styles.[38] According to Inglehart, "the peace movement . . . is in large part a Postmaterialist phenomenon. . . . In West Germany . . . the impact of values held was especially pronounced . . . Postmaterialists were more than *twenty* times as likely to be members [of the peace movement], as were Materialists."[39] See Tables 2.1 and 2.2 for data on the relationship in the European Community (EC) between postmaterialist values, and support for and membership in the 1980s peace movements.

The dialectical nature of the new movements' identity formation processes, of their challenges to dominant cultural codes—the tension observed by Foucault between individualization and communal urges—can lead, say critics, to "political tribalism," narcissism, and a replacement of political commitment by an apolitical egotism. Ironically, the desire for self-realization is encouraged by the increase in education and skill levels characteristic of postindustrial society. Melucci conceded this danger and suggests that the need for individualization was frustrated in the sixties by restrictive youth policies, inadequate educational reforms, and other weak responses of the system. Bolstering civil society, he thinks, can prevent the overpowering of self-actualization by communal solidarity. L.A. Kauffman considered the search for new identities and the principle that identity should be central to the vision and practice of radical politics the most distinctive feature of contemporary movements.[40] While highly aware of the benefits of consciousness-raising for feminists and cultural reconstruction for people of color, she expressed concern that "the personal is political" thrust of identity politics can devolve into viewing self-exploration as a political process itself. When this happens move-ments become mere scattered groups who have lost the

TABLE 2.1   Support for Peace Movements by Value Type (Percentage "Approve Strongly")

Question: "Can you tell me whether you approve (strongly or somewhat) or disapprove (somewhat or strongly) of the anti-war and anti-nuclear weapons movements such as the Campaign for Nuclear Disarmament?"

Value Type	France	Belgium	Nether-lands	FRG	Italy
Materialist	31	40	35	20	73
Mixed	38	53	36	26	72
Postmaterial	53	64	61	66	79
	Greece	Ireland	Denmark	UK	EC*
Materialist	78	56	42	25	43
Mixed	81	56	42	28	47
Postmaterial	88	72	58	44	63

* Weighted according to population of each EC member-state.

Source: Euro-Barometer, no. 17 (May 1982); adapted from Table 1 in Ronald Inglehart, "Generational Change and the Future of the Atlantic Alliance," *PS*, vol. 17, no. 3 (1984), p. 531. Used by permission.

TABLE 2.2   Membership in Peace Movements by Value Type (Percentage Saying They "Are a Member")

Question: "Can you tell me whether you are a member, or are likely to join, or would certainly not join . . . the anti-war and anti-nuclear weapons movements, such as CND?"

Value Type	France	Belgium	Nether-lands	FRG	Italy
Materialist	0	0.2	1.0	0.5	0.8
Mixed	0.4	0.6	1.1	4.1	2.7
Postmaterial	3.3	3.2	5.5	10.4	5.6
	Greece	Ireland	Denmark	UK	EC*
Materialist	0	0.8	0.9	0.6	0.5
Mixed	0.8	1.6	1.1	1.1	1.4
Postmaterial	4.7	0	4.3	5.6	5.0

* Weighted according to population of each EC member-state.

Source: Euro-Barometer, no. 17 (May 1982); adapted from Table 2 in Ronald Inglehart, "Generational Change and the Future of the Atlantic Alliance," *PS*, vol. 17, no. 3 (1984), p. 532. Used by permission.

sense of solidarity necessary for progressive politics. Paralleling the loss of cohesion is the inability of movements to think strategically, to differentiate between the relative importance of various forms of power: when everything is political, how do movements create effective political strategies? Kauffman applied her analysis to the case of an anti-trade union organic food market and its ostensibly progressive patrons who considered green consuming a substitute for political action.[41] When the essence of identity politics moves from individualization as overture to political action to self-actualization *as* political action, then we have, argued Kauffman, an anti-politics or a depoliticization of identity.

New Organizations and Action

The third proposition about the extent to which contemporary movements are different from their predecessors centers on the issues of organization and action. NSM organizations tend to be decentralized and leaderless; they have no strong center and simple, temporary divisions of labor.[42] Luther Gerlach coined the acronym SPIN to describe them: organizations that are segmented, polycentric, ideologically integrated networks.[43] Claus Offe distinguished them from the "formal organization[s] [and] large-scale representative associations" of old political actors.[44] These new formations first arose in large numbers during the 1960s (with precursors appearing as early as the 1930s) and have since spread across various movements and throughout society. They require enormous expenditures of time and energy to manage and maintain. Great stress is put on grassroots participation and democracy with the organizations (again) a way of experiencing collective action itself. It is in this sense that Melucci considered the actual forms of the movements—their models of interpersonal relations and decisionmaking processes—to operate as signs or messages for the larger society. New groups are, according to Michael Welton, "particularly privileged sites for the organization of enlightenment and emancipatory praxis."[45] The NSM are, goes the claim, living laboratories practicing the future today.

Such fluid and relaxed structures contribute to NSM suspicion of those established institutions practicing the past: corporations, trade union hierarchies, political parties, and state bureaucracies. New movements emerge largely outside and "underneath" these dominant institutions and comprise what Melucci called "invisible" networks of small groups "submerged" in everyday life. These submerged or "latent" networks, characterized by an emphasis on individual needs, collective identity and part-time membership, constitute the laboratories in which new experiences are invented and dominant codes of societal routine challenged. NSM rarely appear as publicly visible phenomena—for instance, during public demonstrations against abortions or for women's rights—and their participation in observable political action is only temporary. New movements spend little time in the public domain because they are busy experimenting with new forms of daily life. Melucci claimed that new movements transcend the distinction common to labor and socialist movements—the more or less sharp divide between private and public life. The affective involvement, cognitive frameworks and modes of life within each sphere were different. For contemporary movements there is instead a complementarity between private life, in which new meanings are directly constructed and encountered, and publicly voiced commitments. Activists may not, after all, be confronted by the choice posed by Richard Flacks between "making history" and "making life."[46]

Conclusion

The discussion of social movement definitions provided an introductory perspective on the issues important to this study: organization, leadership, origins, constituencies, strategy, tactics and mobilization. While abstract definitions cannot do more than outline the nature of movements, they are necessary as a starting point for deeper investigations. It is too early to tell whether the 1980s West German peace movement was an NSM. Whether it acted in new arenas of conflict, displayed new forms of identity and consciousness, and employed new types of organization and action, are questions to which we return in Chapter 9.

Notes

1. Rudolf Heberle, "Types and Functions of Social Movements," in David L. Sills, ed., *International Encyclopedia of the Social Sciences*, vol. 14 (New York: Free Press, 1968).

2. Luther P. Gerlach and Virginia H. Hine, *People, Power, Change: Movements of Social Transformation* (Indianapolis: Bobbs-Merrill, 1970), p. xvi.

3. William Bruce Cameron, *Modern Social Movements: A Sociological Outline* (New York: Random House, 1966), p. 7.

4. John Wilson, *Introduction to Social Movements* (New York: Basic Books, 1973), p. 8.

5. John D. Mc Carthy and Mayer N. Zald, *The Trend of Social Movements in America: Professionalization and Resource Mobilization* (Morristown, NJ: General Learning, 1973).

6. Theodore Lowi, *The Politics of Disorder* (New York: Basic Books, 1971).

7. Joseph R. Gusfield, ed., *Protest, Reform and Revolt: A Reader in Social Movements* (New York: Wiley, 1970), p. 2 and p. 453.

8. Roberta Ash Garner, *Social Movements in America*, 2nd ed. (Chicago: Rand McNally, 1977), p. 1.

9. Roberta Ash, *Social Movements in America* (Chicago: Markham, 1972), p. 2. See also, Mayer N. Zald and Roberta Ash, "Social Movement Organizations: Growth, Decay and Change," *Social Forces*, vol. 44 (1966).

10. Piven and Cloward, *Poor People's Movements*, p. 5.

11. Charles Tilly, "Social Movements and National Politics," in Charles Bright and Susan Harding, eds., *Statemaking and Social Movements* (Ann Arbor: University of Michigan Press, 1984), p. 306.

12. Tilly, "Social Movements and National Politics," p. 311.

13. Tilly, "Social Movements and National Politics," p. 313.

14. Jean Cohen, "Strategy or Identity: New Theoretical Paradigms and Contemporary Social Movements," *Social Research*, vol. 52, no. 4 (1985).

15. David Plotke, "What's So New About New Social Movements?" *Socialist Review*, vol. 20, no. 1 (1990).

16. Thomas R. Rochon, "The West European Peace Movement and the Theory of New Social Movements," in Russell J. Dalton and Manfred Kuechler, eds., *Challenging the Political Order: New Social and Political Movements in Western Democracies* (Oxford: Oxford University Press, 1990).

17. Richard Stöss, "Vom Mythos der 'neuen sozialen Bewegungen:' Neun Thesen und ein Exkurs zum Elend der NSB-Forschung," in J.W. Falter, C. Fenner, M.T. Greven, eds., *Politische Willensbildung und Interessenvermittlung* (Opladen: Westdeutscher Verlag, 1984).

18. Barbara Epstein, "Rethinking Social Movement Theory," *Socialist Review*, vol. 20, no. 1 (1990).

19. See Donald Hodges, "Old and New Working Classes," *Radical America* vol. 5, no. 1 (1971).

20. On the former, see Michel Aglietta, *A Theory of Capitalist Regulation: The US Experience* (London: Lowe and Brydone, 1979); on the latter, see Samuel Bowles, David M. Gordon, and Thomas E. Weisskopf, *Beyond the Wasteland: A Democratic Alternative to Economic Decline* (New York: Anchor, 1983); and Samuel Bowles and Herbert Gintis, *Democracy and Capitalism: Property, Community, and the Contradictions of Modern Social Thought* (New York: Basic Books, 1986).

21. Rüdiger Schmitt-Beck, "A Myth Institutionalized: Theory and Research on New Social Movements in Germany," *European Journal of Political Research*, vol. 21 (1992).

22. Joachim Raschke, *Soziale Bewegungen: Ein historisch-systematischer Grundriss* (Frankfurt: Campus, 1985).

23. Offe, "New Social Movements."

24. Karl-Werner Brand, *Neue soziale Bewegungen: Entstehung, Funktion und Pespektiven neuer Protestpoentiale* (Opladen: Westdeutscher Verlag, 1982).

25. Dieter Rucht, "Themes, Logics, and Arenas of Social Movements: A Structural Approach," in Bert Klandermans, Hanspeter Kriesi, and Sidney Tarrow, eds., *From Structure to Action: Comparing Social Movement Research Across Cultures* (Greenwich, CT: JAI, 1988).

26. Alberto Melucci, *Nomads of the Present: Social Movements and Individual Needs in Contemporary Society* (Philadelphia: Temple University Press, 1989); and Alberto Melucci, "A Strange Kind of Newness: What's 'New' in New Social Movements?" in Enrique Laraña, Hank Johnston, and Joseph R. Gusfield, eds., *New Social Movements: From Ideology to Identity* (Philadelphia: Temple University Press, 1994).

27. Michel Foucault, "The Subject and Power," in Hubert L. Dreyfus and Paul Rabinow, eds., *Michel Foucault: Beyond Structuralism and Hermeneutics* (Chicago: University of Chicago Press, 1983), p. 211.

28. Zsuzsa Hegedus, "Social Movements and Social Change in Self-Creative Society: New Civil Initiatives in the International Arena," in Martin Albrow and Elizabeth King, eds., *Globalization, Knowledge and Society: Readings from International Sociology* (London: Sage, 1990), p. 274.

29. Laraña, et al., eds. *New Social Movements.*

30. Alberto Melucci, "The Symbolic Challenge of Contemporary Movements," *Social Research*, vol. 52 (1985), p. 793.

31. Melucci, *Nomads of the Present*, p. 35.

32. Verta Taylor and Nancy Whittier, "Collective Identity in Social Movement Communities: Lesbian Feminist Mobilization," in Aldon D. Morris and Carol McClurg Mueller, eds., *Frontiers in Social Movement Theory* (New Haven: Yale University Press, 1992), p.105.

33. Bert Klandermans, "Transient Identities? Membership Patterns in the Dutch Peace Movement," in Laraña, et al., eds. *New Social Movements*, p. 169.

34. Foucault, "The Subject and Power," p. 212.

35. Cohen, "Strategy or Identity," p. 664.

36. On ethnolocalism, see Luther P. Gerlach, "Territorial and Cultural Borders and the Role of New Stakeholders in the Management of Global Resources," unpublished manuscript, March 1990.

37. See his "The Silent Revolution in Europe: Inter-generational Change in Post-industrial Societies," *American Political Science Review*, vol. 65 (1971); *The Silent Revolution*; and, Ronald Inglehart, *Culture Shift in Advanced Industrial Society* (Princeton: Princeton University Press, 1990).

38. Franz-Urban Pappi, "Neue soziale Bewegungen und Wahlverhalten in der Bundesrepublik," in Max Kaase and Hans-Dieter Klingemann, eds., *Wahlen und Wähler: Analysen aus Anlass der Bundestagswahl 1987* (Opladen: Westdeutscher Verlag, 1990).

39. Ronald Inglehart, "Generational Change and the Future of the Atlantic Alliance," *PS*, vol. 17, no. 3 (1984), p. 531.

40. L.A. Kauffman, "The Anti-Politics of Identity," *Socialist Review*, vol. 20, no. 1 (1990).

41. L.A. Kauffman, "Tofu Politics in Berkeley," *The Nation* , September 16, 1991.

42. Gerlach and Hine, *People, Power, Change.*

43. Luther P. Gerlach, "Protest Movements and the Construction of Risk," in B.B. Johnson and Vincent T. Costello, eds., *The Social and Cultural Construction of Risk* (Amsterdam: Reidel, 1987), pp. 114-17.

44. Claus Offe, "Challenging the Boundaries of Institutional Politics: Social Movements since the 1960s," in Charles Maier, ed., *Changing Boundaries of the Political* (New York: Cambridge University Press, 1987), p. 73.

45. Michael Welton, "Social Revolutionary Learning: The New Social Movements as Learning Sites," *Adult Education Quarterly*, vol. 43, no. 3 (1993), p. 152.

46. Richard Flacks, "Making History vs. Making Life: Dilemmas of an American Left," *Social Inquiry*, vol. 46, no. 3-4 (1976).

3

Movement Origins

One germane problem now remained, a problem towering over all others: how to prevent the human race from being destroyed by its demoralized but reputedly sane leaders. That problem has still to be solved.

—Lewis Mumford, *The Pentagon of Power*

My intention in this chapter is to review six social movement theories for their insights on movement origins. The review is the first part of a two-part assessment of which individual theory or combination of theories best explains the rise of the peace movement. Are the roots of the movement exposed by the spade of social movement theory? If movement organizations spring from irrational fears about nuclear war, then elected officials would be prudent to disregard the organizations' prescriptions for building a safer world. If, on the other hand, the arrival of new peace movement organizations on the political scene can be explained by reference to changes in social structure or individual values, a policymaker would be unwise to ignore such developments. I assess the value of the six theories in Chapter 9. By then, it is possible to determine the explanatory power of the theories.

Theories are bodies of interrelated variables and propositions designed to explain phenomena. More specifically, social movement theories aim to explain why movements originate and why people participate in them. Even more specifically, social movement theory propositions link variables such as strain, deprivation, powerlessness, ideology, the organization of discontented groups, and the structure of the economy and the political system into theories of the "middle range" that emphasize only a few variables and try to explain but a limited range of behavior. Scholars are divided as to the most theoretically parsimonious and empirically valid models for conceptualizing the flowering of (new) social movements and have categorized the theories in various fashions. Charles Tilly cataloged movement theories by their roots in social theory: Millian, Marxian, Weberian, and Durkheimian.[1] Another approach assigned the various theories to one of three paradigms: the social-structural, the social-psychological, and the psychological. Alberto Melucci talked of a traditional focus on "action [irrationality, contagion] without actors" (psychological approaches) versus a focus on "actors [classes] without action" (Marxist approaches). By the 1970s, Melucci considered the dominant approaches to be three: "structural" (broadly what I call new social movement theory), "resource mobilization" (I also use this term), and "political exchange" (what I call political process theory).[2] My intention is not to devise yet one more typological scheme. Rather, I simply distinguish between six clusters of theories—party failure, fear of war, collective behavior, resource mobilization, political process, and new social movement. These labels are not mine, although I take liberties in defining their boundaries.

Party Failure

The protest movements of the sixties and seventies ushered in a new era for the party systems of the advanced industrial democracies. The New Left on both sides of the Atlantic demanded a greater role for the average citizen in public affairs. Students for a Democratic Society's Port Huron decree in the United States, and the numerous manifestoes of young German radicals and the French "May 68" students, blasted their parents' generation for its failure to provide creative and humane outlets for the selfless energy of its progeny. Rejecting the promise of a job in the city, house in the suburbs, and vacations by the seashore, this "successor generation" opted for an activist life, devoted to the raising of consciousness (and less rarified pursuits) in order to allow the disadvantaged and alienated to make their own history.[3] But the cold, impersonal nature of Establishment political institutions dictated that their cause be taken to the streets. Demonstrations and marches were the vehicle most amenable to the issues raised by postmaterialist students. Those student activists who took part in the "long march through the institutions" during the seventies were back on the streets again in the so-

cial movements of the early eighties. The student movement opened political space for a whole series of new protest movements: womens' and
gay liberation, grassroots citizen initiatives, ecological and anti-nuclear,
alternative and Green, peace and disarmament. These groups have operated largely outside the traditional bounds of political conflict. Although
many have utilized the civil and administrative courts, and lobbied legislatures and executives, it is partly the perceived inadequacy of these
measures that led to the rapid growth and unconventional tactics of citizens' groups.

As a concept, "party failure" aims to capture the polity's response to
social and economic change.[4] It tries to explain how governments' have
lost the trust of their citizens.

> EMNID polls taken in October 1981 revealed the depth of [West Ger-
> mans'] distrust toward the traditional parties and politicians: 61 percent
> of respondents under 21 years, 69 percent under 25, and 64 percent un-
> der 29 considered the traditional parties "incapable of solving prob-
> lems." Further, 79 percent of those under 21, 86 percent under 25, and
> 77 percent under 29 believed that politicians no longer know what the
> people think. In a later INFAS poll only 43 percent of respondents be-
> tween the ages of 16 and 23 believed that "politicians' decisions are
> made in the interest of the people."[5]

Party failure theses followed the fragmentation of the postwar economic
growth consensus that accompanied the oil shocks, stagflation, and malaise of the 1970s.[6] They are also a product of attempts to explain the cor-
responding social trends toward voter dealignment and realignment in
advanced capitalist polities.[7] The decline of unquestioned American
global hegemony paralleled the loss of economic momentum. The failed
U.S. aggression in Vietnam, the Grand Coalition in Bonn, and the Water-
gate scandal were formative experiences for a new generation of West
Germans. They grew up in an era of unprecedented economic success,
the famed Wirtschaftswunder (economic miracle), that created a mass
consumption society and unprecedented levels of affluence. Structural
constraints on growth were exacerbated by citizens' groups which
sought to put an end to unrestrained environmental destruction; continued industrial advance was seen by many as pernicious for both humans
and the planet. Political parties that clung to the crumbling growth consensus could no longer agree on the policies needed to reinvigorate their
sagging economies and pacify their discontented youth.[8] Thus dawned
the "age of ungovernability" accompanied by left and right squabbling
over the relative merits of Keynesian pump-priming versus monetarist
and supply-side cures.[9]

A prime component in the discussion of policy alternatives is the role of political parties and the state. With the spread of information technologies and growing global interdependence, government assumed greater responsibility for macroeconomic management and welfare state transfer payments. Increasing bureaucratization was deemed necessary to insure efficiency, while further worker safety and health regulations were enacted, and pollution control and environmental protection issues rode to the fore on the backs of the "citizens' initiatives" (Bürgerinitiativen). The tide of "rising expectations," so bemoaned by neoconservatives on both sides of the ocean, forced new demands upon the state, which responded with further centralization and hierarchical rigidity. Policymaking came to be dominated by planning boards and tripartite institutions ruled over by experts and technocrats.[10] As neocorporatism reigned supreme, parties became less relevant as interest aggregators and policy formulators, and the Social Democratic "Modell Deutschland" (policies and institutions that supported both social welfare programs and capital accumulation) became ever more dependent on global markets. The Grand Coalition of the second half of the sixties typified the dual phenomena of growth consensus and bureaucratic centralization. But Otto Kirchheimer's thesis of the "vanishing opposition," a product of "catch-all" strategies and policy homogenization, would, however, fall out of step with reality shortly after its genesis. The tendency toward ever-increasing government intervention lost its allure shortly after West German economic dynamism dissipated. The end of rampant growth illuminated the all-encompassing nature of the state machinery (the state apparatus, in this sense, includes the established political parties as well as local and federal level administrations). It is this Leviathan that "failed" with which citizen movements, of whatever hue, do battle.

Theories of party failure aim to comprehend both change and continuity.[11] They typically have a twin purpose: to explain what has become of contemporary parties, and to understand the political formations that have arisen to challenge the once tight grip of parties on citizen loyalty.[12] It is the second purpose that is of primary concern here. To investigate the relevance of party failure theory for an explication of the roots of the West German peace movement, the best place to start is with the volume edited by Kay Lawson and Peter Merkl.[13] Party failure theses need to explain against what standard they measure parties; by what criteria can parties be said to fail? Lawson and Merkl's contributors were not of one mind in defining party failure, but a majority agreed that parties have failed when they can no longer perform their traditional functions: mediating major group interests, structuring elections, managing states, and devising public policy. The duration of failure is an allied concern; although most authors concurred that struggling parties may recover, this does not mitigate their past failure.

Lawson and Merkl identified four types of alternative organizations that arose to challenge parties as mediating institution between state and citizen: environmentalist, supplementary, communitarian, and anti-authoritarian. Lawson and Merkl's sample of anti-authoritarian groups arose in party systems operating at the pleasure of strong militaries (Poland, Taiwan, Ghana). These are groups that "direct their attention to 'the masses,' to the rights and interests of people at large, especially when these are denied by the selfish rule of a narrow elite."[14] Anti-authoritarians, it is argued, are unique to party systems considered authoritarian or totalitarian (in the sense these terms were once used by Jeane Kirkpatrick). The peace movement is assigned to the environmentalist grouping (due to its new politics, participatory, action-oriented profile).

A magnified view of the act of peace movement birth is available through the lens of "linkage failure."[15] Linkages are those mechanisms scholars of party systems have employed to describe the interconnections between citizens and policymakers. Students of international relations have used a linkage concept to explain foreign policy reciprocity of a Kissingerian sort, or the processes of aggregation James Rosenau observed between different geographical levels (local, state, national, international) and diverse organizational units (parties, interest groups, movements, legislatures).[16] Lawson suggested four possible linkage forms between parties and citizens: participatory, electoral, clientelistic, and directive. It is the first two that the SPD has traditionally practiced and which have suffered in recent years. Rank-and-file Social Democrats, and especially those active in the peace movement, complained about the dearth of opportunities for meaningful participation in setting the party program and holding candidates and incumbents to settled programs. Instead, they complained, the SPD concentrated on electoral linkage which many movement sympathizers see as little more than leadership manipulation of the grassroots on behalf of the parliamentary party.

Rosenau identified two linkage processes which have implications for citizen-party-state connections: penetrative (actors from one level of aggregation participate in the politics of another level) and reactive (one organizational unit responds to the actions of another). As the SPD appeared less and less capable, from the perspective of peace-minded citizens, of successful penetrative and reactive linkage, the greater became the need for alternative organizations. The peace movement created penetrative links by forming networks of individuals and organizations that operated at and across local, state, national and even transnational levels. German pacifists forged reactive links by pressuring state, parties and public opinion to respond to their demands. This follows Lawson's general hypothesis that alternative organizations result when parties fail to provide adequate forms of linkage.[17] Robert Bellah observed that "the strength of our voluntarism seems to be positively correlated with the concurrent weakness of our political parties."[18] Suzanne Berger too found evidence of party and linkage failure in:

> the declining capacity of political institutions to produce a widespread reaction against the state, at the same time that they promote high levels of participation in politics. It is this disjunction between the growing politicization of everyday life and the decay of the parties that in the past articulated and aggregated demands that best characterizes the current phase of West European politics. The principal manifestation of these shifts can be found in the antiparty and antistate values of virtually all new political movements . . . in Europe today.[19]

An unrelated but relevant observation of Charles Tilly's suggests another perspective on party failure. He found that social movements as concept and reality arose during the nineteenth century alongside parties, labor unions, and other associations contending for power. Movements are "parallel streams of people . . . which overflowed the narrow channels of elections or labor-management negotiations which were being dug at the same time."[20] Movements and parties remain parallel streams in the 1990s. The tough problems that go unresolved, and other charges lodged against parties as evidence of failure were always fair to make. Parties, in this view, have probably failed recently no more or less than they did in the past. The case of the Democratic party in the United States is instructive. The badly divided party, which had elected but one president in a generation, verged on collapse following the 1924 election.[21] Some observers now claim the Republican and Democratic parties to be stronger than ever before.[22] The apparent reconstitution and resurgence of the main parties in the United States does not, however, contradict the concept of party failure as employed in this section. When failure means inability to cope with some intransigent problem like militarism or racism, then the parallel stream of movements runs as if after the spring thaw. It might then return to its banks, or even to a trickle, should superpower tensions relax or the state respond to race-based claims. The crux here might be, to continue the metaphor, one of ebb and flow, of tides and lunar cycles. Perhaps one stream (parties) or the other (movements) is stronger depending on the weather, season and phase of the moon (economic, social and political conditions). When the conditions are right, peace movements may overflow the narrow channel of party systems.

Fear of War

Governments have traditionally touted the strength or inhumanity of their enemies in order to relieve taxpayers of sufficient funds (and bodies) to provide for the common defense. Once defenses are engaged, once war breaks out, support for it must be marshaled and maintained. British propaganda about German atrocities in Belgium during the First World War (later determined to have been false), was an attempt to maintain flagging support for the war of attrition in the trenches of Flanders. U.S. demonization of its communist foes in the Cold War, and in two hot wars, Korea and Vietnam, was absorbed and transmitted by popular culture industries and worked for decades to sustain widespread support for a permanent war economy and for intervention overseas. Demonization proceeds to dehumanize enemies through either racist or ideological appeals. Thus, in the case of U.S. foes, the Japanese were "Japs" or "Nips," bucktoothed and wearing spectacles. The Koreans and Vietnamese were "Slants," "Gooks," and "Zips," obsequious but treacherous. And the Russians were "godless atheists," "Commies," and "Reds," drab amoral robots. Little thought is given to the possibility that building up the enemy or inflating the threat might eventually result in citizens uneager to part with their wages or to supply the uniformed services with their young male kin. Failed campaigns to drum up support for wars can lead to ugliness, the New York City draft riots in the midst of the U.S. Civil War are a case in point. Or they can lead to more focused resistance, such as the transnational anti-war movement of 1965-1973.

Cacophonous and anxiety-producing government rhetoric on behalf of a particular war, or the growing frequency of telegrams delivered to homes by military officers and the proliferation of Gold Star families, are not the only sources of public disenchantment with states' military mobilizations. Preparations for war and the prosecution of Cold Wars also generate fearful opposition. "Peace through strength" policies can give rise to fears prompting active or passive citizen responses. Passivity can take the form of resignation, apathy and withdrawal into privatism, or quiet support based upon trust and the belief "the President knows what he's doing," a reaction common to the "silent majority." Those less certain of official omniscience may take active measures of two primary sorts—offensive and defensive. Defensive responses include the construction of backyard fallout shelters, a practice peaking about the time of the Cuban missile crisis, or the purchase and provisioning of survivalist retreats in the mountains of Idaho, the preferred approach of those

who could afford it in the 1980s. Offensive responses to potential or actual consequences of Cold War policies include German reactions to rearmament in the early 1950s, British responses to nuclearization in the
Ban the Bomb movement of the late fifties-early sixties, U.S. protests of
above-ground nuclear testing prior to the Partial Test Ban Treaty, and
mobilization in the U.S. against possible invasion of Central America
through much of the eighties. Those opting for defensive measures rarely
engage in offensive action as well, and vice versa. Fears sparking offensive action stem from either memories of past wars, as in the case of the
German anti-rearmament movement, or from concern about the prospects of a new war, as in the case of the West German anti-Euromissile
movement. A mature Briton photographed while protesting outside the
gates of the U.S. Air Force base at Greenham Common (a Cruise missile
site) symbolized the merger of fear from the past and for the future. Her
placard complained that having lived through two world wars she was
afraid she would not survive a third.

There is in the dialectic of fear—fear of war and fear of the "enemy"—a paradox for peace movements. Fear of war may be necessary for
movement mobilization, but militarists are able to manipulate the same
fear and to transform it into anti-communism, or some other fear of the
enemy. Fear may simultaneously accelerate the arms race via increased
defense spending and, perhaps, stimulate a peace movement. Former
Assistant Secretary of Defense Richard Perle was forthright about the
importance of fear of the enemy for the Reagan administration:

> Cosmetic agreements [on arms control are] in the long run fatal for the
> democracies of the West. Democracies will not sacrifice to protect their
> security in the absence of a sense of danger. And every time we create
> the impression we and the Soviets are cooperating and moderating the
> competition, we diminish that sense of apprehension.[23]

It was therefore imperative for the Reaganites to traffic in fear. Fear
was the hinge upon which the superpower arms race depended, and its
locus was in "the threat." Kermit Johnson made clear the importance of
elite threat construction:

> 1) the intensity and scope of "the threat" is defined differently at differ-
> ent times, according to domestic political considerations; 2) militarily
> "the threat" is also defined variously, depending on the availability of
> defense dollars and the extent of the "defense consensus." At one time
> the military has said we must be geared to fight 1 1/2 wars simultane-
> ously . . . at other times the figure is 2 1/2 wars, and at other times the
> scope is anywhere and everywhere. This change . . . can take place quite
> rapidly, particularly with the change of political parties in power; 3) left

to its own devices, the military considers the "enemy threat" on the basis of worst-case analysis.[24]

Crafty politicians and their intellectuals were able to transform a tense political relationship between the United States and the Soviet Union into an increasing "threat" (see Figure 3.1). While Soviet aggression in Afghanistan and heavy-handedness in Poland definitely worsened the relationship with the U.S., the Soviet military threat was not appreciably greater than it had been prior to these crises. Indeed, entanglements in

FIGURE 3.1   The Fear of Enemy Cycle

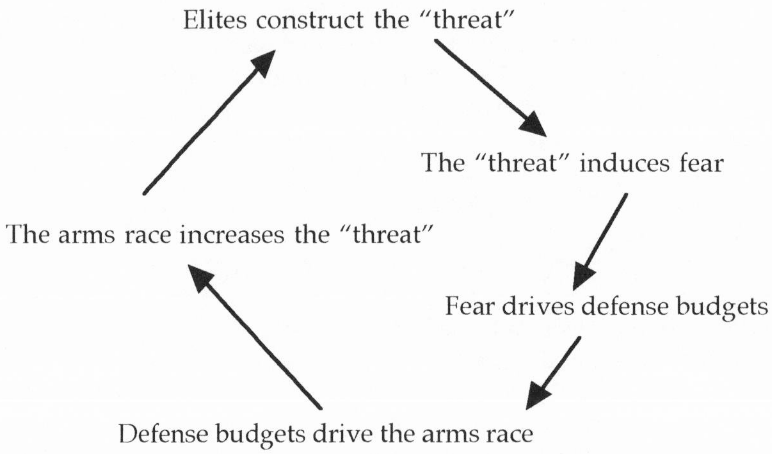

Elites construct the "threat"

The "threat" induces fear

The arms race increases the "threat"

Fear drives defense budgets

Defense budgets drive the arms race

Source: Adapted from Johnson, *Realism and Hope in a Nuclear Age*, p. 33.

Central Asia and Eastern Europe reduced the Soviets' ability to intervene elsewhere, as was true for the United States in Vietnam.[25] Healthy patriotism was manipulated by elites into a lubricant for the wheels of the cycle. What really matters is that this was a complex geopolitical process out of control. Even when politicians did not want to play the game, it was very difficult to halt the cycle, to restrain those forces materially or psychically benefitted by its revolutions.

Jürgen Straub and his colleagues identified five types of fear of war relevant to participation in and thus the genesis of peace movements:

1) that resulting from a cognitive wrestling with existing security policy and its implications (which is what most people mean, argued the authors, when they refer to fear of war);

2) that considered a species of a more general "catastrophic fear" which worries about "day X" when the world will suddenly come to an irradiated end (a possibility the authors do not completely rule out)—this is a more diffuse fear than the first type, and is less likely to lead to collective action;

3) that related to the Freudian concept of neurotic fear, thought to be a product of childhood;

4) that considered an element of a general fear of life or the future— this type can be mixed up with fear of ecological destruction or unemployment and thus lose its distinctiveness; and finally,

5) that related to a fear of individual death, of the death of loved ones, or the death of life on earth.[26]

Whether the 1980s West German peace movement exhibited one or more of these types of fear within its ranks is a question to which we return in Chapter 9. But what is clear at this point is that some variety of war fear was not limited to peace activists. According to Russett and Deluca,

Expectations of war are not significantly linked to specific segments of the population. . . . they are about as common among men as among women, and equally prevalent among the various age groups. Nor are they related to political opinion, either on a standard "left-right" political spectrum or on a scale of foreign-policy preference ranging from pro-NATO through neutralism to a pro-Soviet orientation.[27]

Collective Behavior

Collective behavior theories, including relative deprivation theories, were for decades the hegemons of social protest studies. Relative deprivation theories share the assumptions of the mass society approach: protest activity, episodic and short-lived, is a result of changes in the psychological state of protesters caught up in rapid social change; protesters are guided by emotions rather than rational calculations; protest activity is abnormal because it is not rooted in institutions, and is fundamentally different from institutional activity. Deprivation theories focus on the links between objective social situations, perceptions of the situations, and the action stemming from the perceptions. When people perceive a gulf between the power and privileges they possess, and the amount they consider just, frustration, anger and movement participation result. Briefly, movements emerge from the changed expectations following rapid social change. Relative deprivation theories were elaborated with materialist protest and rebellion in mind; they have been employed to explain urban ghetto violence in the United States and political unruliness in the Third World.[28] Both method and substance of relative deprivation studies have been criticized.[29] To characterize postmaterialist peace movement emergence in relative deprivation terms distorts or even caricatures the approach. Affluent West Germans were not deprived of goods relative to some other national group, but only in relation to an ideal-type of participatory democratic citizen.

Collective behavior theories explain the origins of social movements by focusing on (1) structural breakdown that spurs noninstitutionalized attempts at social change; (2) the psychology of movement adherents; and (3) the role of beliefs in movement action. I follow Aldon Morris and Cedric Herring in discerning two primary camps in the collective behavior paradigm, the Chicago School and the work of Neil Smelser.[30] My account of the Chicago School draws on their concise treatment. Ralph Turner, a Chicago School theorist, suggested in an interview that the inclusion of Smelser in the paradigm is mistaken. One major difference is that where Chicago School theorists are symbolic interactionists, Smelser is a Parsonian structural-functionalist. Nonetheless, Smelser and the Chicago school have enough in common to justify examining them in tandem. Collective behaviorists borrowed from and extended the arguments of the crowd psychologists like LeBon about the irrationality of collective action. Collective behavior for Herbert Blumer, a leading Chicago theorist, is "not based on the adherence to common understandings or rules," but rather is "formed or forged to meet undefined or structured situations."[31] A central theme of the paradigm is cultural or structural breakdown. Collective behavior—panics, fashion trends, revivals, riots, revolutions, and social movements—consists of efforts to repair shattered social structures and to create a new shared meaning system.[32] This frequently leads participants, through the communication processes of contagion, suggestibility and imitation, to spontaneous, emotional or irrational behavior. Turner and Killian moved beyond the emphasis on irrationality to focus on a hypothesized emergent norm to explain collective behavior. An "emergent norm"—in direct opposition to some established practice or belief—allows participants to structure meaning and to work for the reform of the practice or belief. These norms are said to develop through rumor, "the characteristic mode of of communication in collective behavior."[33]

While not denying the role of organizations in the growth of movements, the Chicago theorists emphasized instead spontaneity, the creation of "meaning frames," and other social psychological processes. The Langs identified core groups that loosely coordinate the contagion and spontaneity of a movement, but these groups also appear unguided.[34] For

Joseph Gusfield, "the unity and coherence of a movement, in its various stages and forms, depend on the similarity of the adherents' beliefs about the legitimacy of a new way of behaving, of their rejection of what has been, and of their demand for adoption of the new."[35] Organization is linked to a movement's spread, but is not seen as a factor in its emergence. No sustained analysis of movement organizations is carried out, despite their admitted importance by some, because SMOs are considered little more than constantly changing and transient phenomena. Turner would later admit that this view limited the usefulness of the Chicago School's perspective to the very early stages of a movement.[36]

The most sophisticated collective behaviorist account of movement origins is that of Neil Smelser.[37] My discussion of Smelser's work draws upon Morris and Herring.[38] Smelser rejected the Chicago School notion that collective behavior is unique and as such deserves its own branch of sociology. Instead, Smelser sought to explain it in terms of a structural-functionalist "value-added" model that was applicable to both norm-oriented movements (aimed at changing the behavior patterns of specific groups) and value-oriented movements (aimed at changing the societal value system). In Smelser's model, collective behavior is produced through the interaction of six variables:

- structural conduciveness (the extent to which a social structure permits protest);
- strains (of four types which occur, in Parsonian terms, through the malintegration of an integrated social system);
- growth and spread of generalized beliefs (by which participants identify the source of strain and suggest ideological solutions);
- precipitating factors (events that draw attention to the source of strains);
- mobilization (process by which participants are mustered for action);
- social control (the reaction of authorities to collective behavior).

The emphasis in the model is on strain, a disabling of the relations among and the resulting faulty functioning of the four components of social action: values, norms, role mobilization, and situational facilities. Existing or newly created organizations speed the rise of a movement *after* its emergence, but strain and generalized beliefs are, for Smelser, the engines of collective behavior.

Collective behavior is "mobilization on the basis of a belief which redefines social action."[39] Participants in collective behavior try to mend a strained social structure and search for solutions to intractable problems by raising the level of generality. This is of itself, of course, quite normal and rational. Beliefs are a basis for mobilization and a criterion by which to distinguish various types of collective behavior. Collective behavior, for Smelser however, is distinguished by the phenomenon of "short-circuiting." Intermediate steps are leaped as the actor moves from a highly generalized and abstract component of action directly to a source of strain. The short-circuit is made by means of a generalized belief. The generalized belief operates like Blumer's "circular reaction," the Langs' "collective redefinition," and Turner and Killian's "emergent norm:" it furnishes the shared meaning that allows actors to act collectively in repairing some aspect of the social order. The generalized belief diverges, however, from the emergent norm or other Chicago School approaches that stress the rationality of collective behavior. Robert Park suggested the possibility that structural breakdown could lead to individual liberation, cosmopolitanism, and enlightenment.[40] Smelser argued, however, that generalized "beliefs differ . . . from those which guide other types of behavior. They involve a belief in the existence of extraordinary forces . . . which are at work in the universe . . . The beliefs on which collective action is based . . . are thus akin to magical beliefs."[41] A generalized belief is a myth by which to mobilize people. It consists of flights of fancy and fearlessness and leads to proposed reforms that "will render opponents helpless, and will be effective immediately. . . Because of this exaggerated potency, adherents often see unlimited bliss in the future if only the reforms are adopted. For if they are adopted, they argue, the basis for threat, frustration, and discomfort will disappear."[42]

Resource Mobilization

Theories arose in the late sixties and early seventies to challenge the dominance of the collective behavior approach. Loosely corralled together in the resource mobilization paradigm, these approaches differ in emphasis and particulars. Resource mobilization theory (RMT) takes as its main purpose the explanation of how organizations acquire resources needed for confronting authorities and how these resources are mobilized to effect social and political change. A resource is anything that allows one social actor to control, benefit or punish another social actor: time, money, labor, experience, skills, etc.[43] Mobilization is the process by which resources become available to a movement. Various RMTs share a number of central assumptions:

1) conventional and unconventional political behavior are not fundamentally different;

2) movement participation is rational;
3) movements pursue interests;
4) grievances alone can not explain the appearance of insurgency as discontent is ubiquitous and uncorrelated with movement life-cycles;
5) mobilization occurs through organizational structures;
6) movement outcomes are products of participant choice;
7) social control also shapes movement outcomes.

The theories necessarily span individual, organizational, and systemic levels of analysis. Following Morris and Herring, RM theories can be analyzed in two separate (but overlapping) clusters: the rational action approach, and the organizational-entrepreneurial approach.

The rational action approach is utilitarian and economistic; it directly contradicts the crowd psychology and the collective behavior approaches that view movement action as irrational. Ultimately traceable to Mill and Bentham, this approach considers challengers of the status quo no less rational, no less effective "utility maximizers" than conventional political actors. According to Anthony Oberschall,

> The individuals who are faced with resource management decisions make rational choices based on the pursuit of their selfish interests in an enlightened manner. They weigh the rewards and sanctions, costs and benefits that alternative courses of action represent for them. In conflict situations, as in all other choice situations, their own preferences and history, their predispositions, as well as the group structure and influence processes they are caught up in, determine their choices.[44]

The lower the ratio of costs to benefits, agree the rational actionists, the more likely people are to participate in social movements. Movements occur because people consider them effective vehicles for the realization of interests.

The organizational-entrepreneurial approach's major claim is that the emergence of movements may be aided by leaders and preexisting organizations. Given sufficient resources, "grievances and discontent may be redefined, created, and manipulated by issue entrepreneurs and organizations."[45] Such was the case of the Free Speech Movement at Berkeley, which arose from existing networks of student activists and organizations.[46] Individuals and organizations may have a personal or professional stake in the social construction of movement activity. In an extension of RMT, Doug McAdam showed that movement-founding individuals and organizations "are themselves embedded in long-standing activist subcultures capable of sustaining the ideational traditions needed to revitalize activism following a period of movement dormancy."[47]

Resource mobilization theory, devised by North Americans to explain the origins and operation of North American movements, focuses on the resources—money, leadership, and long-lived movement organizations—provided various movements by the affluent middle class. Movements are able to surmount the "free rider" problem because the resources necessary for mobilization are solicited from the affluent sympathetic to but outside "oppressed groups."[48] Movements themselves are seen as preference structures for change. Preferences for change are mobilized through SMOs that operate in social movement industries (SMI) that are part of a social movement sector (SMS). A social movement industry consists of movement organizations struggling to attain the preferences of a social movement. Social movement industries need not be dependent on particular movements, however, because organizations within industries may manufacture products useful to other industries and movements. An SMS takes in all the SMIs of a society. The resources available within an SMS determines the genesis and prospects of SMIs and SMOs. The SMS must compete for resources with other sectors of society, and is seen by McCarthy and Zald as a frequent loser in the competition as it can bloom only after the satisfaction of other needs and desires. Their account parallels Abraham Maslow's concept of the human needs hierarchy adopted by Inglehart and others. It is the discretionary resources of the affluent that are available for investment in the SMS.

McCarthy and Zald stress the importance of "conscience constituencies" for the creation and maintenance of movements.[49] Conscience constituents are direct supporters of an SMO who do not stand to benefit directly from the organization's success. The benefit for conscience constituents is psychic satisfaction, the sense of having helped a worthy cause, and of taking part in a noble effort. It is such big-hearted people who provide the resources needed by professional (permanent) movement organizations. Professional organizations are cast in a leading role by the organizational-entrepreneurial approach and, with some exceptions, evince the following features:

- they direct appeals for resources to conscience constituencies.
- they employ few constituents for movement work.
- they include a small professional entrepreneurial cadre that provides leadership and labor through "transitory teams."
- they have a tiny or nonexistent membership.[50]

McCarthy and Zald's sample of SMOs consists of what are essentially economic interest groups: AFL-CIO lobbyists, the National Union for Social Justice, and the National Council for Senior Citizens. Movement entrepreneurs may be crucial for the formation of movements for they, as suggested above, are able to advertise and market grievances, create organizations, and mobilize support. Movement entrepreneurs are, in this view, political entrepreneurs much like party politicians.[51] McCarthy and Zald argued that the selective incentives Olson thought necessary to induce participation in mass action are expendable for the affluent individuals and organizations that comprise the outside resource base of most contemporary American movements. Numerous other studies have either modified or completely rejected Olson's famous thesis about the necessity of selective incentives for collective action.[52]

Political Process

The political process model can be seen as part of the effort of political sociology in the U.S. to "bring the state back in."[53] The model, elaborated by McAdam (from whom my account borrows), examines the collective structures and processes through which movements pursue power. Posited as a conscious alternative to collective behavior and RMT perspectives, the process model considers social movements primarily political rather than psychological phenomena. It views movement mobilization as a continuous process rather than as distinct steps on a developmental ladder. Because it was initially developed in opposition to RMT and classical social movement theories, the early formulations did not position the model in relation to NSM theory. We can say now that perhaps the central contention of the political process approach—at least in comparison to NSM theory—is that politics matters more for the rise and mobilization of social movements than does social structural or cultural change.[54] Of course social change is important, but it impinges indirectly on protest through a restructuring of political power relations. According to political process theorist Sidney Tarrow,

> [T]he 'new' social movements that arose in the 1970s and 1980s are not best understood as a new cultural paradigm, but as a product of the cycle of mobilization of the previous decade, which left a heritage of new forms of action and new ideological themes for the next period of history. Like their predecessor, the 'old' labor movement, these new movements, however radical or flamboyant they seemed at the time, were part of a general cycle of mobilization. They are best understood in relation to the political system.[55]

And as Christian Joppe argued, "Locating social movements at the institutional level of national political structures and traditions provides a desired middle-ground, which helps to avoid the country-blind abstractions of new social movement theory and the rational actor allusions of resource mobilization theory."[56]

The process perspective also reflects its practioners concern about what they consider the overemphasis on external financial resources and professional manipulators of the organizational-entrepreneurial RMT approach. It focuses instead on the process of political struggle and the collective action political struggle generates.[57] McAdam found that early in the U.S. civil rights movement blacks were able to rely on indigenous sources of support rather than the resources or skills of outsiders. Outside assistance only became important to black SMOs after their own initial activity rather than prior to it as suggested by the organizational-entrepreneurial approach.[58] As compared to collective behaviorists and other classical approaches, process theorists are interested in political collective action rather than the full gamut of collective action including fads, panics, cults, and religious revivals. By focusing on political struggles, political process scholars are able to examine both conventional and unconventional political behavior within the same model; they are able to reject some collective behaviorists' need for special theories and concepts, and the claims of other collective behaviorists about protester irrationality.

Where collective behavior theories are founded on a pluralist conception of power, and RMT stems from the elitist perspective, the political process model combines elitist and Marxist notions of power. It sees political arenas with unfair advantages for the rich and well-connected as high but not insurmountable barriers to popular mobilization. And, also paralleling Marxist scholarship, the process model stresses the importance of shifts in human consciousness. The will to personal and group agency can bloom and flag. Consensus-building is essential because what people think is possible could be made actual through their collective efforts. State structure, political culture, temporal opportunities, and movement organizations are, consequently, key features of political process accounts of movement mobilization.[59] Movement life cycles are a complex product of adherents' energy (skill, commitment, resources) and authorities' social control (repression, facilitation). The extent to which internal or external factors determines a movement's course varies with the movement. The political process model locates movement origins in three areas: (1) the level of organization; (2) the level of potential adherent consciousness; and (3) the political opportunity structure.

Organization is indispensable for both movement emergence and collective action. Challengers must construct or have access to internal organization—a common identity and unifying structure. Strong organizations provide five crucial resources: members, leaders, a communication network, solidary incentives, and "enterprise tools" (office space, lawyers, photocopy machines).[60] Internal organization may include established institutions, informal and professional networks, and more or less formal SMOs. Many of the organizational forms involved in the generation of a movement may exist prior to it, and may be deeply involved in later movement mobilization. Contrary to collective behavior models, preexisting organization and not its breakdown aids the formation of movements. Challengers are generally excluded from routine, low cost access to state-controlled resources and decisions that affect them. The state responds to claims only of established, "legitimate" members of the polity; the interests of insurgents must be pursued outside conventional channels of power. Impolite tactics and strategies—rational methods for marginalized groups—are necessary to gain the attention of the state and established polity members. The model looks also to the responses of authorities to budding movements. Pervasive repression of challenging groups can snuff out movements before they have a chance to take root. The costs of mobilization and collective action can be raised to such a level as to force insurgents to withdraw their challenge. Blocking access to resources, arrest of leaders, and disruption of organizations are some of the varied means open to those in power to forestall movement challenges.

On the question of consciousness, McAdam considered "cognitive liberation" necessary for individual participation in movements.[61] For Christian Smith, "insurgent consciousness is a collective state of understanding which recognizes that social change is both imperative and vital."[62] It is not merely a self-interested, rational calculation, but includes emotion and will. Grievances are crucial to insurgent consciousness, but are not seen by process theorists as either unnatural or automatically giving rise to social movements. For Piven and Cloward, protest movements emerge after changes in both consciousness and behavior. Consciousness change occurs through three sequential stages: (1) the system and its leaders lose legitimacy; (2) people's fatalism gives way to assertions of their "rights" that imply demands for change; and (3) a new sense of efficacy develops.[63]

Movement emergence is also, finally, a response to expanding political opportunities, to a particular, dynamic political opportunity structure (POS).[64] As McAdam explained, "*any* event or broad social process that serves to undermine the calculations and assumptions on which the political establishment is structured occasions a shift in political opportunities. Among the events and processes likely to prove disruptive . . . are wars, industrialization, international political realignments, prolonged unemployment, and widespread demographic changes."[65] While mass society and other theories also stressed the importance of such events in protest etiology, the process model makes clear that social processes are filtered through the existing power structure. For Tarrow, the POS consists of four components: (1) the degree of openness of the polity; (2) the stability of political alignments; (3) the presence of allies; and (4) divisions within the elite and its tolerance of protest.[66] Political opportunity is subject to interpretation by the actors involved—opportunities are not always recognized and, even when visible, are not always seized. And political opportunity is subject to political space as constructed in struggles over the interpretation of what is possible. Thus, political opportunity calculations and cognitive liberation go hand in hand. See Figure 3.2.

FIGURE 3.2   A Political Process Model of Movement Origins

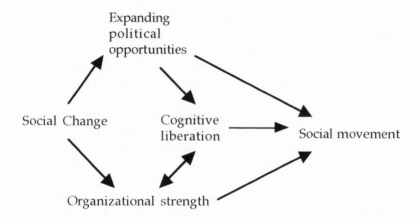

Source: Adapted from McAdam, *Political Process and the Development of Black Insurgency*, p. 51. Used by permission.

New Social Movement Theory

As we saw in our introductory discussion of NSMs in Chapter 2, a new stream of theorizing about social movements arose in Western Europe in the 1970s. The term "new social movement," now widely accepted, began as a modest "provisional collective term."[67] NSM theory shares with the collective behavior paradigm the conviction that social movements are the products of social change. It breaks with its New World predecessor in finding a theoretical base not in structural-functionalism or symbolic interactionism but in (neo) Marxism. Much NSM theory is situated in the specific context of debates about the transformation of twentieth-century capitalism. Because of its grounding in Marxism, it is able to raise broader questions about social movements than resource mobilization theory.

Alberto Melucci has worked to fundamentally rethink the conventional social science interpretations of social movements. His framework for analyzing movements in complex societies was founded on a rejection of both the nineteenth century view of movements as actors (heroic or villainous) on the stage of world history. It rejected too twentieth century views informed by Marxism, Freudianism and theories of deprivation that emphasized either the objective sources of collective action—the structural contradictions and crises of capitalism—or its subjective sources, people's psychological motivations, and the preferences that draw them together into a social movement. Melucci did not reject the totality of Marxism—he retained, for example, the "point that we live within a system which has a definite logic and definite limits."[68] But both nineteenth and twentieth century views, he thought, were founded upon the problematic assumption that movements are a personnage and that collective action is a unified empirical entity whose teleology can be discovered by analysts. Movements, he argued, have neither personalities of their own, nor are they the product of either institutional processes and "interests" generated by "the system" or the psychological preferences of their participants.

As we have seen, the term "social movement" has its roots in the nineteenth century and thus carries over a century's worth of heuristic and political baggage. Melucci provided a dual critique of the concept. First, he was critical of its metaphysical nature; it "expresses the idea that there is a central actor whose every action is caught up in a linear process of motion towards a final goal." Second he connected it to totalitarianism: "the vision of a new system of transparent power replacing the old and unjust system has claimed too many victims in our century. At the very least, respect for the victims obliges us not to feed such grandiose and dangerous illusions any longer."[69] Despite these qualms, Melucci still occasionally employed the term (though with refurbished meaning). These old views should be discarded in part, Melucci thought, because of the increased mobility and differentiation of the conflicts, actors and forms of action in contemporary societies. They need to be replaced by a view of movements as socially constructed composite action systems. Social movements must be considered delicate and heterogeneous social constructions. Collective action is always 'built' by people and takes place within the field of possibilities and restrictions presented them by social institutions. Movements emerge through the processes by which individuals communicate, negotiate, produce meanings and make decisions within these fields. Movements never function in a vacuum.

They establish relations with other actors, and through these interactions they produce meanings, express needs and constantly rework the context of these relationships. From these processes actors construct a "collective identity." Such identities, according to Karl Japp, involve flexible self-definitions of the actors, their social world, the goals of their collective action, and a loosely shared understanding of the social field of opportunities and constraints within which they act.[70]

Conflicts in complex societies are most likely in those arenas with the heaviest pressure on people to fall in line with institutions that manage information and symbolic codes. Corporations and the state are no longer the lone loci of power in postindustrial society. Power relations became more diffuse and less stark. They are now permeated with symbolic codes produced for the very purpose of veiling the flexing muscles of power. Consequently, societal control over its members' lives extends beyond the business and government office to areas formerly left more or less autonomous. Administration reaches into people's personal relationships, their health, safety and sex lives, the birth of their children and the death of their parents. And yet the same giant organizations which try to regulate and control the full range of citizens' lives also provide the resources—knowledge, money, communicative skills—which can facilitate individual autonomy. Here Melucci went beyond Habermas who stressed the long reach of institutions without explaining the means by which citizens might struggle against them. While superorganizations may not contain the seeds of their own destruction, they do, argued Bergmann, produce malcontents, dissidents and those who would pose a challenge to their control.[71]

In his explanation of the rise of peace movements during the 1980s, Melucci pointed to the "changing political and military situation . . . [and] the further deployment of nuclear weapons in Europe."[72] Melucci opted for the term "mobilization" rather than movement to describe peace protest since peace movements are not unified entities but, like other recent collective actions, "multi-dimensional realities which converge, only in a specific conjuncture, on the ground staked out by peace mobilizations."[73] Military policy change provided the conditions for the appearance and crystallization of various dimensions of collective action into peace mobilizations. Melucci highlighted two key facets of the popular reaction to these changes. The first followed the political process model and saw the new peace mobilizations "explained almost entirely within the framework of national political systems." The anti-missile campaign was, argued Melucci, used by the Communist Party in Italy and by what remained of the New Left in West Germany to breath new life into their organizations. The second popular reaction to military policy change could be explained by Straub's Jürgen fear of war approach (type one) that stressed the objective worsening of superpower relations as a stimulus to movement mobilization but, at the same time, Melucci thought fear-inspired peace mobilizations could "be analyzed following classical analyses of crowd or aggregative behavior . . . as the sum of the atomized behavior of individuals."

The rise and occasional coherence of peace protest was more, for Melucci, than a reaction to changed military policies.

> Peace mobilizations also display a form of *moral utopianism*. This is not just a contemporary phenomena [sic]. Every social system contains a certain number of moralizing and totalizing expectations for happiness, justice and truth. These claims do not reside in specific social groups, and they do not involve specific interests or practical-historical projects. They live on the fringes of great religions or great cultural and political trends, in the form of small sects, heretical cults and theological circles. The great collective processes, such as the emergence of new social and cultural patterns, provide a channel for expressing this moral utopianism, which otherwise would survive only in marginal enclaves. . . . The contemporary international conjuncture provides a social and cultural opportunity for a form of collective action which has only casual links with the precipitating military situation.[74]

Third, argued Melucci,

> peace mobilizations are not only a reaction to recent military policies. Political actors have only a minor role in mobilization. The fear of the bomb does not explain the patterns of solidarity, organization and identity of recent collective action. These patterns of collective action are very different from aggregative behavior such as a panic. Moral utopianism would remain marginalized if it were not effected by collective processes which have their roots elsewhere.[75]

Melucci would have us look beyond the fear of nuclear war to "the whole planetary system" for an explanation of the 1980s peace movements.

This planetary system is marked by the centrality of information for the survival and development of complex societies. Life is socially constructed and artificial: witness the increased importance in daily life of the mass media. Space and time are redefined. Space loses it limits when whole libraries end up on CD-ROMs and anyone with a television can visit the outer reaches of the solar system thanks to planetary probes. The changing nature of power in complex societies, where it consists more and more of access to information and the ability to manipulate it, where it is found increasingly in the operational rationality of computer languages, organizational science, and electronic media techniques, makes, for Melucci, "the possibility of integrating individual experience above and beyond the standards of operational rationality . . . more and more difficult: there is no place [or time] for questions concerning individual destiny and choices to do with life, birth, death and love. The nuclear situation, which entails the possibility of total destruction, has to be considered within the framework just outlined."[76]

This consideration, for Melucci, proceeds in four points. First, the nuclear dilemma is paradoxical: it is the ultimate example of society's ability to intervene on itself, to artificially construct a self-reflexive social life. The root issue for peace mobilizations is the *"the self-production of the human species* at the individual and collective level [his italics];" it is the battle over the production and quality of life. Peace movements would give global society the power to determine its own existence in "a new set of relations among its diverse constituents (groups, interests, cultures, 'nations')." Nuclear war presents humanity with an unprecedented time-space conjuncture: instantaneous and global destruction. And the irreversibility of nuclear information mandates state confrontation with citizens and attempts at social control. Second, the problem of war and peace has for the first time ever become a truly global social question. Again a paradox surfaces: while in technological terms war is increasingly the domain of experts, its potential consequences make it a general social problem of universal concern. Third, problems of war and peace have transcended the limits of the state system which no longer has a monopoly of control over them. The struggle for peace unmasks the transnational character of the problems and the interdependence of the global system. A 'New World Order' becomes a realizable aim with the arrival of global interdependence. The decline of the state system is, for Melucci, "perhaps the fundamental message of contemporary pacifism." Fourth, the advent of nuclear weapons moved the threat of war to the realm of information, especially to the symbolic arena. As nuclear war means the end of life on earth, confrontation short of war is a symbolic battle for the control of information. Nuclear deterrence itself functions primarily as a symbol: "it intervenes in the information and representations of opponents by creating a mirror game in which every player tries to influence the other and to take advantage of the enemy's misperception."[77]

Conclusion

Whether the six clusters of social movement theory reviewed in this chapter can help explain the origins of the 1980s West German peace movement is problematic. Party failure theories emerged from the political and economic crises of the 1970s. They try to understand the new political formations which have arisen to challenge parties' traditional role in structuring participation and making policy. The deterioration of détente and growing superpower confrontation were further developments perhaps conducive to the emergence of the peace movement. The prospects of nuclear apocalypse may have contributed directly to protest potential. The memory of past wars combined with anxiety about possible future war may have helped create a large constituency for offensive action against the sources of fear: nuclear weapons and the governments who control them. The collective behavior paradigm's use of generalized beliefs, emergent norms, and meaning frames to explain movement origins holds promise. Smelser's concepts of precipitating factors, mobilization, and social control too seem necessary for a movement political sociology. RMT makes several claims about movement rationality, normality, and the central importance of organizations that are worthy of further investigation. The rational action approach within the RM paradigm makes clear that movements spring not from spontaneous emotional outbursts but from more or less refined calculations about the costs and benefits of collective action. The organizational-entrepreneurial RM approach helps to explain the importance of entrepreneurs and professional organizations in the creation and manipulation of discontent.

The political process model considers social movements primarily political rather than psychological phenomena, and claims that politics matters more for the rise and mobilization of social movements than does social or cultural change. Movements spring up when the levels of organization and potential adherent consciousness are sufficiently high, and when the political opportunity structure is conducive. NSM theory finds the roots of recent movements in social structural change: urbanization, rapid transportation and communications, and politically skilled citizens. NSM are reactions to deep social contradictions and unsolved problems. Taken together, the six perspectives appear to supply the wherewithal for understanding social movement origins. It is still too early, however, for conclusions about the usefulness of these theories in our particular case. Only after examining the West German anti-missile movement's organization, leadership structures, and some constituencies (Chapter 4), spectrums (Chapter 5), strategy and goals (Chapter 6), tactics (Chapter 7), and mobilization (Chapter 8), can we return, in Chapter 9, to assess the degree of fit between theories and movement.

Notes

1. Charles Tilly, *From Mobilization to Revolution* (Reading, MA: Addison-Wesley, 1978).

2. Melucci, *Nomads of the Present*.

3. For a generational analysis of changes in the world views of postwar West Europeans, see Stephen F. Szabo, ed., *The Successor Generation: International Perspectives of Postwar Europeans* (London: Butterworth, 1983).

4. My use of the party failure concept parallels the purpose to which Kriesi, et al., put the concepts of "national cleavage structures," "institutional structures and prevailing strategies," and "alliance structures." See the first three chapters of Hanspeter Kriesi, Ruud Koopmans, Jan Willem Duyvendak, and Marco G. Giugni, *New Social Movements in Western Europe: A Comparative Analysis* (Minneapolis: University of Minnesota Press, 1995).

5. Wayne C. Thompson and Peter Wittig, "The West German Defense Policy Consensus: Stable or Eroding?" *Armed Forces & Society*, vol. 10, no. 3 (1984), p. 339.

6. On the decline of political consensus see Lauber, "From Growth Consensus to Fragmentation in Western Europe;" and William E. Paterson and Alastair H. Thomas, eds., *The Future of Social Democracy: Problems and Prospects of Social Democratic Parties in Western Europe* (Oxford: Clarendon, 1986).

7. See Dalton, Flanagan, and Beck, *Electoral Change*.

8. On the decline of parties as governmental policymakers, see Peter H. Merkl, "Mapping the Temporal Universe of Party Governments," *Review of Politics*, vol. 47, no. 4 (1985).

9. For a review of the "ungovernability" or "crisis" literature, see Anthony H. Birch, "Overload, Ungovernability and Delegitimation: The Theories and the British Case," *British Journal of Political Science*, vol. 14 (1984).

10. Philippe L. Schmitter and Gerhard Lehmbruch, eds., *Trends Towards Corporatist Intermediation* (London: Sage, 1980); see also, Michael Noller, "Neocorporatism and Political Protest in the Western Democracies: A Cross-National Analysis," in Jenkins and Klandermans, eds., *The Politics of Social Protest*.

11. Peter Lösche, ed., *Parteien in der Krise: Das Parteiensystem der Bundesrepublik und der Aufstand des Bürgerwillens* (Munich: Beck, 1986).

12. Oskar Niedermayer and Richard Stöss, eds., *Stand und Perspektiven der Parteiforschung in Deutschland* (Opladen: Westdeutscher Velag, 1993).

13. Lawson and Merkl, *When Parties Fail*.

14. Lawson and Merkl, *When Parties Fail*, p. 9.

15. See Kay Lawson, "When Linkage Fails," in When Parties Fail.

16. James N. Rosenau, ed., *Linkage Politics* (New York: Free Press, 1969), and James N. Rosenau, "Theorizing Across Systems: Linkage Politics Revisited," in Jonathan Wilkenfeld, ed., *Conflict Behavior and Linkage Politics* (New York: McKay, 1973).

17. Lawson, *"When Parties Fail,"* pp. 17-18.

18. Robert Bellah, "Populism and Individualism," *Social Policy* (Fall 1985), p. 30.

19. Berger, "Politics and Antipolitics in Western Europe in the Seventies," p. 34.

20. Tilly, "Social Movements and National Politics," p. 310.

21. Alan Dawley, *Struggles For Justice: Social Responsibility and the Liberal State* (Cambridge: Harvard University Press, 1991).

22. Xandra Kayden and Eddie Mahe, Jr., *The Party Goes On: The Persistence of the Two-Party System in the United States* (New York: Basic Books, 1985).

23. Quoted in *Newsday*, February 23, 1983, p. 6.

24. Johnson, *Realism and Hope in a Nuclear Age*, p. 30.

25. Johnson, *Realism and Hope in a Nuclear Age*, p. 31.

26. Jürgen Straub, Hans Werbick and Walter Zitterbarth, "Friedensbewegung und Kriegsängste: Über einige Aspekte der Motivationalen Hintergründe Friedenspolitischer Aktivitäten," in Klaus Horn and Volker Rittberger, eds. *Mit Kriegsgefahren Leben: Bedrohtsein, Bedrohungsgefühle und Friedenspolitisches Engagement* (Opladen: Westdeutscher Verlag, 1987), pp. 95-98.

27. Bruce Russett and Donald R. Deluca, "Theater Nuclear Forces: Public Opinion in Western Europe," *Political Science Quarterly*, vol. 98, no. 2 (1983), p. 180.

28. See, for example, Ted Gurr, *Why Men Rebel* (Princeton: Princeton University Press, 1970); and Samuel Huntington, *Political Order in Changing Societies* (New Haven: Yale University Press, 1968).

29. See Anthony Orum, *Introduction to Political Sociology: The Social Anatomy of the Body Politic* (Englewood Cliffs, NJ: Prentice-Hall, 1978).

30. Aldon Morris and Cedric Herring, "Theory and Research in Social Movements: A Critical Review," *Annual Review of Sociology*, vol. 2 (1985).

31. Cited in Morris and Herring, "Theory and Research in Social Movements: A Critical Review," p. 146.

32. Joseph R. Gusfield, "The Reflexivity of Social Movements: Collective Behavior and Mass Society Theory Revisited," in Laraña, et. al, eds., *New Social Movements*.

33. Ralph H. Turner and Lewis Killian, *Collective Behavior* 2nd ed. (Englewood Cliffs, NJ: Prentice-Hall, 1972), p. 32. The first edition was published in 1957.

34. Kurt Lang and Gladys Lang, *Collective Dynamics* (New York: Crowell, 1961), p. 497.

35. Joseph R. Gusfield, "The Study of Social Movements," in Sills, ed., *International Encyclopedia*, p. 446.

36. Turner and Killian, Collective Behavior; and Ralph Turner, "Collective Behavior and Resource Mobilization as Approaches to Social Movements: Issues and Continuities," *Research in Social Movements: Conflicts and Change*, vol. 4 (1981).

37. Neil Smelser, *Theory of Collective Behavior* (New York: Free Press, 1962).

38. Morris and Herring, "Theory and Research," pp. 150-54.

39. Neil Smelser, "Social and Psychological Dimensions of Collective Behavior," in *Modern Sociological Explanation* (Englewood Cliffs, NJ: Prentice-Hall, 1968), p. 8.

40. Robert Park, "Human Migration and the Marginal Man," *American Journal of Sociology*, vol. 33 (1928).

41. Smelser, *Theory of Collective Behavior*, p. 72.

42. Smelser, *Theory of Collective Behavior*, p. 117.

43. McCarthy and Zald, "Resource Mobilization and Social Movements," p. 1220.

44. Oberschall, *Social Conflict and Social Movements*, p. 29.

45. McCarthy and Zald, "Resource Mobilization and Social Movements," p. 1215.

46. Max Heirich, *The Spiral of Conflict: Berkeley, 1964* (New York: Columbia University Press, 1968).

47. Doug McAdam, "Culture and Social Movements," in Laraña, et. al, eds., *New Social Movements*, p. 43.

48. Morris and Herring, "Theory and Research," p. 161. On the free rider problem, see Mancur Olson, Jr., *The Logic of Collective Action* (Cambridge: Harvard University Press, 1965).

49. McCarthy and Zald, "Resource Mobilization and Social Movements," p. 1222.

50. McCarthy and Zald, The Trend of Social Movements in America, p. 20.

51. Oberschall, Social Conflict and Social Movements, p. 69.

52. See especially James Q. Wilson, *Political Organizations* (New York: Basic Books, 1973); Terry Moe, *The Organization of Interests* (Chicago: University of Chicago Press, 1980); and Edward Muller and Karl-Dieter Opp, "Rational Choice and Rebellious Collective Action," *American Political Science Review*, vol. 80 (1986).

53. Peter Evans, Dietrich Rueschemeyer, and Theda Skocpol, eds., *Bringing the State Back In* (New York: Cambridge University Press, 1985).

54. Hanspeter Kriesi, Ruud Koopmans, Jan Willem Duyvendak, and Marco G. Giugni, "New Social Movements and Political Opportunities in Western Europe," *European Journal of Political Research*, vol. 22 (1992).

55. Tarrow, "Struggle, Politics and Reform," pp. 4-5.

56. Christian Joppke, "Explaining Cross-National Variations of Two Anti-Nuclear Movements: A Political Process Perspective," *Sociology*, vol. 26, no. 2 (May 1992), p. 326.

57. Representative works include McAdam, *Political Process and the Development of Black Insurgency*; Tilly, "Social Movements and National Politics;" Gamson, *The Strategy of Social Protest*; William Gamson, Bruce Fireman, and Steven Rytina, *Encounters with Unjust Authority* (Homewood, IL: Dorsey, 1982); and, to some extent, Oberschall, *Social Conflict and Social Movements*.

58. McAdam, Political Process and the Development of Black Insurgency; see also, Aldon D. Morris, *The Origins of the Civil Rights Movement* (New York: Free Press, 1984).

59. Joppke, "Explaining Cross-National Variations of Two Anti-Nuclear Movements."

60. McAdam, *Political Process and the Development of Black Insurgency*, pp. 44-48.

61. McAdam, *Political Process and the Development of Black Insurgency*.

62. Christian Smith, *The Emergence of Liberation Theology: Radical Religion and Social Movement Theory* (Chicago: University of Chicago Press, 1991), p. 62.

63. Piven and Cloward, Poor People's Movements, pp. 3-4.

64. Sidney Tarrow, "National Politics and Collective Action: Recent Theory and Research in Western Europe and the United States," *Annual Review of Sociology*, vol. 14 (1988); see also Hanspeter Kriesi, "The Political Opportunity Structure of New Social Movements: Its Impact on Their Mobilization," in Jenkins and Klandermans, eds., *The Politics of Social Protest*.

65. McAdam, *Political Process and the Development of Black Insurgency*, p. 41.

66. Tarrow, "Struggle, Politics and Reform," p. 34.

67. Dieter Rucht, "The Study of Social Movements in West Germany: Between Activism and Social Science," in Rucht, ed., *Research on Social Movements: The State of the Art in Western Europe and the USA* (Frankfurt: Campus, 1991), p. 178, fn. 6.

68. Melucci, *Nomads of the Present*, p. 186.

69. Melucci, *Nomads of the Present*, pp. 188-189.

70. Karl P. Japp, "Selbsterzeugung oder Fremdverschulden: Thesen zum Rationalismus in den Theorien sozialer Bewegungen," *Soziale Welt*, vol. 25 (1984).

71. W. Bergmann, "Was bewegt die soziale Bewegung? Überlegungen zur Selbstkonstitution der 'neuen' sozialen Bewegungen," in D. Bäcker, ed., *Theorie als Passion* (Frankfurt: Suhrkamp, 1987).

72. Melucci, *Nomads of the Present*, p. 81.

73. Melucci, *Nomads of the Present*, p. 81.

74. Melucci, *Nomads of the Present*, p. 82.

75. Melucci, *Nomads of the Present*, pp. 82-83.

76. Melucci, *Nomads of the Present*, p. 84.

77. Melucci, *Nomads of the Present*, p. 85.

4

Organizations and Constituencies

Amongst the laws which rule human societies there is one which seems to be more precise and clear than all the others. If men are to remain civilized . . . the art of associating together must grow and improve.

—Toqueville

Social movements transcend the organizations which are their skeletons; they are not unified empirical entities, but fragile, heterogeneous coalitions, composite social constructions. There is much more to a movement, in other words, than its constituent organizations. Yet, organizations as parts of skeletal support networks are the generators of movement action. Movements can be seen as organizations of organizations or as networks of networks. These networks, in the case of the West German anti-missile movement, were local, regional, national and transnational in scope. Movement organizations and the networks of which they are part, some grassroots and some overarching, are necessary objects of analysis for a political sociology of the peace movement. In the following section, I assess the general nature of the movement's organizational structure and leadership, and analyze the movement's decisionmaking and leadership structures. Section two examines some movement constituents: peace researchers, professionals and workers. I conclude with some reflections on movement organizations, structure, leadership and constituencies.

Organizations and Leadership

Movement leadership usually occurs in the context of organizations. Leaders of individual organizations can at the same time be leaders of the broader movement. Weber's concept of charisma can help clarify the roles of certain peace movement leaders. Two clearly charismatic peace movement leaders in the 1980s were Helen Caldicott and Petra Kelly. Caldicott, an Australian pediatrician and a founder of Physicians for Social Responsibility (PSR), became a leader of the global peace movement due to the acuity of her analyses of the arms race, her unflagging energy, and the power of her rhetoric. She is probably responsible for recruiting more activists in more countries than any other single movement leader. Kelly was a leading figure in both the Greens and the peace movement. She was a moving speaker and gained international prominence due to her attractiveness to the media. The aura of these women's leadership ranged beyond that of any specific organization. They came, over time and to the consternation of some, to speak for national and even transnational movements. But the movements and organizations these women led were not dependent on their leadership. PSR chapters around the world, and the Federal German peace and ecology movements, including the Greens, were quite capable of soldiering on in the absence of these charismatic leaders. In this way, new movements stand in sharp contrast to authoritarian or totalitarian "strong man" movements.

Gusfield suggested that movements may be either or both "undirected" and "directed." The undirected (or "new") movement or movement organization uses informal personal interaction to alter norms, values, and outlooks.[1] New SMOs tend to be decentralized, diversely organized, and "leaderless" with simple, temporary divisions of labor.[2] Gerlach's SPIN concept—segmented, polycentric, ideologically integrated network—describes groups of the "new" type.[3] By segmented or segmentary he means that an organization is a multicellular organism, it consists of different grouplets, committees, campaigns and initiatives of varying size, scope, aims, capability and duration. Polycentric refers to the decentralized, heterogeneous character of organizational leadership and decisionmaking. Structural, personal and ideological links integrate segments and leaders into reticulated systems or networks. Networks have fuzzy boundaries that extend outward as new nodes are added to the network. Networks usually lack a single headquarters but have nodes of special influence where a number of segments intersect.[4] Groups come and go with considerable frequency, and this is often either acceptable to or even the intention of organizers. Indeed, new groups may be seen as "disposable" by those who organize them.

The directed (or "old") movement or movement organization has structured groups with identifiable programs, formal leadership, definitive ideology, and clear goals. Directed groups also tend to be centralized and strongly led, with a sharp division of labor. Today, old groups can be found mostly in labor movements. And the model is under siege even there with the rise and success of groups like Teamsters for a Democratic Union (TDU) in the United States and the Workers Party (PT) in Brazil. The bureaucratization characteristic of directed movements helps prevent factionalism, but the most common impetus for the development of centralized organizational structures is the need for money. Foundations and other funding bodies prefer to support groups that appear solidly grounded. Construction of governing boards, of committee structures, and the appointment of officers is seen as evidence for such grounding. My experience during the late eighties as a participant in LABWATCH, a student group opposed to University of California management of the nuclear weapons laboratories at Livermore and Los Alamos, confirmed the tendency of groups to adapt their structures to the exigencies of grantsmanship. We appointed "officers," created a committee, shuffled the requisite papers, attended meetings, and otherwise conformed so as to qualify for funding from the student government, colleges, departments, and the campus-wide administration. While the organization would have been considerably less active without the money (to pay honoraria for invited speakers, travel costs, event preparation, etc.), we were able to rationalize the involuntary bureaucratization through our belief that 'playing the money game' had not negatively affected us. We held the same views and retained the same consensus decisionmaking style, did not moderate our goals, were not coopted by the University, and refrained from 'selling out.' The point is that the successful procurement of funding (and we were wildly successful by campus standards) need not lead a group down the path of unwieldy bureaucracy, authoritarian leadership, or institutionalization. The funding imperative need not lead inexorably to the creation of old-style groups. Many of the largest and most influential of the West German peace organizations were connected directly or indirectly to larger parents which were sources of funding—trade unions, parties, churches, and professional associations.

The Federal German peace movement of the 1980s consisted of both new and old groups. The numerous smaller, grassroots citizen peace initiatives tended toward the new model. The larger, longer-lived, professionally-staffed groups shared characteristics of the old model. Numerically, the new groups predominated; nary a German town or city neighborhood was without one. In organizational capacity and muscle, the old groups were clearly superior. They were the moving forces behind the major campaigns, the mass demonstrations, and large-scale public education. The media reported the action and views of both types of organizations, although those recognized as national spokespersons of the movement emerged from the big groups. In practice, many activists participated alternately or simultaneously in the work of both types of organizations.

Four key concepts—grievances, resources, opportunities, and meaning—which arise from social movement theory are useful for an examination of Federal German peace movement organizations, their strategy, and their mobilization. As we have seen, the collective behavior tradition and the fear of war approach (and NSM theory to a lesser extent) focused primarily on grievances. Resource mobilization theory is alert to resources and opportunities. Meaning (and identity as one component of meaning) has recently been the concern of new social movement theorists. Party failure theses encompass all four concepts. The theoretical model deployed in this chapter stems from these four central concepts and is quite simple.[5] The nature of a peace movement organization is determined by its internal and external environments. Features of the internal environment—leadership and decisionmaking structures—regulate the mobilization and allocation of resources, the interpretation of grievances, and the evaluation of opportunities. Allies and antagonists (which circulate in the external environment) condition the organization's political opportunity structure, and aid an organization's construction of meaning. Answers to the questions of how and why resources are accumulated and invested (questions that are functions of both internal and external organizational operation) determine organizational effectiveness in pursuit of internal and external goals.

As it developed, the movement gave rise to and experienced both centripetal and centrifugal forces. The tendency to simultaneously centralize and decentralize was a source of tension within the movement while at the same time one of its greatest strengths. The centripetal force stemmed from the natural desire on the part of major organizations and their leaders to coordinate and combine their efforts in order to maximize movement mobilization. The imperatives of media management (press conferences and releases, interviews, etc.) also encouraged bureaucratization and professionalization. Forging coalitions and alliances between like-minded groups is generally sound organizational policy. The movement grassroots (die Basis) can be seen as one source of centrifugal force. While in some cases eager for direction from the center, many local peace initiatives (Friedensinitiativen) were just as likely to operate happily independent of the core. The Greens and the Independ-

ents were another decentralizing source. Ideologically opposed to centralization, these two groupings fought what they considered the will to
power of the center.

The German peace movement is not unique in undergoing, at once,
these contradictory tendencies; they can be observed in most new movements of consequence. The question of which organizational path a
movement should take—toward the periphery or toward the center—is
ultimately unresolvable. Directional decisions, if made at all, are usually
unenforceable and may contribute to factionalism. To further compound
the dilemma, if perennially postponed, the tensions framed by the question can lead to a decline in political effectiveness. One means by which
to manage the problem, to live with if not answer the question, is to create intermediary links between core and periphery, and this the movement eventually did. The Coordinating Committee (Koordinationsaus-
schuß, Koordinierungsausschuß or CC) was the movement's central
communications and decisionmaking body. One step up from the grassroots were the Regional Peace Assembly Action Conferences at the big
city and state level (Regionale Aktionkonferenzen Friedensversammlun-
gen). Above the regional conferences were three Action Conferences—
South, West and North—at the inter-state level. The next step toward the
center were the national Action Conferences which elected the Coordinating Committee which in turn elected an Executive Committee
(Geschäftsführung) which sometimes appointed a Speaker. See Figure
4.1. Although provisionally developed during the campaign against the
Euromissiles, this structure was not formally adopted until 1984.

The Executive's power was two-fold: the preparation of strategy papers for discussion, and direct contact with the news media.[6] All press
releases had to be cleared by the CC and appeared as unsigned collective
products. Some 28, focused on substantive issues, were released between
May and December 1983 (during peak movement mobilization). The idea
was to counter the media's taste for stories directly related to events. The
movement leadership's concern about "transparency" led it in 1983 to
issue an open invitation to reporters to attend CC meetings. Despite efforts to prevent the "personalization of leadership," media requirements
for dealings with articulate and charismatic spokespersons led to the
creation of "media stars," a source of never-ending controversy on the
CC. Jo Leinen, a leader of the BBU and its representative on the Coordinating Committee and Executive, became just such a familiar face on
television due to his qualities as "the man every mother would love to
see as her son-in-law" (Volkmar Deile). The high profile of some movement leaders relative to other activists understandably caused some tension within the movement. The CC alternated between leaving important
decisions to the Executive and the postmaterialist distrust for appara-

FIGURE 4.1   The Movement's Decisionmaking and Communications
Structure

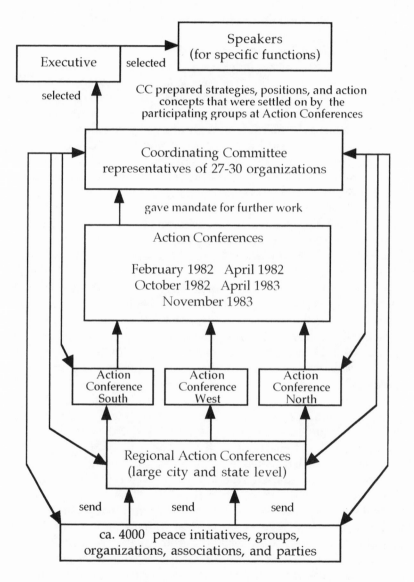

Source: Adapted from Leif, *Die Strategische (Ohn-) Macht der Friedensbewegung*, p.
140. Used by permission.

tchiks. Considered to have overstepped its authority, the Executive gave rise by December 1983 to a "negative coalition" on the CC led by the Greens and Independents. It was replaced that month by a Task Force (with essentially the same if slightly expanded membership). The ineffectiveness of the new body led to its replacement by a new Executive in July 1984.

Action Conferences were the Coordinating Committee's organizational means to prepare for large events, exchange information, and coordinate strategy. The Action Conference as peace movement organizational device was pioneered in 1968 by 'old' pacifist groups who participated in the Extraparliamentary Opposition. It was an Action Conference in Kassel in 1979 that first brought the old peace and new ecology movements together—led by the DFG-VK and the BBU—into the new peace movement. This sparked the first joint demonstration (Bundeswehr Day) in October 1980. The BBU and the Greens cooperated in an Action Conference in June 1981, and the first national Action Conference of the new peace movement was held in February 1982.

A centralized organizational overview is available through an examination of the CC at the height of mobilization in 1983.[7] Officially open to any and all interested parties, in practice meetings were attended only by "insiders" and a "everyone-knows-everyone-else climate" prevailed. It was clubby and insular. Grassroots activists paid little attention to the meetings of the CC, were apprehensive about central attempts at control, and suspicious of the imperfect transparency of CC meetings. The minutes of these meetings were not published. The CC sprang up as the structurally fluid successor to the "Bonn Breakfast Rounds" or "breakfast club" (Frühstückrunde) held to exchange information and plan the massive October 1981 demonstration. The breakfast club developed out of networks constructed at and after the nineteenth Protestant Church Convention in Hamburg during June 1981. Two leading Christian pacifists, Ulrich Frey and Volkmar Deile, sent personal invitations to representatives of 22 organizations to discuss the potential for transnational cooperation.[8] These early meetings during the summer of 1981 included two representatives from the Dutch "Stop de Neutronenbom" campaign and the Interchurch Peace Council (IKV). They were present to "internationalize" the movement, an ongoing effort that found its origins here during the early stages of the German national movement. The self-conception of the West German anti-Euromissile movement always included a transnational dimension in addition to its local and national character. To work for peace was for many German pacifists an inherently human task that transcended cleavages of race, creed and ideology. German activists made trips abroad and created networks that spanned the Atlantic and crossed geopolitical lines. The German-Dutch connection was the oldest and the closest. The autumn 1981 events were to take place in the Netherlands and Belgium as well as the Federal Republic. The Germans present at the early meetings included Leinen, Lukas Beckmann, Roland Vogt, Deile, Gregor Witt, Achim Maske, Manfred Kühle, Frey, Eva Quistorp and representatives of various Christian groups. These individuals were or would become leaders in their own organizations and in the Coordinating Committee. These organizations are listed in the Appendix, and their relative representation on the CC is illustrated by Figure 4.2.

By early 1984, the spectrums had become institutionalized to the degree that the CC assigned each a representative to plan Action Conferences. The organizational diversity of the Committee naturally gave rise to conflict. According to Diana Johnstone,

> Relations between individuals and groups . . . are often stormy and quarrelsome. Yet somehow the thing does not fly apart, and the work gets done. The idea seems to be that for conflicts to be resolved, they must first be brought out into the open and clarified. This is very demanding both intellectually and emotionally.[9]

Johnstone thought the "Coordinating Committee was both more authentically democratic in the way it was put together and more efficient in the work of coordinating than the somewhat 'more self-appointed' leadership of comparable American structures such as the anti-war mobilization committees during the Vietnam war." This assessment, one I share, is a consequence of the experience of the lead members of the CC. They were veterans of the new social movements of the sixties and seventies and had learned from previous mistakes. In the tug and pull of everyday activism, coalitions among the spectrums on specific strategic questions shifted. Majorities were fleeting, and an organization normally content in one spectrum might find itself in agreement with groups in another. Generally, the Greens and Independents found themselves together on issues. The Christians could be found between the positions taken by the Social Democrats on the one hand, and the Greens/Independents on the other. A "traditional spectrum" made up of all groups besides the Greens, Independents and some Christian organizations most frequently put together majorities in the CC.

Members of the CC represented both their individual organizations and diverse tendencies within the movement. The influence of individual groups within the CC was a function of several factors: size of membership, organizational capacity, programmatic strength, media coverage, and the credibility of their political positions.

FIGURE 4.2   Representation of Groups on the Coordinating
               Committee

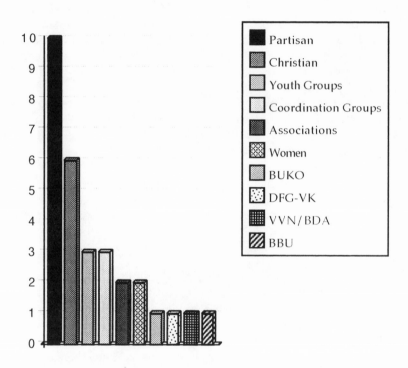

Source: Adapted from Leif, *Die Strategische (Ohn-) Macht der Friedensbewegung,* p. 31. Used by permission.

Peace Researchers, Professionals, Workers

Groups organized along occupational lines played a significant and visible role in the peace movement. Perhaps the most important were peace researchers, but numerous doctors, lawyers, teachers, and others could be found in the front ranks of the movement. Many of the professionals were typical new social movement members: young, highly educated, left-libertarian and affluent.[10] Others were older veterans of previous peace, civil rights, environmental, or student campaigns, or were initiated into extraparliamentary politics by the anti-missile movement in the early eighties. Professionals may be distinguished from their fellow concerned citizens and opinion leaders in that they brought their particular skills and specialized knowledge to the problem of peace in the eighties. Due to the respect shown the masters of technique in advanced industrial societies, physicians could hold forth credibly on the medical consequences of nuclear war, attorneys were paid heed on the legality of nuclear weapons, and psychologists could lecture about the psychic price paid for living in the shadow of the bomb. This section examines the role and character of the peace research, professional, and other occupational contributions to the movement.

Peace Researchers

The peace movement drew on the expertise of independent "counter-experts" and those from peace research institutes in its attempts to diagnose security policy problems, pose solutions to them, and inform the public of the findings. Research results were integrated into the prodigious output of topical defense policy books pouring forth from the typewriters and word processors of journalists and other movement sympathizers during the early eighties. Peace researchers performed an enormously important service for the movement.[11] Without the alternative strategies proposed by researchers—nuclear-free-zones, no first use of nuclear weapons, nonoffensive defense, social defense, conversion of defense industries—the movement would have remained simply a negation. It would not have been able to present genuine, workable alternatives to real, existing NATO doctrine. The alliance between movement and peace researchers was indispensable, and one of the movement's greatest strengths.

Some (neo)conservatives were critical of the marriage of the movement and certain sectors of the peace research community. Peace research has since its infancy been charged with producing "politicized science;" these charges, heard again while peace researchers aided the anti-nuclear power, environmental and women's movements during the 1970s, resurfaced once more during the Euromissile years. Yet, Karl Heinz Koppe—former director of the national peace research organization—describes one of the goals of peace research as developing ways in which "the interest of public opinion in the problem of peace could be awakened."[12] As circulated and popularized by the movement, peace research findings helped do just that. Karl Kaiser, former chairman of the German Society for Peace and Conflict Research (DGFK) and a scholar with impeccable Atlanticist credentials, described the goal of peace research as "research into the deep seated social, psychological and technological conditions of peacelessness and the presuppositions for creation of a more peaceful world."[13] According to a report of an academic council which was instrumental in procuring public funding, peace research was to be:

> engaged [in] aiming at a transformation of existing relations to the degree to which they are characterized by non-peace and the conduct of conflicts with violence. . . . Among the tasks of peace research is the elaboration of conceptual models which are directed not only at the overcoming of immediate causes, but also aim at the transcendence of deep-seated grounds for violent conflict through development of new forms of human order and interaction. The presuppositions, plausibility and practicability of such utopias must be examined in light of all available knowledge and methods.[14]

There can be little doubt that peace researchers, perhaps especially when in league with the movement, lived up to Kaiser and the council's mandate.

West German peace researchers have several homes and are of several persuasions. A handful of institutes are long-lived, well-funded and prestigious such as the Frankfurt Peace Research Institute (HSFK), and the Institute for Peace Research and Security Policy (IFSH) in Hamburg. Researchers at these two facilities, both founded in 1971 as manifestations of the increased concern about war and peace raised by, on the one hand, the student movement, and on the other hand, the onset of superpower détente, tend to pursue what might be called "mainstream" research; that with a focus on armed conflict, arms control, weapons systems, and defense doctrines. Research findings tend to be mildly critical of established policy; concern about scientific objectivity and credibility with policymakers caused these researchers to keep it at arm's length a movement with which they sometimes sympathized.

Others, including the relatively new but widely-known Research Institute for Peace Policy, also known as the Starnberg Institute, are considerably closer to the movement. Alfred Mechtersheimer, the founder and head of the Starnberg Institute, published several highly influential critiques of NATO policy, as well as a peace policy news service for subscribers and the media: MEDIATUS. Sometimes pursuing research agendas not much different than the state-supported institutions, findings tend to be more critical of the defense status quo. There may also be differences in methods and underlying philosophy. "Critical" peace research, a radical variety of inquiry into the problems of war and peace, makes no attempt to curry favor with the powerful, is committed to a fundamental overhaul of liberal democratic society, and is typically housed in universities.

The alliance between peace researchers and the movement, sometimes close, sometimes uneasy, is similar to that between specialists and non-specialists found in other movements. Disputes among contending technical experts—government and corporate versus movement—was a feature the West German peace movement shared with the anti-abortion, anti-fluoridation, and anti-nuclear power movements in the U.S.[15] These disputes among experts display four common characteristics: opposing experts sometimes address different questions, talking past each other, a practice that can confuse the uninitiated; "facts" (policy goals, the number and quality of armaments) are ambiguous; experts often exaggerate the strength or significance of their findings and views; a given "fact" may be variously interpreted, and experts tend to choose the interpretation that favors their side. Debates between established security policy authorities and the counter-experts of critical peace research networks and the peace movement displayed these four attributes at various times.

Counter-experts were no doubt aided in the sometimes fierce discourse with the authorities by the atmosphere of generalized distrust in government, by their lack of a personal stake in the controversy (their political futures did not ride on the outcome), and by the marked lack of public confidence in the peaceful intentions of the Reagan administration. Nonetheless, the huge success the movement had in mobilizing active support, evidenced by mass demonstrations, blockades, and petition campaigns, as well as passive support as registered in public opinion polls, was perhaps a sign that the counter-experts more than held their own against the specialists from the NATO politico-military complex and the strategic studies community.

Peace researchers, journalists and other professional friends of the movement worked to bridge the knowledge gap between the experts and the masses in the anti-missile movement.[16] "Everyone an expert" was an unofficial slogan of the movement. European citizen expertise on defense issues during the early-1980s typically came after these citizens had already been mobilized by the threat of new nuclear weapons. Tens of thousands of citizens knew enough initially to oppose the Euromissiles; what they later learned from sympathetic experts about launch-on-warning, MIRVs and circular error probable "rationalized" their fears and made many of them extraordinarily articulate and thus more effective challengers of elite decisions. The transformation of a significant sector of the West German populace into specialists capable of taking on politicians and strategic technocrats—the result of an unprecedented public education campaign—was one of the two main contributions of peace researchers to the movement's cause (the other was the formulation of alternative security strategies discussed above).

Professionals

A partial list of professionals involved in the movement includes: physicians, pharmacists, architects, soldiers, computer scientists, journalists, jurists, teachers, mathematicians, philosophers, physicists, psychologists and psychoanalysts, authors, social scientists, athletes, and employers.[17] Professional participation shared five common features: organization along occupational lines; a sense of responsibility for peace based on professional ethics; the performance of a legitimation function; the introduction of occupation-specific technical expertise into the security policy debate; and controversy within and without the profession as to the rectitude of participation. Examples illustrating each of these five characteristics follow.

Physicians were probably the best organized and funded of professionals' peace organizations. Their message during the Euromissile years was loud, frightening and influential. Concerned particularly with the medical consequences of nuclear war, doctors were unambiguous about the outcome: demolished hospitals, no electricity or water, no emergency vehicles, personnel, or medicine, unparalleled death and pestilence. Organized on several levels (local through global), the world's peace-minded doctors were found most frequently in national sections of two groups: Physicians for Social Responsibility (PSR), an established group which mobilized in support of the 1963 Partial Test Ban Treaty, and the International Physicians for the Prevention of Nuclear War (IPPNW), formed in response to the nuclear predicament of the eighties, and recipient of the 1985 Nobel Peace Prize. Sponsoring numerous conferences and seminars to propagate their dread message, West German physicians marched in demonstrations, wrote an open letter to Youth, Family and Health Minister Heiner Geissler, and issued declarations. A specifically Federal German organization, Doctors Warn Against Nuclear War, published a popular pamphlet detailing the horror of nuclear war and explaining the fate of the medical community and facilities of Hiroshima. Following deployment, this group grew impatient with meetings, marches and appeals and counseled its members to "become more political," to "become more personally engaged," and to "lose our fear of civil disobedience and its consequences."[18]

Many members of Judges and Prosecutors for Peace were moved to participate in the movement out of a sense of ethical responsibility. For Ulf Panzer, a moving force behind the group and a Hamburg criminal law judge,

In a democratic state, law, justice and peace are different terms with the same meaning. In enforcing the law we work for justice, and justice and peace go together. There is no justice without peace, and no peace without justice. So judges in a democratic state must speak out if they see peace in danger, even if it's their own government that endangers the peace. That doesn't make any difference. We have to speak out.[19]

Panzer thought this a special responsibility of German judges, who were docile instruments of the Third Reich:

We feel that by being silent today we judges would be guilty again. . . . We feel we are right at the point of being used again to legitimate instruments of mass murder, of omnideath, really. We do that in our courts by declaring [nuclear weapons] to be legitimate property, which they are not. Or we do it by jailing or at least in Germany by fining people who try to stop those weapons from destroying us. We don't want to be part of that legitimating process any more.[20]

Journalists too relied on their ethical codes in justifying their opposition to the arms race. Journalists Warn Against Nuclear War specifically referred to the laws governing their profession in its call to tell the truth about the dangers of the Euromissiles, nuclear deterrence, and enemy images. The Media Peace Initiative saw its mission as the conversion of a majority of the public to movement values and goals. The power of the media to set the premisses of debate, influence public opinion, and publicize alternative social constructions of the peace problematic made newsrooms important fronts in the struggle for cultural hegemony.

Judges and Prosecutors for Peace organized in the fall of 1981 with a newspaper advertisement condemning the morality, legality and constitutionality of the Euromissiles sponsored by 140 jurists in West Berlin. Similar ads popped up elsewhere in Federal German papers; after a Munich judge wrote to the signatories, the organization began to take shape. These were lawyers who rejected the model of the disinterested or apolitical judge. They saw jurisprudence as inherently political and activist whether one supports or rejects nuclear weapons or private property. Judges played a significant role in defending the movement against criticism—emanating from the government and conservative media—that it was criminal, anti-democratic and an agent of Moscow. Panzer's group held a march through downtown Bonn complete with banners, bands and songs. Citizens were amazed to find judges and prosecutors demonstrating for peace. While representing a small minority of jurists—Panzer estimates ten percent took part in his group—the refusal of a vocal few to cooperate in the further militarization of society was impressive.

Natural scientists' interventions into the public debate over the missiles were also significant. Held in high esteem by both state and civil society, the pronouncements of mathematicians, physicists, biologists and chemists grabbed the attention of the media, put the government on the defensive, and affected the aura of technical expertise. Initially spurred to action by the example of the atomic scientists movement in the U.S., dissident scientists in the Federal Republic were not new to political controversy. The "Göttingen 18," whose members included renowned nuclear physicists Born, Gerlach, Hahn, Heisenberg, and von Weizsäcker, expressed their reservations about nuclear deterrence in a meeting with Chancellor Adenauer in 1957. And German scientists were eager participants in Pugwash conferences.[21] Professors Dürr, Starlinger, and von Ditfurth led scientific opposition to the Bomb in the 1980s through various organizations, including Natural Scientists for Peace, the International Physicists' Appeal for an End to the Arms Race, and several Max-Planck-Institutes. Their critique of nuclear deterrence, the Euromissiles, and NATO security policy was essentially indistinguishable from that of many other professionals and lay citizens. But the mantle of authority conferred on scientists in technocratic societies (especially those working in esoteric fields and discoursing on arcane matters) gave their pronouncements helpful to the movement a high profile.

Movement participation could be hazardous to one's career. Dozens of judges received reprimands from the Secretary of Justice and court presidents for their political activities. An administrative court in Kiel, however, reversed one disciplinary finding. Its ruling upheld the independence of the judiciary and the freedom of expression of individual jurists. Panzer was

> convinced that if the judges in . . . our country would unite and say we are so glad to have nuclear arms, no government official would say a word because it would reflect official opinion. . . . But as soon as you oppose certain things, then they come and say you have violated a judge's neutrality. There is no such thing as a neutral judge.[22]

Nor a neutral professional of any sort, and controversy over activism flared in other fields too. Engineers and scientists who refused to take Star Wars or other military research and development funds were roundly criticized by less discriminating colleagues and by state functionaries for tearing the sheer (but still symbolic) veil of scientific objectivity. Journalist Franz Alt was removed as lead editor of the Südwestfunk program "Report" for his sympathetic portrayals of the movement. Editor Norbert Pfister of the *Heidenheimer Zeitung* was disciplined for his commentary "We Have Only One Chance: Peace and the Renun-

ciation of Force." Teachers who marched in the street or developed pacifist curricula were set upon for polluting young minds. Architects who
railed against the idiocy of fall-out shelter construction were told to return to the drawing board. Intra-professional disputes, media attacks,
and bureaucratic condemnations did not, however, deter thousands of
knowledge workers from taking part in the movement.

Workers and Farmers

Workers whose jobs left dirt under their fingernails were also abun-
dant in the movement's ranks, though as Peter Glotz argued "the bulk of
the working class were more interested in their paychecks than in [arms
control proposals]." Many workers sympathized with the peace movement according to Glotz; "they thought it better kids were demonstrating
against war rather than for it," but would never themselves participate in
a demonstration or vote for the Greens. Unsurprisingly, a "smaller group
of workers resented the peace movement and people like [SPD leader
Erhard] Eppler" (who did not "act their age").[23] Hundreds of farmers
objected to the "Agricultural Assessment Decree" issued by the federal
farm minister Ignaz Kiechle in April 1983 and initiated Farmers Against
the Rearmament. The decree required all farmers to provide the state a
detailed list of their livestock and foodstuffs in preparation for a national
emergency. Older farmers recalled that similar measures were taken just
prior to the invasion of Poland in 1939; said one, "First came the laws,
then came the war."[24] The farmers insisted it was lunacy to think the
Federal Republic could feed itself if imports of petroleum, fertilizers, and
animal feed were cut off. They found it interesting that the new decree
was promulgated in the "rearmament year," without a reason given as to
why a new law was necessary, and complained that whereas the previous regulation of this sort—in force for fifteen years—had at least
seemed defensive, the new program could be also be activated "in
'alliance matters' without the consent of our Parliament."[25]

The German Trade Union Federation (DGB) pressed trade union
concerns about peace, although not as vigorously or honestly as many
members would have liked. Early peace movement attempts to reach out
to labor leaders were, according to long-time labor activist Wolfgang
Abendroth, rebuffed by the latter.[26] Abendroth recalls how the labor elite
verbally opposed the 1960s Emergency Laws (Notstandsgesetz) but
when the anti-Notstands movement scheduled a march through Bonn,
the DGB hierarchy scheduled a parallel event in Dortmund. Labor's aim
was to support SPD policy on the issue. Nonetheless, numerous labor
functionaries attended the demonstration in Bonn. Abendroth thought

the best time for a coalition between labor and NSMs was during the so-cial-liberal coalition years. But he thinks labor elites let opportunities slip away; the promise of a labor-peace movement coalition was unrealized. Due to pressure from its parent organization, the DGB-Youth had a diffi-cult time helping organize peace events, and some young workers were disciplined by the union federation. Abendroth considered the DGB's 1981 "Peace through Disarmament" proclamation a direct pro-govern-ment response to the challenge of the movement-sponsored Krefeld Ap-peal.[27] But the rapid mobilization of the anti-missile movement was more than most labor leaders could or wanted to resist. Workers, especially the young, flocked to the movement. Their participation helped over time to move labor unions closer to the peace movement. The DGB put forward a solidly pro-peace platform at its congress in May 1982. Defense spending was to be capped, new weapons programs ended, the German government was to more vigorously push the superpowers toward prog-ress in Geneva, and no new INF were to find their way to European soil. Later, at the period of peak movement mobilization in autumn 1983, the DGB hierarchy urged the rank-and-file to participate in protest actions. Individual unions also grew outspoken as the peace movement grew. The executive board of IG Chemie-Papier-Keramik sought to minimize any distinctions between labor and other peace constituencies: "Our en-gagement for peace in East and West stems from the same sense of social responsibility of all social groups."[28]

Conclusion

The analytically tidy boundaries between new groups and old groups tended to blur in their regular interactions. And the definitions of what was new and what was old also became murky. Grassroots concern with democratic process and egalitarian ideology spread to the older or-ganizations, and the federal-level concern with organizing huge rallies, publishing anti-missile propaganda, and influencing politicians trickled down to the local level. Moreover, several seemingly large organizations were actually coalitions of hundreds of autonomous local groups. Both types of organization considered the other parts of the same movement, working toward similar ends, if perhaps through different perceptual prisms and with possibly divergent means. The movement would have been a very different phenomenon—less broad, less deep and less visi-ble—without the combination of and cooperation between the new and old groups. Without the large organizations the movement would have wielded considerably less clout. Without the thousands of grassroots initiatives the movement would have lost its verve, its spontaneity and flexibility, as well as much of its local base. Each type had strengths and weaknesses; each made contributions appropriate to its organizational structure and leadership.

Centripetal and centrifugal forces within the movement were both strength and weakness. Leadership bodies were constructed to coordinate the action of the several levels of the movement. The various organizations that made up the Coordinating Committee represented the tendencies within the movement. Individual group influence within the CC was a function of size, organizational capacity, programmatic coherence, media coverage, and the credibility of their political positions. Movement communications and decisionmaking structure paralleled the federalism of the West German political system.

Peace researchers and professionals brought credibility and occupation-specific perspectives to the movement. Activists pointed to the opposition of natural scientists and said, "See, even the inventors of the Bomb oppose it." Sympathetic journalists covered IPPNW conventions and filed reports detailing the medical horrors of nuclear war. Publicists reviewed peace research institute publications and stressed the existence of alternatives to the security policy status quo. A public constantly bombarded with the appeals, open letters, advertisements, and entreaties of professionals it respected was a public more apt to identify with and participate in the movement. The substantive expertise of most professionals, with some notable exceptions, was of considerably less practical assistance to the movement than the symbolic power of that knowledge. Chemists and physicians were not necessarily more effective propagandists and organizers than sales people or social workers. Lawyers and professors were no better at painting signs and gathering signatures than farmers or housewives. While professionals arguably have an edge in areas like strategic planning, they were less likely to be found in the upper reaches of movement leadership than were the *other* sort of professionals (the political entrepreneurs discussed by resource mobilization theorists) who made dissent a career. But the mere presence of professionals, with their respected ethical codes, lent the movement a degree of legitimacy and credibility it would not have had otherwise. The state could not easily brand judges outlaws, physicians hysterical fear mongers, or biologists shiftless hippies. Farmers were not do-nothing drop outs, machinists lazy students, nor chemists dangerous subversives. These were solid citizens with specialized knowledge who came to the movement as personifications of that expertise. Most citizens came to the movement without the paraphernalia attendant to their means of making a living. They organized themselves along other familiar lines: political party identification, gender, ideology, connection to other new social movements and preexisting organizations.

Notes

1. Gusfield, "The Study of Social Movements," in Sills, ed., *International Encyclopedia*.

2. The original major study of new SMOs, a work which remains highly useful, is Gerlach and Hine, *People, Power and Change*.

3. Gerlach, "Protest Movements and the Construction of Risk," pp. 114-117.

4. John Lofland (with Michael Jamison), "Social Movement Locals: Modal Member Structures," in John Lofland, *Protest: Studies of Collective Behavior and Social Movements* (New Brunswick, NJ: Transaction, 1985).

5. My framework borrows from that presented in Bert Klandermans, ed., *Organizing for Change: Social Movement Organizations in Europe and the United States* (Greenwich, CT: JAI Press, 1989), p. 11.

6. This paragraph draws on Joyce Marie Mushaben, "The Struggle Within: Conflict, Consensus, and Decisionmaking Among National Coordinators and Grass-Roots Organizers in the West German Peace Movement," in Klandermans, ed. *Organizing for Change*, pp. 280-282.

7. My treatment of the CC and its constituent members owes much to Thomas Leif, *Die Professionelle Bewegung: Friedensbewegung von innen* (Bonn: Forum Europa, 1985), pp. 24-67.

8. Mushaben, "The Struggle Within," p. 276.

9. Diana Johnstone, "Peace," *In These Times*, September 21-27, 1983, p. 22.

10. Manfred Küchler, "Die Anhänger der Friedensbewegung in der BRD: Einstellungsmuster, Wertorientierung und Sozialdemographische Verankerung," in Anselm Skuhra and Hannes Wimmer, eds., *Friedensforschung und Friedensbewegung* (Vienna: VWGÖ, 1985).

11. Ulrike C. Wasmuht, ed., *Ist Wissen Macht? Zur Aktuellen Funktion von Friedensforschung* (Baden-Baden: Nomos Verlagsgesellschaft, 1992).

12. Herf, Jeffrey, "War, Peace and the Intellectuals: The West German Peace Movement," *International Security*, vol. 10, no. 4 (1986), p. 190.

13. Herf, "War, Peace and the Intellectuals," p. 186.

14. Herf, "War, Peace and the Intellectuals," pp. 188-189.

15. For details, see Peter Leahy and Allen Mazur, "A Comparison of Movements Opposed to Nuclear Power, Fluoridation, and Abortion," *Research in Social Movements: Conflicts and Change*, vol. 1 (1978).

16. This paragraph borrows from my "Knowledge as Power: Ecology Movements and Global Environmental Problems," in Ronnie D. Lipschutz and Ken Conca, eds., *The State and Social Power in Global Environmental Politics* (New York: Columbia University Press, 1993).

17. See Klaus Gerosa, ed., *Grosse Schritte Wagen: Über die Zukunft der Friedensbewegung* (Munich: List, 1984), for a compilation of materials from the professionals' peace organizations.

18. Excerpts from a pamphlet entitled "Ärzte warnen vor dem Atomkrieg," reprinted in Gerosa, *Grosse Schritte*, p. 108.

19. Quoted in James Douglass, "Judges Must Speak Out For Peace: An Interview With West German Judge Ulf Panzer," in Arthur J. Laffin and Anne Montgomery, eds., *Swords into Plowshares: Nonviolent Direct Action for Disarmament* (San Francisco: Harper & Row, 1987), p. 199.

20. Douglass, "Judges Must Speak Out for Peace," pp. 201-202.

21. See Helmuth Springer-Lederer, "Die Pugwash-Bewegung," in Skuhra and Wimmer, eds., *Friedensforschung und Friedensbewegung*.

22. Quoted in Douglass, "Judges Must Speak Out for Peace," p. 201.

23. From an interview with Peter Glotz.

24. Gerosa, ed., *Grosse Schritte*, p. 118.

25. Gerosa, ed., *Grosse Schritte*, p. 118.

26. Quoted in Frank Deppe, ed., *Friedensbewegung und Arbeiterbewegung: Wolfgang Abendroth im Gespräch* (Marburg: Arbeiterbewegung und Gesellschaftswissenschaft, 1982), p. 72.

27. Quoted in Deppe, ed., *Friedensbewegung und Arbeiterbewegung*, p. 73.

28. Gerosa, ed., *Grosse Schritte*, p. 134.

5

Spectrums

It is mind-boggling to think of the public expression of hope as a way of subverting the dominant royal embrace of despair.

—Walter Brueggemann, *The Prophetic Imagination*

The movement itself employed the concept of spectrums to distinguish between its various political and ideological tendencies. While imprecise (not all organizations neatly fit in one or another spectrum), the concept is still useful; an understanding of the diversity and internal politics of the CC, and consequently the leading organizations of the movement, is advanced through such categorization.[1] My concern with the sociology and origins of the movement mandates a focus on the larger, more influential groups. But this concern also makes an in-depth investigation of individual organizations impossible.[2] What follows is an analysis of the "membership" and politics of the five spectrums—Christian; Independent; KOFAZ (Communist); Social Democratic/Young Socialist; and Green—and of several nonspectrum groups (see Figure 5.1). The aim of these sections is to make clear the leading groups and tendencies of the movement. This is necessary for two reasons. First, to make clear the diversity within the movement. And second, to set the stage for future chapters, where in contrast to the relatively "still picture" of movement organizations presented here, I construct a "motion picture" of groups striving to set goals, formulate strategy, coordinate action, and mobilize resources.

FIGURE 5.1   Representation of Spectrums on the Coordinating
Committee

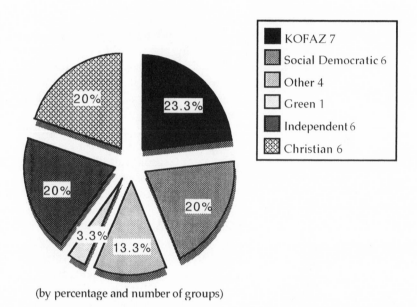

KOFAZ 7
Social Democratic 6
Other 4
Green 1
Independent 6
Christian 6

(by percentage and number of groups)

Source: Adapted from Leif, *Die Strategische (Ohn-) Macht der Friedensbewegung,* p. 34. Used by permission.

Christians

Protestants were more numerous, more active, and more visible in German peace movements than their Catholic brethren.[3] The Protestant church suffered more deeply from the rifts over peace and security issues among its congregants and was more open to discussion of these issues than its Catholic counterpart. Protestants took to heart theologian Karl Barth's views on war and peace.

The most important contribution that Christian ethics can make is to lift the whole problem inexorably out of the indifferent sphere of general

> political and moral discussion and to translate it into the personal question. . . . Killing is a very personal act, and being killed a very personal experience. It is thus commensurate with the thing itself that even in the political form which killing assumes in war it should be the theme of supremely personal interrogation.[4]

These were not the innocuous theological musings of impotent preachers, as claimed by movement critics, but a wake-up call for many Christians. As Kermit Johnson reminded us, "All theological reflection has a net effect of legitimizing or disestablishing the world as it is."[5]

Religious affiliation did not much affect people's attitudes toward the Euromissiles but made a significant difference in the propensity to participate in the movement against the weapons. A 1981 Emnid survey conducted for *Der Spiegel* found that 70 percent of the activists in the movement were Protestant, 17 percent Catholic, and 13 percent unaffiliated.[6] This contrasts with the religious affiliation of West Germans as a whole: 51 percent Protestant, 43 percent Catholic, and 5 percent unaffiliated. Four Protestant organizations were represented on the CC to two for the Catholics. There were also some joint Catholic-Protestant peace groups although none was so large or active to participate in the leading bodies of the movement. Steps toward Disarmament, one of the ecumenical groups, worked out a "gradual disarmament strategy" that counseled small unilateral phases in order to initiate momentum for greater progress. These were three: a ban on new nuclear deployments and reductions in current potential; a restructuring of the Bundeswehr into a genuinely defensive force; and a ban on weapons exports outside of NATO.

German Protestants, organized into the Protestant Church in Germany (Evangelische Kirche in Deutschland or EKD), had a dual impact on the peace movement. First, Protestants were a large presence within the movement both at its highest levels and at the grassroots. Organizations represented Protestants on the Coordinating Committee and at the Action Conferences, and local churches provided the structural focus for a large number of grassroots initiatives. The church was "penetrated" by the movement and the movement by the church. This was possible to a great extent because of the EKD's loose organizational structure and lack of concern for doctrinal purity. The church has three central bodies: a council, a church conference and a synod. The synod is of special interest because a number of leading peace activists were among its members during the Euromissile years, including Helmut Gollwitzer, Erhard Eppler and Theodor Ebert. The synod has 120 appointed members, half clergy, half laity. The synod may decide both ecclesiastical and public matters, and its annual meetings, events of great import to the church, provide for free-wheeling exchanges between clergy and laity. Peace issues came to dominate synod meetings during the early eighties. Individual pastors were able to take far more initiative and to more freely hold dissenting views than Catholic clergy.[7] The decentralized and relatively nonhierarchical character of the EKD stemmed from its difficult reconstitution immediately after the war. And the EKD itself was able to probe deeper than the Catholic church during the missile controversy. It could ask and pursue the more subversive questions. It wrestled with precisely those issues—the ethics of nuclear weapons, the morality of military service—that bedeviled it over two decades earlier during the first controversy over stationing nuclear weapons in the Federal Republic. And with the passage of time, the church and its adherents became less patient with the continued arms spiral and the growing threat to world peace. They could not ignore the fact that a moral situation only provisionally tolerable in the late fifties had worsened in the interim.

Second, despite the seemingly limited context of the debate over the double-track decision—ostensibly a controversy over the necessity of new nuclear missiles—a number of other difficult questions resurfaced during the imbroglio: the place of West Germany in the world, the question of religious socialism, the place of morality in politics, and the balance between political and military factors in the defense equation.[8] Christian peace activist Dorothee Sölle worked overtime to put these larger issues on the public agenda. Sölle, a widely known Protestant theologian, first came to prominence as an advocate of religious socialism during the height of the student movement in the 1960s. She was also a leading personality in the 1980s peace movement, delivered powerful speeches to the Hamburg church convention (Kirchentag) in 1981 and the June 1982 mass demonstration in Bonn, and became one of the movement's international emissaries. The "moralization" of the debate over the missiles provided Protestants a special role. Present in the peace discussion on both sides of the Atlantic, questions about the morality of nuclear deterrence were especially sharp for the EKD, a considerable part of which thought that security policy must never be separated from the moral cloud hanging over the successor state to the Nazi regime.[9] Opposition to nuclear missiles in the eighties, as rearmament and nuclearization before it in the fifties, furnished Protestants with an opportunity to atone for the sins of their fathers and grandfathers.

The EKD's numerous statements on peace during the missile controversy, although carrying substantial moral force, were not binding on individual Protestants. This is due to the fact the EKD is not a unitary church but a federation of autonomous provincial churches.[10] A wholly reformed institution from that which prevailed from the Reformation through the Wilhelmine, Weimar and Nazi eras, the EKD only loosely gathers Lutheran, Reformed and United sects together. Formerly closely linked with the German Empire, German Protestantism added a skeptical attitude toward the state as one consequence of its coming to grips with its generally shameful behavior during the Third Reich. The willingness to critically confront political power, the legacy of the heroic "Confessing Church" during the thirties and forties, made the EKD a natural forum for discussions of security policy. Each declaration was the product of fierce debate within the church and represented a concerted effort to compromise between congregants on both sides of the missile divide. Again, the church relived the conflicts it experienced during the debate over nuclear weapons in the fifties.[11] These carefully-honed pronouncements typically portrayed both sides' positions as legitimate and morally derived from Christian principles, although many critics claimed the EKD had gone over to the pacifists.[12] There is some validity to the critics' charge as we shall see. A backlash group of Protestants mobilized during the summer of 1980 to minimize the influence of peace groups within the Church. Safeguarding the Peace (Sicherung des Friedens) garnered signatures for its own petition which reiterated the state's right to defend its citizens against threats from within and without, and supported disarmament on the foundation of a military balance. Live Without Weapons (see below) was Safeguarding the Peace's nemesis in the battle for the allegiance of German Protestants on the missile question. The church directly if not fully lent its considerable social weight to the cause of the peace activists, giving the movement a moral aura vexing to the government.

Reconciliation Action/Peace Service (Aktion Sühnezeichen/Friedensdienste or ASF), the largest of the Protestant peace groups, was one of the most influential groups in the movement (its ideological mate in the U.S. is the Fellowship of Reconciliation). Formed in 1958 during the previous wave of anti-nuclear protest, ASF concentrated on several major activities during the Euromissile years. Thousands of ASF volunteers have participated in "peace service" work around the world including Israel and the U.S. Every November since 1980, Aktion Sühnezeichen sponsors its nationwide Peace Week under the theme "Create Peace Without Weapons" (Frieden Schaffen Ohne Waffen). ASF conducts antifascist work in the Federal Republic, publishes various informational pamphlets and press releases, and employed 25 in its Berlin office and in foreign countries. Opposed to the logic and practice of deterrence, ASF opposed the Euromissiles and was open to careful unilateral steps to end the arms race.[13] One of ASF's primary slogans in the campaign against the missiles was "No new nuclear weapons in the Federal Republic." It justified this unilateral formula as a first step toward mutual disarmament. Reconciliation Action, and its leader Volkmar Deile, first came to prominence in the new peace movement on account of its role—together with AGDF—in preparing the huge October 1981 demonstration in Bonn. It played a coordinating role among other Christian peace groups and a leading role in the movement as a whole because of its strict adherence to nonviolence, favorable assessment in the media, and willingness to take the initiative.

Service for Peace Action Community (Aktionsgemeinschaft Dienst für den Frieden or AGDF) was an umbrella organization for 18 Christian member groups, including ASF. Founded in 1968 and active in the Extra-parliamentary Opposition, AGDF stressed public education for peace and to this end organized seminars, conferences and courses. The organization churned out a large volume of books and other informational material for its members and other groups during the Euromissile years. Its member organizations came from a number of German Protestant traditions, including pacifists like the Quakers, anti-Fascists such as Reconciliation Action, and Third World aid groups like the International Christian Peace Service. Action Community rejected the formula "Peace service with and without weapons" arrived at during the 1967 Church Convention. The Church Convention is a biennial lay assembly which drew tens of thousands of German Protestants when it focused on peace issues in the early eighties. A compromise between those who thought the church ought to take a stance for conscientious objection and those who argued that one could wear a uniform, bear (nuclear) arms, and remain a good Christian, the 1967 agreement broke down by the early eighties. In its place AGDF substituted this pledge:

> I will do everything within my power to prevent the deployment of U.S. intermediate-range missiles in our country. I am prepared to discuss the question of nuclear weapons in my community. I declare myself for further calculated unilateral disarmament steps, beyond this first step, on the path to the abolition of all nuclear weapons.[14]

The formation of Live Without Arms (Ohne Rüstung Leben or ORL) was inspired by the 1975 statement of the World Council of Churches against militarism, and is intent on injecting pacifist themes into religious discussions. The World Council of Churches (WCC) also weighed in during the missile controversy. Like the German Protestants, the WCC moved from division over the extent to which a nuclear war could ever be considered just, to a position closer to traditional Christian pacifism.[15] Relying on ethical and moral arguments against war and its preparations, ORL was the hub of a network of 120 local groups who focused on witnessing for peace, fasting, and training for nonviolent direct action. ORL members signed a statement declaring their willingness to live without military protection and to do all they could to see that they got just such an opportunity.

The Protestant Student Associations (Evangelische Studentenge-meinden or ESG) was the Protestant college student voice on the CC and a major player in the June 1981 demonstration at the Hamburg Church Convention and in preparations for the demonstrations greeting President Reagan on his 1982 visit.[16] It was active too on the local level in university towns. Concerned with the connections among churches, universities and society, the ESG took progressive political stands on current issues: for alternative energy and against nuclear power, against the abuse of foreigners, on the side of internationalism and citizen initiatives, against the arms race, and so on. It remained true to the legacy of resistance of the Confessing Church (Bekennende Kirche), the circle of Protestants inspired by Karl Barth and organized by Dietrich Bonhöffer and Martin Niemöller during the Third Reich.

The Catholic church strongly supported Konrad Adenauer's defense policies in the 1950s.[17] Closely allied to the CDU/CSU, the church followed a postwar path widely divergent from its Protestant counterpart. Despite the church's early support for Hitler, its latent (and sometimes open) anti-Semitism, and its opposition to the Weimar Republic, it spent little time in moral confrontation with twentieth century German history. Prior to the Second World War, the church was monarchist and the (Catholic) Center Party had unanimously voted for the infamous Enabling Act of 1933, cheering Hitler's assumption of dictatorial power. Only a relative few individual clergy and laity were exceptions to this generalization.[18] While never incorporated into the Nazi-created "German Christians" as had been some Protestants, the church preached accommodation with the National Socialist regime, with the support of the Vatican and with few exceptions, even after Hitler violated the terms of the church-state modus vivendi, the Concordat.

Only since Vatican II and the papal encyclical *Pacem in Terris* has a more significant number of Catholics been drawn to peace protest. This is not, once again, to say that there was no Catholic presence in peace movements prior to the Second Vatican Council, only that it was far less extensive than that of socialists or Protestants.[19] The church changed in two discernible ways during the papacy of John XXIII: it became less hierarchical and more democratic; and it began to rethink the doctrine of just war and the role of nuclear weapons in defense and deterrence. Absent during the popular mobilization against rearmament and during the late fifties Struggle Against Atomic Death (Kampf dem Atomtod—the popular campaign against emplacement of the first nuclear weapons on German soil), radical Catholics organized into base communities (Basisgemeinden, modeled on those of the popular church in Latin

America), and took part in the 1970s battles against the Brokdorf nuclear facility, and the expansion of the Frankfurt airport. And yet by 1982, there were only three or four dozen such grassroots communities.[20]

Debate over the Euromissiles divided German Catholics as it had Protestants. The Central Committee of German Catholics, the federal organization for lay Catholic associations, took the side of the government in the dispute. The missiles were necessary to combat the Soviet push for hegemony in Europe, to right the military balance, and to shore up deterrence.[21] The Catholic youth organization (BDKJ), on the other hand, opposed the missiles on the grounds that fewer rather than more weapons were the answer to the security dilemma. Peace could only come about through education and confidence-building, not an arms race.[22]

Pax Christi represented German Catholics on the CC. The 80 or so Pax Christi groups in the Federal Republic stood for disarmament, nonviolent conflict resolution, and international understanding. Founded after the Second World War in France, Pax Christi began as people working for Franco-German reconciliation. Open to civil disobedience, the organization insisted during the missile years that participants undergo nonviolence training. Throughout the controversy, Pax Christi was a source of alternative security policy thinking within the church. It published a series of pamphlets with titles such as "What Can the Church Do For Peace?" and "Nonviolent Action and Citizen Initiatives," as well as a bimonthly journal *Problems of Peace Info.*

Radical Catholics found a home in the Church From Below Initiative (Initiative Kirche von Unten or IKvU) which also had a seat on the Coordinating Committee. A cousin to the base communities of the popular church in Latin America, the IKvU subscribed to a politicized Catholicism characterized by liberation and feminist theology, and worked for internal church reform.[23] Some fifty groups unconnected to the church hierarchy make up the IKvU, created in 1980. It took a strong stand against the missiles, and like Pax Christi, contended that security springs not from military hardware but from dialogue, cooperation and trust. The IKvU claimed the allegiance of some ten percent of the participants at the Catholic Church Convention in 1986. At this same convention, the chairman of the German Bishop's Conference, Cardinal Höffner of Cologne, declared that a good Catholic could not vote for the Greens (in the January 1987 election) because of their stands on abortion, premarital sex, and homosexuality. This brought the IKvU to the measured defense of the Greens, and caused a stir among Green Catholics like Hessian Environmental Minister Joschka Fischer who called the Bishops "pitiful cowards."[24]

Independents

The Unabhängigen or Independents (sometimes called the Autonomous peace movement) came together as individual activists and representatives of numerous initiatives and groups in the Federal Conference of Independent Peace Groups (Bundeskonferenz unabhängigen Friedensgruppen or BUF; the grouping formerly called itself Bundeskongreß autonomer Friedensinitiativen or BAF). Their union did not, however, extend much beyond this loose organizational coupling. Split into two wings—the Anti-militarists and the Anti-imperialists—their political differences were such that cooperation within the spectrum was problematic. One fundamental question divided the wings: can violence be used to combat the state? The Anti-imperialists, also known as "Autonomen," were those who met visiting American dignitaries with a hail of paving stones, and employed ball bearing-armed sling shots and Molotov Cocktails in their pitched battles with German police over vacant housing and nuclear power plants. Apart from the Communists (about whom more below), the Autonomen gave the peace movement a "bad name" with much of the press and public. The Greens came under fire for their general alliance with the Anti-imperialists.[25] Red Greens, former Communists who had undergone at least partial ideological conversions, had some sympathy for the young rioters. Green Greens and others from a spiritual or New Age background thought the party ought to have nothing to do with rowdies wearing ski masks, leather jackets and combat boots. Autonomen excesses provided critics with a welcome club with which to flail the otherwise nonviolent anti-missile movement.

In the run-up to the events of fall 1983, the Civil Disobedience Coordination Office (Koordinationsstelle Ziviler Ungehorsam or KOZU) coordinated the activities of the 1600 or so peace initiatives that constituted the BUF through the publication of a *Rundbrief* which provided dates of rallies and meetings, proposals for action, and discussions of strategy for the Independents. Based in Kassel, the office of the Coordination Office grew increasingly powerful as it generally stayed free of the wrangling within the BUF. The Greens provided financial assistance for the office prior to deployment, a task taken up by several leading Independent organizations in 1984. Dieter Schöffmann was the moving force behind the office and by 1984 had become the representative of the Independents within the CC's Executive.

The Federation of Nonviolent Action Groups (Föderation gewaltfreier Aktionsgruppen or FÖGA) had as its goal fundamental social change—a "nonviolent revolution"—leading to the end of the domination of human by human, the end of the destruction of nature, the creation of a decentralized and self-sustaining economic order, and to grassroots democracy. Suspicious of "parliamentary ways," the Federation had little trust in disarmament negotiations or appeals to governments. Instead, the demilitarization of society must be organized by the people themselves. The FÖGA ran nonviolence training sessions prior to actions and looked after conscientious objectors who also objected (for political reasons) to civilian service (Totalverweigerer). Its journal, *Grassroots Revolution*, listed during the missile debate the addresses of some 100 nonviolent action and "collective nonviolent resistance" groups (what in the U.S. anti-nuclear power and peace movements are known as "affinity groups").

The Women's Incitement for Peace Initiative (Initiative Anstiftung der Frauen für den Frieden or FfdF) came into being following the campaign of the Scandinavian Women for Peace to gather signatures on a petition condemning the superpower arms race for presentation to the UN-sponsored World Women's Conference. FfdF women and their sisters across North America and Western Europe linked the issues of gender liberation, the demilitarization of society, peace, and social justice.[26] The achievement of any one goal depended, they argued, on the achievement of the others. Active on the international scene, Women's Incitement for Peace took part in the peace camps at the Comiso Cruise missile site in Sicily and at Greenham Common air force base in Great Britain. Women's Incitement was one of the few autonomously organized women's peace movement groups to participate in the leading bodies of the West German peace movement. It became the representative of women on the executive board of the CC in 1982.

Issues of war and peace were among the various concerns of the Committee for Constitutional Rights and Democracy (Das Komitee für Grundrechte und Demokratie). The Committee was founded in 1980 to take part in the preparations for the Russell Tribunal on the situation of human rights in the Federal Republic. Many civil libertarians were alarmed at what they considered creeping authoritarianism accelerated by efforts to combat terrorism during the 1970s. In the anti-missile struggle, the Committee had a special interest in devising and publicizing alternative security policies through widely-circulated and influential books.[27] The Committee had a high profile in the movement during its peak period of mobilization as attested to by the publication of the widely-read "Peace Manifestoes" of 1982, 1983 and 1984. Numerous prominent citizens on its Council (including Heinrich Albertz, Walter Dirks, Helmut Gollwitzer, and Robert Jungk) provided the Committee with significant influence both within the movement and outside it in the larger public debate over the missiles. The Committee received outstanding coverage in the pages of the *Frankfurter Rundschau*—due to the group's excellent contacts at the paper— and was able to have its various policy prescriptions and texts published in the series *FR—Dokumentation*.[28] Apart from its Council, which represented the Committee to the outside world, its internal organizational structure included an advisory board of 80 prominent people and experts, 550 nonvoting supporting members, an eleven person executive board, and a secretariat in Sensbachtal headed by Hanne and Klaus Vack. The Committee created a Working Group to attend to its peace movement participation and it cooperated with a couple of other civil liberties organizations—the Gustav-Heinemann-Initiative and the Humanistischen Union—to publish the biweekly newspaper *Vorgänge* .

The heterogeneous West German Third World solidarity movement had a place in leading pacifist circles, and essentially merged with the larger peace movement during the early 1980s. A significant part of the Independent spectrum, the Federal Congress of Development Action Groups (Bundeskongress entwicklungspolitischer Aktionsgruppen or BUKO) was formed in 1977 to coordinate the activities of hundreds of local and regional solidarity groups. Throughout the 1980s, BUKO mobilized against U.S. intervention in Central America. Its presence at peace rallies ensured that the problems of El Salvador and Nicaragua were aired. Central American refugees were invited to retell their horror stories to the assembled, and hundreds of Germans volunteered to do development work in the region. BUKO actively opposed German arms exports to the Third World and criticized the activities of German multinationals in the developing world. BUKO's influence within the Independent spectrum was considerable and this carried over to the group's work within the Executive of the CC (which it entered in 1984). The BUKO journal, *Third World Information Center Papers*, was one of the solidarity movement's leading journals, widely-read in Austria and Switzerland as well as the Federal Republic.

KOFAZ

The important and well-organized Communist presence on the CC was known as the Committees for Peace, Disarmament and Cooperation (Komitees für Frieden, Abrüstung und Zusammenarbeit or KOFAZ) spectrum. The Committees coordinated the activities of organizations more or less close to the German Communist Party (DKP), and formulated and publicized the political proposals of the spectrum. Programmatic declarations of KOFAZ were quite unremarkable: there were calls for an end to the arms race, a deepening of détente, and greater understanding between states. Formed in 1974, its members during the anti-missile movement included Martha Buschmann (executive board of the DKP), Klaus Mannhardt (former chairman of the DFG-VK), Horst Trapp (German Peace Union), Christoph Strässer (former chairman of the Young Democrats), and anti-fascist pastor Martin Niemöller. KOFAZ described itself as a citizens' initiative committed to "public and concrete activities." KOFAZ came early to the 1980s peace movement—it is a classic example of a preexisting professional group—and organized a demonstration and rally in Bonn on the fortieth anniversary of the German invasion of Poland for which some forty thousand people turned out.

During CC strategy sessions KOFAZ always came out for mass actions versus other protest forms. According to Achim Maske, a KOFAZ leader, "the most radical actions are those with the most participants."[29] Other preferred KOFAZ instruments for public education were the mass leaflet and the mass newspaper. These appeared with titles such as "Are Disarmament and Social Reform Compatible?" and "Do Armaments Secure Jobs?" KOFAZ members went to great lengths during the missile controversy to assuage concerns about the Communist presence in the peace movement. According to KOFAZ leader Gunnar Matthiesen,

> The KOFAZ spectrum is not very different from the SPD at the moment, we have a somewhat further developed political understanding, i.e., the foundation of peaceful coexistence and a critical argument against anti-communism. That is what is really specific to the KOFAZ spectrum and why it is described as "Moscow directed." And accordingly this spectrum will always, as I see it, be only a part of the peace movement. It can thus never make a claim to leadership and does not want to anyway. . . . We have always been counted as partisan because we assigned the Americans primary responsibility [for the arms race] and not the superpowers. This alone among our positions is suspect.[30]

KOFAZ defended this position in strategy sessions and communiques of the CC, in its own publications, and in regular interviews with reporters of the DKP's daily, *Our Time*.[31]

The KOFAZ spectrum sponsored seminars, action conferences and public meetings. By the summer of 1984, KOFAZ was concerned about its inability to reach local peace initiatives. The institutionalization of the CC and its office in Bonn—which KOFAZ cheered—appeared to come at the price of far left influence over grassroots groups. Competition with the Krefeld Initiative (about which more later) for contact with neighborhood-based groups made outreach all the more difficult. KOFAZ efforts to mobilize the masses and to bring about the unity and coordinated action of the movement were always paralleled by efforts to cooperate within KOFAZ itself, an alliance within the larger coalition of the movement. Many differences existed within the organization, differences which while not outweighing the common views of the membership about the need for peaceful coexistence, cooperation with socialist states, and rejection of new NATO missiles, were sufficient to complicate its workings.

Closely allied to KOFAZ was the Socialist German Worker Youth (Sozialistische Deutsche Arbeiterjugend or SDAJ), the political youth organization of the German Communist Party. The SDAJ was typically more vigorous in its support of the "peace policy of the Soviet Union" than was KOFAZ. It made a point of trying to eliminate, within the movement, criticisms of East European regimes and declarations in support of the East German peace movement. Like KOFAZ, SDAJ considered mass rallies and the broadest possible peace movement sound strategy. Like its mother party, the SDAJ represented the position that the socialist states were the greatest allies of the peace movement in the capitalist world.

Women had their own organization within the KOFAZ spectrum. Women in the Armed Forces? We Say No! (Initiative Frauen in die Bundeswehr? Wir Sagen Nein!) was headed in the early eighties by Mechthild Jansen, a functionary of the DKP-oriented Democratic Women's Initiative and a member of KOFAZ. For Jansen, women had "become the motors of the peace movement." Opposition to the Euromissiles and to discrimination against women "are two sides of the same coin."[32] Of special concern to this group was the possibility women might, at some point in the not-so-distant future, be conscripted into the Bundeswehr. A topic for discussion on the op-ed pages of newspapers in the early-middle 1980s, it was a contingency that hinged upon the changing demographics of the West German population. Military planners feared that by early in the next millennium too few young men would be available for the draft and that the Bundeswehr would slowly but surely shrink below its half-million men force level. The problem was seen by some pundits as yet another unforeseen side-effect of the Pill. Pacifist feminists were not amused by the irony. Cheap, safe contraception had freed women from the iron cage of involuntary motherhood. Now it appeared the patriarchy would exact an additional price for women's liberation.

The Union of Nazi Regime Survivors/League of Antifascists (Vereinigung der Verfolgten des Naziregimes/Bund der Antifaschisten or VVN-BdA) fits neatly into the KOFAZ spectrum. Strongly opposed to the missiles, the group claimed that stopping deployment of the U.S. missiles would create the conditions to revoke Soviet countermeasures: the emplacement of SS-22s and SS-23s in Czechoslovakia and the GDR.

The Antifascists campaigned for what became standard movement fare: a nuclear-free-zone (NFZ) in Central Europe; acceptance of the Warsaw Pact's offer of a no-first-use (NFU) agreement; a nonaggression pact with the Pact; and massive reductions in conventional forces and defense budgets in Europe.

The Federal Pupils' Representation (Bundesschülervertretung or BSV; formerly the Konferenz der Landesschülervertretungen or KdLSV) can be counted among organizations close to the DKP because it was represented on the Coordinating Committee by representatives of KOFAZ. Elsewhere, the BSV took a course independent of any established political grouping. These junior high and high school students took most seriously the pledge (which became a mantra for most peace activists): "War must never again emanate from German soil." During the early eighties, the BSV favored détente, disarmament, economic conversion, a peace dividend (to be shared with the Third World), a nuclear-free Europe, and a ban on weapons of mass destruction. A regular target of pacifist student wrath were Youth Officers, those Bundeswehr personnel assigned to propagandize on behalf of the military in schools. The BSV worked to extend to schools the plebiscite on the missiles envisioned by the movement after deployment, and to recruit students for the annual Easter Marches.

The United German Student Associations (Vereinigte Deutsche Studentenschaften or VDS) represented the vast majority of college students—over 170 student associations—during the missile controversy. The VDS was a coalition of the most important political organizations in the student movement: the Young Socialists College Groups, the Marxist Student League Spartakus (MSB), the Socialist College Association (SHB), and the Liberal College Association (LHV). Despite this diverse membership, the VDS belongs in the KOFAZ spectrum because the MSB was the lead student organization on the CC. The VDS took part in the actions against the neutron bomb, helped collect signatures for the Krefeld Appeal, organized a demonstration around the theme "BAFÖG instead of Pershing" (BAFÖG is the federal student financial aid program) and participated in the giant Bonn rally of October 1981.

The German Peace Society (Deutsche Friedensgesellschaft or DFG), founded in 1882, is the oldest peace organization in Europe. In 1974 the DFG merged with the German affiliate of what is called the War Resisters League (International) in the United States, the United War Service Opponents (Vereinigte Kriegsdienstgegner or VK). The DFG-VK has long been the leading German organization working on behalf of conscientious objectors. Indeed, the organization hoped in 1983 to incite levels of conscientious objection high enough to practically and directly affect the Bundeswehr and Defense Ministry. Its approximately 20,000 members were organized into 200 locals during the early eighties. A chairperson oversaw an eight-person executive board and the group employed 15 in its business office in Velbert. Among the most visible, vocal and important of peace groups, the DFG-VK strenuously opposed the Euromissiles and hoped to make the double-track decision politically impossible to implement. The organization labored under the motto "Let us make our country nuclear-free, street by street, city by city" during the preparations for the large actions in which it took a leading role. The DFG-VK was among the most "realistic" during the INF negotiations, preferring incremental negotiated steps toward disarmament rather than utopian conceptions. Not all tendencies within the organization were pleased with this realist stance. During the height of the movement a "radical pacifist opposition group" regularly sought to have the organization change course; these radicals, especially strong in Baden-Württemberg, were far less patient with the negotiations than their parent organization. I was struck by their lack of faith in nuclear arms negotiations between the superpowers during interviews with some of the radicals in Freiburg in 1986.

Social Democrats

Left-wing SPD members and Young Socialists made up the bulk of the Social Democratic spectrum of the peace movement. The Jusos were among the first groups in the spectrum to reject the Euromissiles, an action taken at their federal congress in 1981. The SPD's youth organization wanted the Schmidt government to work within NATO to have the double-track decision cancelled. Like the DFG-VK and their mother party, the Jusos placed great store by the INF negotiations. The Jusos were obviously better situated to influence the SPD's stance toward the missiles than other peace movement organizations. And they tried to take full advantage of their status as (at least partial) insiders by directing most of their anti-missile activities at their own party. This internal pestering reached a high point at the Juso and Falken demonstration during the SPD's 1982 convention (Bundesparteitag) in Munich. The Jusos took part in the planning of the big demonstrations and were solidly in favor of movement unity, a position which manifested itself in opposition to any fragmentary tendencies that appeared in the movement and in the willingness of the Jusos to regularly switch coalition partners within the CC so as to prevent the solidification of blocs. Similarly, many Jusos thought it good for the peace movement to broaden its focus to include the 35-hour work week, the major goal of the DGB in the mid-eighties.

The Social Democratic Women's Working Community (Arbeitsgemeinschaft Sozialdemokratischer Frauen or AsF), an association of leftist women in the SPD, was closely aligned to the Jusos. They too had come out against the missiles as early as 1981 and worked to convert other Social Democrats to this position in opposition to their own parliamentary caucus and their own Chancellor.

The Initiative for Peace, International Compromise and Security (Initiative für Frieden, internationalen Ausgleich und Sicherheit or IFIAS) acted essentially as the organizational vehicle for left-wing Social Democrats within the movement. IFIAS found its roots in the Berliner Verband, formed in 1980, and populated by various prominent Social Democrats and other leading citizens. It took part in strategy sessions and discussions at the highest levels of the movement and its Director, Wolfgang Biermann, was welcome at the headquarters of the SPD while Peter Glotz was the party's business manager. In an issue of its periodical, *Peace and Disarmament*, IFIAS declared itself for a mutual, verifiable and immediate superpower nuclear freeze as the first step toward disarmament; for Western responses to Soviet INF negotiating proposals that, unlike "unacceptable 'Zwischenlösungen'" (interim solutions between full deployment and no missiles at all), would not automatically lead to the deployment of new intermediate-range missiles; against any nuclear doctrine which viewed nuclear war as manageable or winnable; for thinning out NATO and Warsaw Pact forces in the immediate vicinity of their shared border; for the recommendation of the Palme Commission to create a battlefield nuclear weapons-free-zone at least 150 kilometers wide on both sides of the East-West frontier.[33] IFIAS was also strongly against any drift toward violent action within the movement.

The Socialist Youth of Germany—the Falcons (Sozialistischen Jugend Deutschlands—Die Falken or SJD), was the SPD's children's and young teen's organization. It lined up with its older siblings, the Jusos, in its security policy stances. The Falcons recommended that the FRG "pursue a policy of détente even against the will of the U.S., not follow the double-track decision, disregard American pressure for increased defense spending, and use all negotiation possibilities and offers of the USSR."[34]

The DGB-Youth was by and large politically independent of its namesake, but played a role vis-à-vis the DGB somewhat like that between the Jusos and the SPD. The Youth held formal observer status in the CC. The Youth's attempts to get the DGB to throw its full weight behind the peace movement finally paid off when the DGB called upon its members to nonviolently participate in the mass demonstration on October 22, 1983 (an effort many thought too little too late). In general agreement with Social Democratic security policy positions, the Youth played a low-key role on the Coordinating Committee. The young trade unionists organized their March 1983 congress around the theme "disarmament is the imperative of the hour," called for participation in the Easter Marches that spring, and in the massive anti-missile actions that fall. The organization had a large presence at the DGB's annual Anti-War Days (held on the first of September), as well as at rallies held in solidarity with Solidarnósc in Poland, and was very active on the regional level. On the sensitive question of the movement's position toward fellow movements in the GDR and Eastern Europe, the Youth took a strong liberal stance. At the same time it declared its support for the unity of the West German movement, a contradictory position not easy to maintain. Accused of trying to split the movement for its support of Solidarity during the Easter activities in 1982, the Youth responded that it had simultaneously been called anti-American, pro-Soviet, anti-Communist, and disoriented. Rejecting such facile labels, Hans Brauser, federal secretary of the organization, called the charges "nonsense."[35] The DGB-Youth was, he argued, evenhanded in its criticism of the superpowers, and like other members of the Social Democratic spectrum, placed much faith in the potential of arms control negotiations to ease regional tensions and lead to disarmament.

The Gustav-Heinemann-Initiative (GHI), founded in 1978 by prominent personalities from politics, society and the churches was named for the highly respected former West German president. Devoted to the advance of civil liberties and human rights, the Initiative's founders included such luminaries as Erhard Eppler, Walter Jens, Carola Stern, Kurt Scharf and Helmut Gollwitzer. The Initiative worked for the democratic rule of law, democratic socialism, social reform, Third World development and other worthy causes. Heinemann resigned as Interior Minister in Adenauer's first cabinet over his opposition to rearmament, and his name connoted the principled rejection of war and violence. While taking a back seat to more aggressive groups in the workings of the CC, the GHI published books, held annual congresses, wrote open letters to politicians and churches, produced a film about the missile controversy, worked on alternative security conferences and saw itself as a forum for internal peace movement discussions.

Greens

The Greens were, since the founding of the federal party early in 1980, closely linked to the peace movement.[36] The early development of the federal party to a large extent overlaps the mobilization of the movement.[37] The Greens were fortunate to piggyback their broader agenda on the wave of peace movement activism. Constructed on the principles of ecology, grassroots democracy, social responsibility, and nonviolence, most Greens firmly believe that a nonviolent society can only be achieved with nonviolent ends. During the early 1980s, the Greens favored abolition of NATO and the Warsaw Pact, cancellation of the double-track decision and removal of the SS-20s, removal of all nuclear, biological and chemical weapons from the world (which could begin with the Federal Republic), removal of foreign troops and weapons from Germany, and long-term abolition of military defense and nuclear deterrence and their replacement by "social defense." These positions were shared by both wings of the party, the Realos, "realists" willing to cooperate and enter into coalitions with established parties and state power, and the Fundis, "fundamentalists" opposed to any compromise with those they saw as responsible for militarism and environmental degradation. By the late eighties, a third faction, the Zentralos, smaller than the other two, appeared. The Zentralos tried to mediate, for a while and with some success, between the antagonistic wings. Their efforts ultimately failed to prevent the splintering of the party with the exit of Jutta von Ditfurth and the most unyielding Fundis.

The Greens played a unique part within the leading bodies of the movement. While poorly represented at Action Conferences, Lukas Beckmann, their veteran representative on the Coordinating Committee, bound them close to the Independent spectrum. Beckmann was able to wield considerable power within the CC on account of the Greens' status as political party and especially because of the media attention focused on them for their unorthodox ways and refreshing flair. The Greens' high profile—Petra Kelly became an international celebrity—led to grumbling within the movement. From the perspective of a number of other organizations, the Greens took credit in the press for the hard work of others. When calling Kelly's office prior to the events of autumn 1983, people found that they could not obtain the anti-missile action information they were after. Instead they had to call the Coordinating Committee whose chair was BBU leader, Jo Leinen. The BUF called on the Greens to more closely coordinate their activities with those of the Independents. A working group on Green peace policy was coordinated by one of the members of its Bundestag caucus. This policy evolved via several party-sponsored meetings including "The Nuremberg Tribunal Against First Strike Weapons and Weapons of Mass Destruction" (February 1983) and "Security Policy Conceptions for Europe After Deployment" (December 1983).

The party preferred resistance to militarism (e.g., civil disobedience) to mass demonstrations and used its position in the Bundestag after the March 1983 elections as a platform from which to bedevil the government with motions, plenary debates and requests for information, and with grueling interrogation sessions.[38] Much of this parliamentary offensive focused on Federal German and NATO security policy, including especially the Euromissiles, Star Wars, and AirLand Battle 2000 (a U.S. Army doctrinal "modernization").

Nonspectrum Groups

The major organization in this pool of groups not easily categorized as belonging to one spectrum or another was the Federal Association of Environmental Protection Citizen Initiatives (Bundesverband Bürgerinitiativen Umweltschutz or BBU), the umbrella association for some 800 ecology movement citizen initiatives. Founded in 1972, the BBU came to the peace movement because of its concern about the destruction of the natural world and the piggish consumption of natural resources by military-industrial complexes. The BBU predicted that wars over raw materials were an inevitable product of industrialism and militarism (an impressive analysis years in advance of the Gulf War). This coalition of grassroots environmentalists pushed for serious progress toward disarmament, opposed nuclear, biological and chemical (NBC) weapons, and the ecological destruction caused by military maneuvers. The wide breadth of the BBU gave rise to internal disagreements over the nature of the organization and its strategic direction. Some thought the mainstream faith in arms control misplaced, others that the BBU should be less willing to interact with state authority and take a stance similar to that of the Green Fundis.

These conflicts were especially sharp in 1983. At the BBU's annual convention, Jo Leinen, the highly respected Speaker of the group (who also had become a media star), declared that he would only continue in office provided the organization continue along the path of nonviolence, nonpartisanship, and willingness to talk with state institutions. Despite Leinen's electoral victory (and those of other board members who supported him) at the convention, the internal disputes continued—and surely contributed to Leinen's decision to accept Social Democratic Premier Oskar Lafontaine's offer of the Environmental portfolio in the Saarland several years later. Near the end of 1983, Leinen's representation of the BBU at the "deescalation talks" between the peace movement and government officials riled some ecology activists, including the editors of *Environment Magazine*, the BBU's widely circulated monthly. The core of the debate concerned the BBU's relations with the SPD, considered too cozy by some critics.

The BBU, perhaps next to only ASF, had the greatest political influence within the leading bodies of the peace movement. This was partly due to its presence, from the very beginning of the new peace movement, at all planning sessions and in the management of the Coordinating Committee. And part of the credit goes to Jo Leinen who was extraordinarily adept at garnering publicity for the BBU. The BBU took an unwavering stance on behalf of nonviolence, was a strong supporter of the East German peace movement, and was open to compromise with other organizations. This ability to cooperate and its high media profile gave the BBU a central role in the movement.

The Liberal Democrats (Liberale Demokraten or LD) split from the FDP to create their own social-left liberal alternative. Organizationally weak and member-poor, the LD was not very influential on the CC. Opposed to the missiles, the Liberal Democrats thought the peace movement could apply pressure to the Geneva arms control negotiations in order to forestall Euromissile deployment.

The Young Democrats (Jungdemokraten or Judos) were the other liberal group on the Coordinating Committee. At one point leaning on the FDP for support, after the Free Democrats' recognition of the Young Liberals as their youth organization, the Judos began to shrivel quickly without the mother party's backing. Many members left for the Greens. Those who remained steered the group into tactical coalitions with the Independents, the KOFAZ spectrum, and the Social Democratic spectrum.

The Democratic Socialists (Demokratischen Sozialistischen or DS) mobilized first as a left-wing opposition group within the SPD as the conflict within the governing coalition heightened early in 1982, and left the party altogether after the demise of the Social-Liberal coalition that autumn. Determined anti-fascists, anti-capitalists, and anti-militarists, the DS came to the peace movement with a decided preference for cooperation with social movements as part of its political work. The DS opposed not only the double-track decision, but also its conventional counterpart, the Rogers Plan. The Democratic Socialists opposed induction of women into the Bundeswehr, weapons exports, and close scrutiny of conscientious objectors. In the 1984 European elections, the DS teamed up with the Communists as part of the Peace List and worked closely with the KOFAZ spectrum within the peace movement. As the DS had few members and a weak organization, its influence on the Coordinating Committee and at Action Conferences was minimal.

Conclusion

The concept of spectrums is a useful means by which to distinguish between the movement's diverse political and ideological tendencies. It is through spectrums that we gain an understanding of the policy positions of the movement's leading organizations and the internal politics of the Coordinating Committee.

Diverse constituencies gave the movement its breadth and depth.[39] Few institutions or social units were left out of the Federal German nuclear debate in the 1980s. From the school to the church to the workplace, grassroots peace initiatives and larger professional organizations pressed their case against the missiles and for a disarmed and demilitarized world. No German was unaware of her precarious position sandwiched between East and West. No German could be oblivious to the presence of foreign troops and military exercises on and above her national territory. With the rise of citizen initiatives and the decline of détente, the failure of parties and the "success" of rapid socioeconomic change, hundreds of thousands of Germans came to actively participate in the peace group of their choice and millions more to sympathize with the movement's cause.

We now understand the movement's structure, leadership, main organizations and spectrums. We move in the next three chapters to round out our sociological portrait with an analysis of movement strategy and goals, tactics, and mobilization.

Notes

1. My account draws on that of Leif, *Die Professionelle Bewegung*, pp. 26-58. Further comprehensive discussion may be found in Aktion Sühnezeichen-/Friedensdienste und Aktionsgemeinschaft Dienst für den Frieden, eds., *Bonn 10.10.81: Friedensdemonstration für Abrüstung und Entspannung in Europa* (Bornheim: Lamuv Verlag, 1981), pp. 197-221.

2. The best comprehensive single-volume treatment of individual movement organizations is Thomas Leif, *Die Strategische (Ohn-) Macht der Friedensbewegung: Kommunikations- und Entscheidungsstrukturen in den Achtziger Jahren* (Opladen: Westdeutscher Verlag, 1990).

3. My analysis of the variations between Protestants and Catholics as peace activists owes much to the account of Alice Holmes Cooper, *The West German Peace Movement of the 1980s: Historical and Institutional Influences* (Ann Arbor: University Microfilms, 1988). This work, Cooper's dissertation, is the single best work in English on the institutional role of the churches in the 1980s peace movement.

4. Karl Barth, *Church Dogmatics*, 4 vols. (Edinburgh: T. and T. Clark, 1961), vol. 3, p. 466; cited in Johnson, *Realism and Hope in a Nuclear Age*, pp. 10-11.

5. Johnson, *Realism and Hope in a Nuclear Age*, p. 57.

6. See the analysis of Peter Nissen, "Prospects for a Realignment of the West German Party System: The Impact of Oppositional Movements and the 'Green Party,'" paper presented to the conference "When Parties Fail: Paths of Alternative Action," Hutchins Center for the Study of Democratic Institutions, University of California, Santa Barbara, May 19-20, 1982.

7. Cooper, *West German Peace Movement*, pp. 204-207.

8. Cooper, *West German Peace Movement*, p. 158.

9. Erwin Wilkens, ed., *Christliche Ethik und Sicherheitspolitik* (Frankfurt: Evangelisches Verlagswerk, 1982).

10. For more on the development of the EKD, see Frederic Spotts, *The Churches and Politics in Germany* (Middletown, CT: Wesleyan University Press, 1973), chapter 1.

11. See "Protestantismus und Pazifismus" in Helmut Donat and Karl Holl, eds., *Die Friedensbewegung: organisierter Pazifismus in Deutschland, Österreich und in der Schweiz* (Düsseldorf: Econ Taschenbuch, 1983), pp. 313-314. On the tensions within the church during the nuclear debates in the early eighties, see Dietrich Strothmann, "Mit der Kirch Über Kreuz: Vom Altar zum Aktionismus—Die Schwierigkeit ein Protestant zu sein," *Die Zeit*, December 31, 1981, p. 7.

12. See, for example, Evangelische Kirche in Deutschland, ed., *Frieden Wahren, Fördern und Erneuern: Eine Denkschrift der EKD* (Gütersloh: Gütersloher Verlagshaus Gerd Mohn, 1981), pp. 37-38.

13. ASF, "Ein Vorschlag zur Auseinandersetzung—Keine neuen Atomwaffen in der Bundesrepublik," in Lutz Plümer, ed., *Positionen der Friedensbewegung: die Auseinandersetzung um den US-Mittelstreckenraketenbeschluss—Dokumente, Appelle, Beiträge* (Frankfurt: Sendler, 1981).

14. EKD, *Frieden Wahren*, p. 37.

15. Michel de Perrot, ed., *European Security: Nuclear or Conventional Defence?* (Oxford: Pergamon, 1985).

16. EKD, ed., *Deutscher Evangelischer Kirchentag Hamburg 1981: Dokumente* (Stuttgart: Kreuz, 1981).

17. This paragraph draws on Spotts, *The Churches*, chapters 2 and 4.

18. For more on Catholic peace activism during this period see the entries on the "Katholische Weltjugendliga" and "Katholizismus und Pazifismus" in Donat and Holl, eds., *Die Friedensbewegung*.

19. Beate Höfling, *Katholische Friedensbewegung Zwischen Zwei Kriegen: Der "Friedensbund Deutscher Katholiken," 1917-1933* (Waldkirch: Waldkircher Verlag, 1979).

20. Thomas Seiterlich, "Basisgemeinden in der Bundesrepublik," *Frankfurter Hefte*, vol. 37, no. 9 (1983).

21. "Zur aktuellen Friedensdiskussion. Eine Stellungnahme des Zentralkomitee der deutschen Katholiken," *Herder Korrespondenz*, vol. 35, no. 12 (1981), pp. 624-630.

22. Hans-Otto Mühleisen, "Grundstrukturen der Friedensdiskussion in der Katholischen Kirche," *Politische Studien*, vol. 33, no. 261 (1982), p. 44. See also Norbert Glatzel and Ernst Josef Nagel, eds., *Frieden in Sicherheit: Zur Weiterentwicklung der Katholischen Friedensethik* (Freiburg: Herder, 1981).

23. See Peter Hertel and Alfred Paffenholz, eds., *Für eine politische Kirche: Schwerter zu Pflugscharen—Politische Theologie und basiskirchliche Initiativen* (Hannover: Schmidt-Kuster, 1982).

24. "Dieses Getto hat der Kirche nie gutgetan," *Der Spiegel*, September 15, 1986.

25. See "'Alles oder nicht—egal, aber storno.' Die Autonomen—der militante Ableger der Friedensbewegung," *Der Spiegel*. no. 39 (1983); and "Ist die Spaltung perfekt? Der Graben zwischen Autonomen und Gewaltfreien wird grösser," *taz*, July 12, 1983.

26. Carolyn Strange, "Mothers on the March: Maternalism in Women's Protest for Peace in North America and Western Europe, 1900-1985," in Guida West and Rhoda Lois Blumberg, eds., *Women and Social Protest* (New York: Oxford University Press, 1990).

27. Klaus Horn and Eva Senghaas-Knobloch, eds., *Friedensbewegung— Persönliches und Politisches* (Frankfurt: Fischer, 1983); and Das Komitee für Grundrechte und Demokratie, *Frieden mit anderen Waffen—Fünf Vorschläge zu einer Alternativen Sicherheitspolitik* (Reinbek: Rowohlt, 1981).

28. See, for example, "Komitee für Grundrechte und Demokratie für eine Menschenkette von Bremerhaven bis München," *FR—Dokumentation*, April 25, 1984.

29. Quoted in an interview in *Hamburger Rundschau*, February 16, 1984.

30. Excerpted from the interview with Matthiesen by Thomas Leif in his *Die Professionelle Bewegung*, p. 40.

31. See, for example, Lorenz Knorr, "Massenbewegung gegen Atomkriegsplanung," *Wissenschaft und Frieden*, vol. 1, no. 2 (1985).

32. Mechthild Jansen, "Rundbrief zur Vorbereitung des Frauentages im Rahmen der Aktionswoche der Friedensbewegung," September 1983, p. 1.

33. *Frieden und Abrüstung*, 7 (no date), p. 42.

34. Verein für Friedenspädagogik, ed., *Friedenserziehung in der Jugendarbeit* (Tübingen: Verein für Friedenspädagogik, 1982), p. 143.

35. See his speech to the DGB-Youth's Easter 1982 rally, organized around the motto "Easter 82—For Peace through Disarmament—Solidarity With All Oppressed Peoples," reprinted in *JW-Dienst*, April 28, 1982.

36. Steve Breyman, "Social Movement Theory, the New Social Movements, and the Greens," paper delivered at the Annual Meeting of the American Political Science Association, New Orleans, August 1985.

37. Ferdinand Müller-Rommel, "Social Movements and the Greens: New Internal Politics in Germany," *European Journal of Political Research*, vol. 13 (1985).

38. E. Gene Frankland, "The Greens: Parliamentary Challenges and Responses," paper delivered at the Annual Meeting of the American Political Science Association, New Orleans, August 1985.

39. Rüdiger Schmitt, "Was Bewegt die Friedensbewegung? Analysen zur Unterstützung des sicherheitspolitischen Protests der achtziger Jahre," *Zeitschrift für Parlamentsfragen*, vol. 1 (1987).

6

Strategy and Goals

The train called "history" is never going to deposit its passengers at the destination of their choice unless they themselves take over the controls.

—Georg Lichtheim

The strategy, tactics, goals and mobilization of movements and their organizations are closely interwoven. Heberle argued that "in politics, the distinction between strategy and tactics cannot be so sharply drawn as in the theory of war, but it is nevertheless important."[1] The former concept stems from the Greek strategia, the office of a general, which is derived from stratos, an army. Even in the art of war it is unclear where strategy leaves off and tactics begin. Military scientists typically use the terms strategy or strategic to refer both to overarching plans to cover all contingencies of a campaign, and to that class of weapons whose use implies the final end of war. The reliance on martial language here invites unintended connotations, and apart from remarking in passing on the irony of drawing on it in a work about a peace movement, these intimations are not of much concern. Euphemisms hold no allure here, and the ancient terms remain useful when thinking and writing about peace movement politics or politics of other sorts.

Peace movement strategy encompasses the communication, planning, and interaction connected to ends or goals. Strategy and goals are tightly linked concepts. I take a catholic approach to the analysis of movement goals. I rely on both the movement's self-understanding of what it was about, and on hermeneutics. No movement sociology would be complete without an analysis of strategy and goals. The treatment of tactics and mobilization would be disembodied without prior clarity as to why the movement acted and mobilized resources.

Strategic Programs

The analytical frameworks of three leading peace movement strategists—Johan Galtung, Theodor Ebert, and E.P. Thompson—serve to outline the strategy and goals of the movement. Ebert put forward a metastrategic analysis of the movement in his 1980 call for an alliance between the peace and ecology movements.[2] It reads (in part) as follows:

1) Decisive changes in the international system stem from domestic political conflicts and structural changes. Social movements are the engines driving these changes.

2) The constitutional founding fathers of the Federal Republic assumed that active citizens would take part in political parties and that these parties and large associations would mediate the will of all citizens. They did not trust social movements.[3]

3) Social movements emerge when the internal contradictions of the basic decisions of a political system become plain. A process of growing social protest is characteristic of social movements.

4) The basic political decisions of the Federal Republic took place in the foreign policy context of western integration and membership in NATO, and in the domestic policy context of reconstruction with market economy methods on the foundation of private ownership of the means of production.[4]

5) The latent internal contradictions of these basic decisions were that (a) western integration also meant the division of Germany; (b) military defense within the bounds of NATO threatened the German people; and (c) progress with the market economy mechanism unfolds at the expense of the Third World and in view of the "limits to growth," must lead to the devastation of the global ecosystem.

6) The established parties and associations of the Federal Republic defend the practicality of these basic decisions against their latent contradictions. At the beginning of the republic the SPD and the trade unions still sought to change these basic decisions (e.g., through the Struggle Against Atomic Death movement).

7) Since then, the large associations and the parties represented in the Bundestag made peace with the basic decisions and references to their latent or already open contradictions were forbidden. The early interest of these established institutions in internal democracy

faded; they were unable to carry through with alternative socio-political concepts. To date, the Protestant Church . . . is the only large institution that offers wide latitude to the criticism of social movements.

8) The first social movements in the Federal Republic took on only single contradictions and failed to overcome them because of the contradiction's particular appendages, to wit, the latency of the other contradictions.

9) The social compass and program of the ecology movement makes it so far the broadest social movement in the Federal Republic. It envelops the points of the peace movement, the movement which brought it foreign and defense policy objectives and the method of nonviolent direct action.

10) The strategic goal of the ecology movement is the ecological in-corporation of our ways of life into the continuation of the human-istic tradition and its ideals of liberty, equality and fraternity. The general goal of protection of life binds it to the peace movement.

This is the macrohistorical and political context of peace movement strat-egy. Useful in placing the movement in a geopolitical moment, this analysis is too abstract to act as more than the most general guide for movement strategy.

Galtung provided a several point program for the movement that recommended investigation of defense alternatives, and narrows the strategic focus.[5] It is useful here in edited, summarized and condensed form:

1) The movement needed to vigorously advocate alternative strate-gies, especially the move from offensive to defensive weapons.[6] For Galtung this was a question about what sort of mix of con-ventional military elements and structures, and what sort of paramilitary and nonmilitary elements one wants in their defense forces. He cited a division on the basis of rank within the military as to openness to these new ideas. Younger, lower and middle ranking officers were, unsurprisingly, more open to decentral-ized, highly mobile small units than were generals.

2) A careful decoupling from the superpowers was a prerequisite for a more peaceful world. This was an option that presented many possibilities but required that some NATO member-state(s) stand up for a NFU policy. Peace movement anti-nuclearism spurred a fiery debate within NATO and strategic studies circles about con-tinued reliance on a first-use policy. While not a new proposal, it was given new life by the movement, and when endorsed by re-spected former officials—the so-called "Gang of Four"—caused a

considerable stir.[7] A key distinction between the Gang of Four and German peace researcher NFU proposals was the question of NATO's conventional forces. The former American officials suggested they required strengthening prior to implementation of NFU, whereas the German peace researchers thought conventional "improvements" unnecessary.[8] For Galtung, NATO's nuclear weapons were not necessary to offset the conventional superiority of the Warsaw Pact. He thought instead the weapons were designed to threaten the other side and to serve as the means for "ideological crusades." The West German peace movement, he argued, helped uncover this "real" purpose of nuclear weapons. The possibility of bloc-freedom or neutrality along the lines of Sweden, Switzerland or Austria could develop from successful superpower decoupling. When echoed by movement members, murmurings about neutralism invited the wrath of defenders of the status quo.[9]

3) Paralleling the call for NFU, the movement needed to popularize special zones of various sorts, especially along either side of the continental divide, free from NBC weapons.[10] The aim was to raise the threshold for the use of these weapons and thus lower the tension throughout the heart of Europe.

4) Staring into the future, Galtung foresaw a time when both the U.S. and USSR had withdrawn their nuclear weapons. Britain would follow suit leaving the French as the sole nuclear power in Europe. Galtung thought the French "still harbor Napoleonic dreams of Continental hegemony." His claim that French nuclear policy under François Mitterand was even more militaristic than under Valéry Giscard d'Estaing was widely shared within the peace movement.

Movement strategy, for Galtung, had to be elaborated within the context of fundamental systemic crises in both superpower empires: economic crisis in the West and political-ideological crisis in the East. Superpowers in fundamental crisis could be dangerous for two reasons: (a) they had a common interest in war to mask their crises; and (b) their common experience that things got better after a war. He meant, for the West, not military Keynesianism but the simple fact that so many commodities were destroyed by war. No more insufficient consumer demand. For the Soviet side it was clear that the Revolution itself was a consequence of the First World War, and the Soviet empire an outcome of the Second World War. How many countries might Moscow acquire with a Third World War? Galtung believed no responsible Soviet would speak in public in this fashion, just as no responsible individual in the

West would wonder out loud how far one could deal with unemployment through war, but he had no doubts there were people on both sides who thought along these lines.

He remarked how difficult it was to describe the dismantling of imperialism as a condition of peace, when the dismantling of empires was so dangerous. And Galtung admitted there was no easy answer to this contradiction. "Perhaps," he wrote, "the solution has something to do with with our need now for one, two or more statesmen, when all we have currently are dwarfs." This appeared to be a prescient call for Gorbachev, still three years away from global prominence. The problem required open discussion, something he thought it had yet to receive. This assessment overlooked, however, the eager but then fanciful speculation on the part of a number of Soviet specialists in the West (including Richard Pipes and Zbigniew Brzezinski) about the consequences of a contraction of Soviet control over the East Bloc. Similar ruminations about the decline of the West had, of course, a long history. They had, however, been the preserve of Marxists, Spenglerians, and neoconservatives until the appearance of *The Rise and Fall of the Great Powers.*[11]

For E.P. Thompson, social movement activists on both sides of the ideological divide in Europe had a serious strategic problem during the Cold War.

> Those who worked for freedom in the East were suspected or exposed as agents of Western imperialism. Those who worked for peace in the West were suspected or exposed as pro-Soviet "fellow travelers" or dupes of the Kremlin. In this way the rival ideologies of the Cold War disarmed those, on both sides, who might have put Europe back together. Any transcontinental movement for peace *and* freedom became impossible.[12]

Thompson nevertheless called for just such a two-pronged strategy, aimed at both East and West. Western activists needed to take risks to establish contacts with Eastern-bloc dissidents and to work hard to keep open channels of communication. Individual troublemakers in the East were to be defended, and attempts made to mobilize ever larger sectors of East European populations: students, churches, professionals, labor unions. At the same time, West European and North American peace protesters should fight the Euromissiles, Reagan's defense programs, and other threatening developments in the arms race. Thompson saw the twinned strategy as self-reinforcing. Each prong would inspire and give strength to the other. Détente made it difficult for the Soviets to crack down on dissidents. Liberalization in the East undercut the case for NATO arms modernization and renewed Cold War. Winding down the Cold War called for a series of reciprocal but unilateral measures; cancellation of Euromissile deployment should lead to withdrawal of SS-20s. Reduction of U.S. troops in Western Europe should move the Soviets to withdraw from Eastern Europe. Nuclear-free zones should give birth to chemical weapons-free zones. Europeans were to play a central role in what looked primarily like a U.S.-Soviet dance. It was Europe's heart after all, rent by the Cold War.

Peace movement strategists were of one voice in calling for the abandonment of nuclear deterrence for a security system rooted in cooperation between East and West. As Kermit Johnson cautioned,

> We must realize that nuclear deterrence has assaulted the moral values and heritage of our nation, locked it into a permanent cold war, subordinated political initiatives to the fixed "balance of terror," seduced our people into being accomplices to the threat of mass death, torn the social fabric of our nation, and distorted the balance of moral, political, economic, military, cultural, and social strength.[13]

"Living with nuclear weapons," wrote the Harvard Nuclear Study Group in 1982, "is our only hope." C. Wright Mills called such views "crackpot realism." Johnson considered the Harvard Group's view an expression of despair rather than hope.

> This is . . . the despair of those who are addicted to nuclear weapons, who feel they cannot live without them. It is the despair of a whole culture that is complicit in and accepting of a collective drive toward death. It is the hopelessness of those who have given up, whose response to the unthinkable is a passive adaptation. In this situation, if despair is to be subverted by hope, that hope must come from a refusal to comply.[14]

Nuclear deterrence made us both potential executioners and victims in waiting. In the words of Adam Roberts, "a policy which could involve us in the roles of Nazi and Jew at the same time has unique moral defects."[15] The crematoria had, however, been replaced by what Arthur Waskow called "instant portable Auschwitzes."[16] Johnson continued,

> By a strange twist of reasoning, those who question the utility of nuclear weapons and the threat system upon which they are based, are often portrayed as idealists who cannot bear to face the reality that nuclear weapons cannot be "wished away." Such a diversionary tactic distracts attention from the "real world" of fantasy, in which nuclear deterrence is depended upon to permanently keep the peace. To think nuclear deterrence will *never* fail is adherence to a wildly romantic and perfectionist view of human nature. It is unreasonable to expect national leaders to regard each other with such enmity that they con-

stantly threaten nuclear destruction and yet never, in the extremity of events, carry out that threat.[17]

As to the ancient Roman precept, the last refuge of the nuclear deterrence addict, "if you desire peace, prepare for war," research has shown that nations that prepare for war eventually go to war. In a study of great power conflict from 1816 to 1965, Michael Wallace found that disputes preceded by arms races "escalated to war 23 out of 28 times, while disputes *not* preceded by an arms race resulted in war only 3 out of 71 times."[18] Peace activists would have no part of a defense consensus that included threats of planetary genocide.

Strategic Dilemmas

Social movements, for Roberta Ash Garner, face a series of strategic choices:

- Between single issue demands and multiple demands.
- Between radical demands and demands that do not attack the legitimacy of present distributions of wealth and power.
- Between influencing elites (or even incorporating movement members into the elite) and attempting to replace elites.[19]

The choice between single issue and more extensive demands comes in for analysis below in the discussion of the anti-missile movement's "minimum consensus." Whether peace movement demands are radical or not is another question saved for discussion below. The "long march through the institutions" of 1960s student radicals straddled the horns of the last dilemma. Upon graduation, former students moved into the schools, the universities, the media, the courts, and the civil service with intent to influence the powerful on their own rise to positions of responsibility, and to become the powerful once they reached these positions. The citizen initiatives, women's and ecology movements of the 1970s, and the peace movement of the 1980s, attested to the marchers' fatigue and the institutional and ideological obstacles in their way.

Garner's choices do not cover the full gamut of strategic issues confronting movements. The constant choice before a movement as to the relative importance of cultural action versus political action cannot be fully subsumed under the rubric of the radical or less radical trade-off. Peace movements encourage people to stop buying war toys, to become pacifists, to renounce violence or threats of violence in their everyday lives. These are campaigns designed to change people's behavior, and consequently, the culture. Movements also typically pursue one or more directly political aims, such as stopping the INF deployment. A perhaps more useful distinction than one between radical and moderate demands is between movement goals and action that may pay off in the short-term versus returns measured in terms of decades or generations. And yet this is probably, at one level at least, a false dichotomy. Cultural action is political action and vice versa. Changing behavior leads to political changes, and political changes can change behavior.

Pam Solo (a Catholic nun, who was an important figure in the Freeze movement, first in Denver, and then in the national effort to bring the arms race to a halt) reframed the dilemma between influencing or replacing elites. Movements must choose between "opting into the power structure and opting out, that is, using the movement to make a symbolic statement of dissent from the larger political system."[20] But, of course, it is more complex than this and various movement organizations within diverse movements can and ought to do both. The movement as a whole opened elites to alternative security policies, alternatives to nuclear deterrence, a questioning of the whole defense structure—the hardware and the software—of NATO. This was one of the movement's most important legacies: its creative security policy thinking, and ability to suggest substantive new ways to provide for the common defense.

Thomas Rochon provided another perspective on the strategic choices facing NSM:

> [Movements'] extended ambitions [a desire for change in both social values and public policy] create acute tactical dilemmas . . . [T]hey sharpen the trade-offs between the activities that would reach the greatest numbers of people and activities that hold the most promise of influencing the government. This tension overlays the classic dilemma between maintaining ideological purity within a movement and diluting the purity in order to widen the breadth of movement support.[21]

He illustrated this tension in the case of the anti-Euromissile movement by opposing the tendency toward mass mobilization (the huge demonstrations) to the attempt to spread "a fundamental critique of militarism and superpower domination of Europe." For the German peace movement, however, there was no real trade-off between reaching people and influencing the government. Masses of people were sought in campaigns like that against the Euromissiles precisely to influence the government.

Rochon's emphasis on ideological purity misconstrues the nature of tensions within the Federal German peace movement. The struggle between the shifting coalitions of organizations and spectrums had far more to do with effectiveness, with what would do the short-term job of forestalling deployment than it did with any ideology, pure or otherwise.

Opposition to the missiles was a feature common to ideologies as diverse as communist, social democratic, and conservative. Ideological differences among the spectrums did give rise to various tensions, but differences over tactics caused most dissension. These tactical differences may have been epiphenomena of deeper ideological cleavages. But even if they were, tensions surfaced as day-to-day disagreements over what would best further the goal of stopping the Euromissiles.

The dilemma posed by Rochon between mass mobilization and a "fundamental critique of militarism and superpower domination" is questionable on another level. The fight against the missiles was implicitly and explicitly a fight against the system of militarism that gave rise to it. By questioning the rectitude of the double-track decision, did not the movement challenge NATO, the bloc system, and nuclearism? The cacophony of voices raised to counter the movement—those of generals and politicians, ambassadors and pundits, bureaucrats and academics—makes it appear so. Saying "no" to missiles deemed necessary by the alliance power structure was to say "no" to deterrence, the arms race, and superpower confrontation. Why, then, the concern a focus on the missiles obscured the more radical critique of militarism? Was it purported fear on the part of movement leaders that people would think once the missiles were stopped everything would be fine and they could go home? That is, victory over the missiles would be self-defeating for the larger purpose of the movement (i.e., to challenge militarism). This is a problem inherent to social movement politics, no matter what the goal or strategy, and it raises a tangle of thorny issues including one of the oldest dilemmas for movements: reform versus revolution. But how many citizens stayed away from anti-missile actions because they addressed alleged symptoms rather than actual causes of militarism; how many remained at home because events were insufficiently radical?

The *state system* itself is a primary cause of militarism, and one of the ways to undermine the state system is to do battle with the choices of one or more of its members. Social movements are not surgeons; they cannot cut out some tumor that is causing pain, or mend a broken bone that is making the patient limp (at least not without endangering the patient's life a lá Bolshevism). Movement intellectuals can write about root causes, they can theorize about what drives the arms race, but they cannot hold a referendum on abolishing the state. Activists can hold a plebiscite on some particular decision of the state and this itself poses both a real challenge to the state (which may not get to deploy missiles) and a symbolic challenge to the state system (states are not all powerful, can err tragically, perhaps need to be supplanted by nonsuicidal arrangements). Alternative security notions like "common security" that overthrow the security dilemma (the zero-sum corollary to realism), a long-lived feature of the state system, were both real and symbolic challenge.[22] With the security dilemma solved perhaps other features of the state system and of individual states themselves can be replaced by superior institutions. This is not to privilege practice over theory but to endorse an understanding of the movement's strategic problematic that fuses theory and practice. The analytical frameworks put forward by people like E.P. Thompson gave people an understanding of what it is they were up against, just how states operated in this realm, what forces confronted the movement. But how to do battle with the state is a different question. Enter practice: this is the realm of E.P. Thompson the activist, the leader of European Nuclear Disarmament (END).

Rochon suggested that as the movement grew and its social breadth increased, its radical critique of militarism was necessarily diluted.

> Although individual activists frequently followed the path of . . . ideological generalization and radicalization, the peace movement as a whole moderated its demands as increasing numbers of people became involved in it. Denuclearization of Europe as goal was replaced by the single goal of preventing deployment of Euromissiles.[23]

This is the common wisdom about the goals of the movement. The main problem with this characterization of its strategic evolution is that, when measured by the content of movement manifestoes, it is simply inaccurate. A comparison of the Krefeld Appeal, first signed in November 1980, or the even earlier Berlin Initiative for Peace, International Compromise and Security (April 1980), with the programs of leading organizations and large coalitions at important junctures—the October 1981, June 1982 or October 1983 mass demonstrations—shows clearly that the movement did not moderate its goals. To the contrary, strategic platforms grew in complexity, length, complaints and alternatives as the movement grew in strength and breadth.

The Krefeld Appeal had a more narrow focus than any of the movement's later pronouncements on what was wrong with the world and what fix was needed. It focused primarily on the double-track decision. It also scored the Reagan administration for failing to initiate arms control negotiations and for refusing to submit SALT II to the U.S. Senate for ratification. There was but one vague reference in it to "an alternative security policy," and a recommendation that disarmament take precedence over deterrence.[24] Documents that issued from the huge Bonn rallies of 1981 and 1982, on the other hand, showed a plethora of concerns beyond opposition to Pershing and Cruise: Afghanistan, Central America, Poland, Turkey, weapons exports, nuclear proliferation, chemical weapons and more.[25] By peak movement mobilization (autumn 1983), movement intellectuals had largely made good on Galtung's charge: proposals for weapons-free-zones, plans for deescalation and disengagement, sophisticated assessments of the value of arms control, elaborate critiques of NATO doctrine and deterrence, fundamental critical understandings of the systemic contradictions of capitalism and communism, well-developed alternative security schemes (nonoffensive defense, civilian-based defense, social defense, common security); the list goes on. The goals of the movement were not only wider-ranging than simple opposition to the missiles but they overlapped, they were common to diverse organizations.

Movement goals can be seen as twinned: a narrow instrumental focus on the missiles and a very broad panorama of alternatives to NATO's security policy dead-end. Both goals were important, but the battle against the missiles was the horse that hauled the cart of alternative strategies. Mass anti-missile mobilization made for dramatic press coverage. The huge demonstrations and myriad other movement activities opened the way for a diffusion of new security policy thinking. Defense alternatives were popularized, and pressure put on politicians to consider them. Rather than describe deployment prevention as a "single goal," it is more illuminating to use the language of the movement itself to characterize its focus: a "minimum consensus" against the missiles. This lowest common strategic denominator was arrived at early in movement decisionmaking and remained throughout the movement's period of high mobilization. The most important determinant of the minimum consensus was the presence of communists in the movement leadership (either actual DKP members or those aligned with various front or allied organizations found in the KOFAZ spectrum). Their presence was especially important for two reasons. It was crucial, first, in the early stage of the movement, when the minimum consensus was settled on, and is typified by the communist role in formulating the Krefeld Appeal. The central role of communists in gathering signatures on the Appeal was undeniable and perhaps irreplaceable. Second, the DKP's critique of nuclear weapons was not even-handed. NATO's weapons were offensive and imperialistic, but the Warsaw Pact's were defensive and existed only as a counter-weight to those of the West.

Thus arises the unity issue, the purported heart of the minimum consensus. Attempts to mobilize around a broader set of goals risked splintering the highly diverse movement. Indefatigable communists might find something else to do. Nuclear pacifists might defect should conventional weapons be targeted for opposition. Evidence of the greater effectiveness of single-issue movements versus those with multiple demands is available.[26] Ironically, the risks to unity stared the movement in the face should it prevent deployment or not. The diversity and differing perspectives of the movement would resurface in the wake of its defeat or defeat of the Euromissiles. But if we see the fight against the missiles as symbolic of the larger critique of society (the way it is run, its logic, the life-chances it affords its young citizens) pointed to by NSM theorists like Melucci, then the minimum consensus appears in a different light. And, as argued above, groups had more in common than the minimum consensus leads us to believe. What appears as a contradiction here—minimum consensus plus numerous ancillary aims—is resolved by recognition that a social movement confronting a problem on the order of militarism, nuclearism, or the war system needs to start somewhere.

Lofty statements of principles and long-term goals are of little assistance to the daily tasks of the practical organizer. We can imagine the views of this organizer: "you can go on about the benefits of a denuclearized world to your heart's content, but what, objectively and politically, are we going to do about it in the here and now? We simply must pick some piece of the larger problem to work on." This will typically be some piece that is tangible (or will be tangible sometime soon), and affects people where they live. This is the service provided by the Euromissiles: they were the piece of the nuclear puzzle that brought the larger threat into plain sight. The missiles were as much a symbol of the greater evils of nuclear deterrence, foreign control over one's destiny, the potential end of all life on earth, as they were a target in and of themselves. This is not to minimize the latter feature, the innate threat posed by the missiles—this was a major theme of movement propaganda—but only to help explain why a diverse movement with more in common than opposition to the latest batch of missiles ended up focusing much of its time and energy on resisting their emplacement. The rockets thus took on a dual character: tangible threat and symbol of "exterminism." Exterminism is a concept developed by E.P. Thompson to explain the structure of abstract research and applied technology directed toward mass slaughter.[27] Although he later admitted the term was "ugly and over-rhetorical," Thompson defended it as a "new category for analysis." He thought it helped explain "something in the inertial thrust and the reciprocal logic of the opposed weapons systems—and the configuration of material, political, ideological and security interests attendant upon them—which cannot be explained within the categories of 'imperialism' or 'international class struggle.'"[28]

Some movement participants argued that the alleged narrow concentration on the missiles was a failing of the 1980s peace movements.[29] But as we have seen, while it had a focus, this was no single-issue movement. Other movement sympathizers complained that dangerous, interventionist foreign policies, not nuclear weapons, should have been the focus of movement action.[30] William Schwartz and Charles Derber claim the "arms race didn't matter" and accuse the 1980s anti-nuclear weapons movements of "weaponitis" (a wrong-headed focus on arms). Superpower bullying of the Third World, they argued, was more likely to lead to war than the nuclear arms race. A focus on nuclear weapons led to obsession with arms control rather than emphasis on disarmament, let alone denuclearization. This is a familiar, if confused, thesis. Kermit Johnson echoed a similar lament:

> All of us would prefer, of course, that a national debate on America's world role could grow out of discussion of our role in Latin America, the Middle East, or Europe, rather than arise from a tragic or dangerous nuclear incident. This debate must go beyond the forty-year stultifying fixation on nuclear weapons and strategies and must become a concerted effort to discover an alternative security system.[31]

Johnson cited the work of George Rathjens who believed that U.S. arms control priorities were completely backwards. The U.S. accorded priority to the problem of Soviet strategic forces, followed by emphasis on Soviet INF, and then conventional forces. Further down the list were confidence-building measures, crisis resolution, superpower intervention in the Third World, and last, improved communications and relations.[32]

Rathjens was right, of course. But peace movements were not responsible for the confused priorities. To argue otherwise assumes a power to set the public agenda, to shape the parameters of debate, far out of proportion to that available to real, existing peace movements. The complaints of Mechtersheimer, and Schwartz and Derber, assumed a naïveté on the part of the movement—"ah, if we only defeat the Pershings all will be well"—that for the most part was not there. Many thoughtful activists realized the missiles were but the newest tip of the nuclear iceberg, that more would follow. NATO, and especially the U.S., already had more gifts in the pipeline, as informed activists knew only too well: Star Wars and anti-satellite weapons (ASAT), AirLand Battle 2000 and Follow-On-Forces-Attack (FOFA). Opening a debate on the American world role was one benefit foreseen by German peace activists through their support for alternative defense proposals. If on one level the movement *appeared* to fall prey to the stultifying fixation on weapons and strategy, on another level, it transcended the fixation by positing ways out of the danger—alternative strategies, principles, and international codes of state conduct. The 1980s West German anti-missile movement was a dialectical phenomenon: the antithesis of nuclear weapons and strategies, it gave rise, through its struggle against nuclearism, to the synthesis of common security.

Part of the problem can be summed up by the question "Where to start ending the arms race or the risks of nuclear war?" Schwartz and Derber berated the anti-nuclear weapons movements for focusing on weapons when it ought to have focused on risky foreign policies. But groups like the Committee in Solidarity with the People of El Salvador (CISPES) *did* battle dangerous interventionist U.S. policy in Central America (I was a charter member). And, as we have seen, a significant constituency of what became the German anti-missile movement came from Third World solidarity groups that were deeply concerned about the perilous course of superpower foreign policy outside Europe. Schwartz and Derber's argument ignores how difficult it was to resist U.S. aid for Cambodian or Nicaraguan "freedom fighters." The restrictions placed on U.S. military intervention in Central America were huge victories. Weapons, and the military forces that wielded them, were the wherewithal for risky interventionist policies in the South. There was a focus on nuclear arms, if not weaponitis, because arms were the currency of international relations, the symbols, the means, the focus of appropriations, the producers of jobs. It was impossible and undesirable to avoid fighting the arms race during the 1980s. Schwartz and Derber's argument is akin to that of the National Rifle Association in the U.S. regarding gun control: guns don't kill people, people do. Just as gun control makes sense (ask most any U.S. police chief) despite the fact guns do not fire without fingers on their triggers, so efforts to stem the usually steady, sometimes torrential flow of new armaments were eminently sensible. We absolutely must change the culture that leads U.S. citizens to gun each down in unparalleled numbers. But part of forcing this cultural change involves making hand guns, assault rifles and other provocative weaponry off limits or harder to get.

There is a reinforcing character between weaponry and strategy that makes a focus solely on one or the other an inadequate peace movement strategy. In practice, weapons developments at the research and development stage precede strategists' understanding about what to do with the new things. But once a purpose has been found for them, they will will be deployed in the field (frequently, in the case of the U.S., on the high seas or on other people's national territory) and resisting the *purpose* to which the arms can or will be put is all the harder simply because they exist, men have been trained to use them, they have been incorporated into operational plans, they are now a given and commanders inevitably can not envision "defense" without them.

Schwartz and Derber appear to forget the existential threat posed to the planet by the Reagan administration. These were people who said and did extremely dangerous things. These were people who doubted the nearly universal view of nuclear war as suicide, the low probability of war in Europe, the silliness of ballistic missile defense and protracted nuclear war, the impossibility of "C^{3}I" (command, control, communications, and intelligence) during a nuclear war, and all the rest. Peace movements did well to oppose the Reaganites at every turn, including every weapons turn. The arms race mattered because by fighting new missiles, activists were fighting extensions of their states, the same states which decide whether to go to war or not. To focus on Euromissiles was not to ignore escalation in Third World or any other "real problem." Instead, it was a way to fight the good fight on one of many fronts. When a belligerent, interventionist administration proposes a whole raft of new weapons, it makes sense to fight the R&D, appropriation, deployment, and testing of those weapons. We may know that escalation of superpower conflict to the nuclear level is nearly a sure thing, and that first strikes are impossible and irrational, but the Reagan administration apparently did not. This shocking fact forced peace movements and researchers to argue against individual weapons systems and against nuclear weapons in general. The prevailing discourse also limited the options available to peace activists. It proved very difficult to conduct a discussion in "foreign policyese" or "interventionese" when the prevailing language of power and influence was "weaponese." To gain access to media, to seem knowledgeable and credible, to catch officials in lies and contradictions, you had to talk the talk.

E.P. Thompson, and other movement strategists, were aware of the pitfalls of weaponitis.

> Some Soviet ideologists have recently been attempting to re-baptise us an "anti-war movement." But that will never be enough. By an "anti-war movement" they intend a movement which is limited in its agenda to matters of military posture and pronouncements only and from which all matters of ideology, polity and culture are excluded. . . . Certainly nuclear weapons are the most odious symbols of our predicament. . . . But the peace movement . . . if it is to *make* peace and not only make protest, must set itself an agenda which extends into every nook and cranny of our culture and our polity. It has to be an affirmative movement of an unprecedented kind.[33]

West German peace movement leaders and strategists considered weaponry but the tools of war. They evinced a political understanding of the roots of war frequently obscured by the arcane discussions of mainstream arms controllers. But they were also aware of the symbolic benefits of arms control and disarmament. And they knew that arms races *have* often mattered throughout history. The most recent cycle of the nuclear arms race mattered because opposition to it was important politically, not technically or militarily, though clearly defeat of some especially problematic weapons system like Star Wars was in the interest of peace forces. German movement strategists knew that the symbolic rituals of superpower negotiations had potentially tangible consequences. Successful arms negotiations can reduce hostility, spur further cooperation in other areas of East-West relations, defuse crises, and help to dismantle enemy images. As such, what may appear to be techniques that merely address the symptoms of bloc rivalry can actually work to uncover the roots of fear and loathing.

Once again, movements need a starting line. This need inevitably narrows their focus. This does not mean there were no short-sighted idealists in the movement who thought defeating the missiles was all the fight was about. But most myopics gained an appreciation of more distant problems in the course of their participation. Surely most activists, sophisticated and simple, truly hoped they would defeat the missiles. It would be a grand victory in its own right, excepting perhaps the possibility of the Carter-era threat of a neutron bomb deployment, an unprecedented defeat of official security policy, that was pushed by two (opposed) German governments. But it might also be the beginning of the end of the nuclear age. Remember the slogan heard in Holland: "Ban all nuclear weapons; let's begin with the Netherlands." The arms race might be halted, a nuclear war in Europe prevented. These are no small accomplishments.

There is something else here, however, beyond the need for an "alpha," a genesis point. It is the shadow of the movement: that set of changed circumstances left in its wake; lessons in democracy learned by formerly insulated policymakers, that shaped future encounters between state and movement. Hopeful activists in the midst of the battle against the missiles said: "If we can beat them here maybe they won't try it again, or maybe we'll be able to get our way on other issues, on the next steps, maybe on some new minimum consensus." It is these next steps that the movement's shadow is cast upon. The longer the shadow, the greater the impact of the previous campaign, and the easier the job of future activists.

Nonviolence and Arms Control Negotiations

Nonviolence was both strategy and tactic for the movement. It was a strategy as it was seen as the overarching concept to guide action by the vast majority of movement adherents—Andreas Zumach, a leading member of the Christian spectrum, estimated that 95 percent of the movement was nonviolent—and as an ultimate goal (a nonviolent society in a nonviolent world).[34] This estimate is confirmed by Ruud Koopman's data on West German social movement protest action for the years 1965-1989 presented in Figures 6.1-6.4.

Whatever else most of the movement might agree on, nonviolence was to shape the political context for the pursuit of that agenda, and was

FIGURE 6.1   Number of Confrontational Actions by Year,
1965-1989

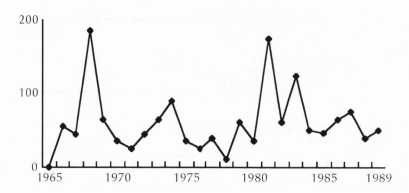

Source: Adapted from Ruud Koopmans, "The Dynamics of Protest Waves: West Germany, 1965-1989," *American Sociological Review*, vol.58 (1993), p. 643. Used by permission.

FIGURE 6.2   Number of Demonstrations by Year, 1965-1989

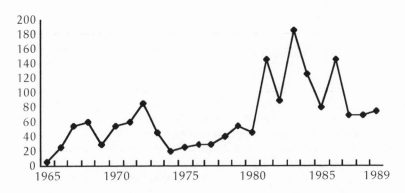

Source: Adapted from Koopmans, "The Dynamics of Protest Waves: West Germany, 1965-1989," p. 643. Used by permission.

FIGURE 6.3   Number of Protests Using Light Violence by Year, 1965-1989

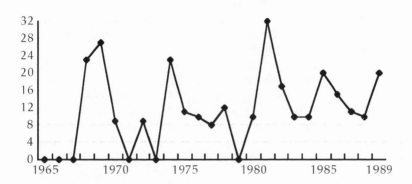

Source: Adapted from Koopmans, "The Dynamics of Protest Waves: West Germany, 1965-1989," p. 643. Used by permission.

FIGURE 6.4   Number of Protests Using Heavy Violence by Year, 1965-1989

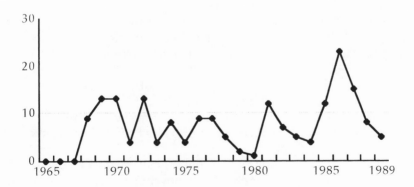

Source: Adapted from Koopmans, "The Dynamics of Protest Waves: West Germany, 1965-1989," p. 643. Used by permission.

to be the leading characteristic of the pacifist utopia following its realization. This is not to minimize the painful and lengthy debates over the
(non)violence and direct action questions within the movement. They
were surely among the most frequently and intensively debated strategic
issues. As late as the summer of 1986, nearly three years after the
Bundestag vote in favor of deployment, movement organizations argued
over the wisdom of blockading a Cruise missile base in Hasselbach for
fear the direct action would be misused by rioters to the movement's discredit.[35] The point is that in its philosophy and in its action the movement
was overwhelmingly nonviolent.

Organizers are never able to fully control actions. Action is, after all,
carried out by individuals, not by "organizations" or "movements."
Violence was never encouraged by the CC, but the Greens and especially
the Independents frequently waffled on the question of counter-violence,
the ability of the movement to defend itself against attacks by the police,
and the definition of resistance to the missiles. And the movement was a
big tent. That brick throwers slipped under it with some regularity was a
source of unending controversy. Photographs and newscast footage of
masked and helmeted youths pummeling police were not conducive to
recruiting efforts, and made it easy for the authorities to cast the missile
opponents as outlaws. Activists knew they had to police their ranks, and
yet feared being authoritarian. Checking identification or conducting
body searches to weed out "anarchist" rowdies (Chaoten) prior to events
was neither desirable nor feasible. To simply disavow such behavior ostensibly committed on behalf of a good cause was the choice for most
movement spokespersons.

Through it all, Gandhi's famous formulation (picked up by A.J.
Muste and Martin Luther King, Jr. in the U.S.) nonetheless remained a
motto for most of the movement: there is no way to peace, peace is the
way. Nonviolence is the obvious difference between peace activists and
armed insurrectionaries. And yet, the movement sympathized with and
supported the popular armed struggles in Central America with as much
gusto as one could find within the solidarity movement in the United
States. Indeed, peace activists easily understand what moves people to
take up arms in their own defense. But nonviolence is the right strategy;
it is both ethically defensible (especially for Christians) and provides the
moral high ground vis-à-vis well-armed authorities. Strategic nonviolence can thus become an ideology. It provides both end game and game
end.

The issues of arms control and disarmament were, like the question
of nonviolence, constant subjects of movement discussion. Activists
clashed over the value to assign negotiations. Was arms control as practiced by the superpowers the best means to prevent deployment or was it
an obstacle to disarmament? A stark reality mooted the argument: arms

control was the only state-sanctioned game in town. Given the virtual impossibility that a German government would cancel its obligations under the double-track decision, the movement had no choice but to play along. So pacifists complained in 1981 that Reagan refused to negotiate with the Russians over the Euromissiles. And when talks began in Geneva, the movement complained the U.S. was not serious, that proposals like the zero option were public relations smoke screens designed to take the pressure off Washington. Then throughout the failed negotiations, to the point of deployment and beyond, peace groups, singly and in combination, applied pressure at all levels of government—local, state, federal, and international—to prevent deployment via successful completion of an arms control treaty.

This pressure was a real test of the movement's political impact. Attempts at influencing the negotiations took two elementary forms: direct and indirect. The two most important avenues of influence were reform of SPD security policy, the indirect route, and interventions in the public discourse surrounding the negotiations, the direct route. The first path was taken with the hope that the party of Helmut Schmidt, a biological father of the double-track decision, would return to the pacifist strand of its interwoven traditions, that it would truly become the "peace party" (Willy Brandt). Because Pershing and Cruise were never popular with the rank-and-file, intraparty wrangling over the missile decision and other controversies provided the movement an opening for influence. The relative weight of party wings shifted after the self-destruction of the Social-Liberal coalition, widening the opening. If the party would not withdraw from nuclear emplacement duties while in power, it might at least work hard toward making the missiles unnecessary while in opposition. This could be effected through intergovernmental lobbying— pressure on Reaganites in the State and Defense Departments, and on more sympathetic Americans in Congress. Should the party regain the Chancellery in March 1983, it would hopefully do so with a refurbished security policy, one with at least the movement's lukewarm seal of approval. And the simultaneous arrival of the Greens in the Bundestag might ensure that the SPD had repressed the fetishism of deterrence and the military balance.

Movement intervention in the domestic and international politics of the INF negotiations proceeded along several lines. Peace researchers and organizations critiqued particular negotiating positions such as the zero option and interim solutions. "The Russians will never buy it. It neglects British and French forces or forward-based aircraft." The dilemma confronting ardent opponents of the bloc system, however, was that nuclear arms control was supposed to shore up the stability of deterrence, not provide its replacement.[36] This was acceptable on one level: most anything that reduced the possibility of nuclear war was fine by German pacifists. But on another level, any result other than complete cancellation of the deployment track—and compromise is the coin of arms control negotiations—raised again the fundamental objection to superpower nuclear bargaining: it legitimizes the arms race and thus rules out disarmament. One possible escape from this paradox was some version of unilateralism: "independent reciprocal initiatives" or "moratoriums" on deployment during the negotiations. If only Bonn or Washington would take the initiative, would take a risk for peace, the log jam might be broken. The irony is that the grand initiative necessary to finally overcome the paradox—unbuckling the Cold War straitjacket—came not from a NATO capital but from parts East.

A plethora of other strategic questions, about which detailed discussions are not possible here, constantly dogged the movement.[37] On the issue of strategic alliances, there were those who thought that unity was not worth any price. Consensual inability to criticize Soviet weaponry, for example, was unacceptable for many.[38] Relations with political parties also caused consternation. In a parliamentary democracy parties are natural targets for influence. But independence from any particular party was a must for the long-term development of the movement. The SPD, the movement's logical ally and friend among the established parties, abandoned the Struggle Against Atomic Death campaign in the fifties.[39] The party launched the extraparliamentary anti-nuclear weapons initiative—aimed at plans to station American atomic bombs in the Federal Republic and at plans to equip the Bundeswehr with nuclear-capable weapons systems—in January 1958.[40] In April 1957, 18 prominent West German physicists issued the Göttingen Appeal that declared their personal refusal to "take part in the production, testing or use of nuclear weapons," and that called on the Adenauer government to reject "the possession of atomic weapons of any kind."[41] April 1957 also saw the bitter nuclear weapons debates in the Bundestag, at which a young Social Democratic representative from Hamburg—Helmut Schmidt—first made a name for himself, opposing nuclear weapons.[42] With public opinion on their side, the SPD tried, as it would again in 1983, to make nuclear weapons a major issue in the September 1957 national election. The party board called on Social Democrats to devote themselves to a broad movement. The movement grew during the spring of 1958 and reached its peak at May Day rallies. The movement exacerbated the party's main fault line. Those still loyal to the pre-war socialist workers' anti-militarist party were strongly in favor of movement mobilization; the "new Social Democrats" including Willy Brandt in Berlin, were wary of it. Shortly thereafter, the party came to grips with the postwar security policy problematique: it accepted the Bundeswehr, nuclear weapons, and

NATO. The electoral opportunism of parties make them potentially important, if fickle, friends of social movements.

There was little strife within the 1980s German movement over the importance of internationalization: outreach to organizations and individuals working for peace and justice in other countries. It was a necessary strategic choice for several reasons: it showed the global, universal nature of the battle against militarism; it helped combat the tendency toward anti-Americanism on the part of some activists; and it helped find allies from other NATO-member states slated for Cruise missile deployments.

Conclusion

Movement goals and strategy involve trade-offs and priorities. Movements can have long-term and short-term goals but a central strategic focus provides a starting point for action and helps guard against threats to unity. The German peace movement had both: a narrow instrumental concentration on a particular weapons system and a lengthy list of alternative strategies, nonviolent methods of conflict resolution, and domestic reforms to remake the country's political culture and relationships with the world. What began as a movement to oppose the Euromissiles blossomed into a far-reaching critique of deterrence, the arms race, and exterminism.

Notes

1. Heberle, "Types and Functions of Social Movements," p. 442.
2. Theodor Ebert, "Zwölf Thesen zur Strategie der Ökologie- und Friedensbewegung," in his *Ziviler Ungehorsam: Von der APO zur Friedensbewegung* (Waldkirch: Waldkircher Verlag, 1984).
3. This point finds support in Peter H. Merkl, *The Origins of the West German Republic* (New York: Oxford University Press, 1965).
4. This point finds support in Wolfram F. Hanrieder, *Germany, America, Europe: Forty Years of German Foreign Policy* (New Haven: Yale University Press, 1989).
5. Johan Galtung, "Die Chancen der Friedensbewegung," in Skuhra and Wimmer, eds., *Friedensforschung und Friedensbewegung*.
6. On alternative strategies and force structures, see Horst Afheldt, "New Policies, Old Fears," *Bulletin of the Atomic Scientists*, vol. 44, no. 7 (1988); Gene Sharp, *Making Europe Unconquerable: The Potential of Civilian-Based Defense*

(London: Taylor & Francis, 1985); Anders Boserup and Andrew Mack, *War Without Weapons* (New York: Schocken, 1975); Adam Roberts, *Civilian Resistance as National Defense* (Harrisburg, PA: Stackpole, 1968); and Burns Weston, ed., *Alternative Security: Living Without Nuclear Deterrence* (Boulder, CO: Westview Press, 1990).

7. McGeorge Bundy, George F. Kennan, Robert S. McNamara, and Gerard Smith, "Nuclear Weapons and the Atlantic Alliance," *Foreign Affairs*, vol. 60, no. 4 (1982). Follow-on endorsements included McGeorge Bundy, "'No First Use' Needs Careful Study," *Bulletin of the Atomic Scientists*, vol. 36, no. 6 (1982); Kurt Gottfried, Henry W. Kendall, and John M. Lee, "'No First Use' of Nuclear Weapons," *Scientific American*, no. 250 (1984); and Robert S. McNamara, "The Military Role of Nuclear Weapons: Perceptions and Misperceptions," *Foreign Affairs*, vol. 62, no. 1 (1983). Two German responses critical of NFU were Karl Kaiser, Georg Leber, Alois Mertes, and Franz-Josef Schulze, "Nuclear Weapons and the Preservation of Peace," *Foreign Affairs*, vol. 60, no. 5 (1982); and Hans Apel, "Zur Diskussion über die Strategie der NATO: Überlegungen zu dem Beitrag, Kernwaffen und das Atlantische Bündnis," *Europa-Archiv*, vol. 37 (June 10, 1982). German peace researchers tended to favor NFU. See, for example, Gert Krell, Thomas Risse-Kappen, and Hans-Joachim Schmidt, "The No-First-Use Question in West Germany," in John D. Steinbruner and Leon V. Sigal, eds., *Alliance Security: NATO and the No-First-Use Question* (Washington: Brookings, 1983).

8. For a comprehensive single-volume analysis of the issues, see Daniel Charles, *Nuclear Planning in NATO: Pitfalls of First Use* (Cambridge, MA: Ballinger, 1987).

9. See Leon Wieseltier, "There Is No Morality in European Neutrality," *Los Angeles Times*, November 1, 1981, section IV, p.1, for a hysterical attack on the peace movements of Western Europe.

10. One such popularization was Arbeitsgruppe Friedensforschung Tübingen, ed., *Atomwaffen-Freiheit und Europäische Sicherheit: Möglichkeiten und Probleme einer anderen Sicherheitspolitik* (Tübingen: Verein für Friedenspädagogik, 1983).

11. Paul Kennedy, *The Rise and Fall of the Great Powers: Economic Change and Military Conflict From 1500 to 2000* (New York: Random House, 1987).

12. Quoted in Michael Bess, *Realism, Utopia, and the Mushroom Cloud: Four Activist Intellectuals and Their Strategies for Peace, 1945-1989* (Chicago: University of Chicago Press, 1993), p. 134.

13. Johnson, *Realism and Hope in a Nuclear Age*, p. 82.

14. Johnson, *Realism and Hope in a Nuclear Age*, p. 44.

15. Adam Roberts, "The Critique of Nuclear Deterrence," Adelphi Paper, no. 183, part 2, IISS, p. 14.

16. Quoted in Johnson, *Realism and Hope in a Nuclear Age*, p. 22.

17. Johnson, *Realism and Hope in a Nuclear Age*, p. 27; see also, Steven Kull, *Minds at War: Nuclear Reality and the Inner Conflict of Defense Policymakers* (New York: Basic, 1988).

18. Michael D. Wallace, "Arms Races and Escalation," *Journal of Conflict Resolution*, vol. 23 (1979), p. 3.

19. Garner, *Social Movements*, p. 230.

20. Pam Solo, *From Protest to Policy: Beyond the Freeze to Common Security* (Cambridge, MA: Ballinger, 1988), p. 180.

21. Rochon, "The West European Peace Movement," pp. 105-106.

22. Palme Commission, *Common Security—A Programme for Disarmament: Report of the Independent Commission on Disarmament and Security Issues* (New York: Simon & Schuster, 1985).

23. Rochon, "The West European Peace Movement," p. 106.

24. The text of the Appeal has been reprinted in numerous works, including Hans Apel, et al., eds., *Sicherheitspolitik contra Frieden? Ein Forum zur Friedensbewegung* (Bonn: Dietz, 1981), p. 145.

25. See Aktion Sühnezeichen/Friedensdienste and Aktionsgemeinschaft Dienst für den Frieden, eds., *Bonn 10. 10. 81*; and Koordinierungsausschuss der Friedensorganizationen, ed., *Aufstehn! Für den Frieden: Friedensdemonstration anläßlich der NATO-Gipfelkonferenz in Bonn am 10. 6. 1982* (Bornheim: Lamuv, 1982).

26. Gamson, *The Strategy of Social Protest*; and Garner, *Social Movements*.

27. E.P. Thompson, "Notes on Exterminism, the Last Stage of Civilization" in his *Exterminism and the Cold War* (London: Verso, 1982).

28. E.P. Thompson, "Exterminism Reviewed," in his *The Heavy Dancers: Writings on War, Past and Future* (New York: Pantheon, 1985), p. 136. For further useful discussion of the "logic" of mass annihilation, see Noam Chomsky, "Intellectuals and the State," in his *Towards A New Cold War: Essays on the Current Crisis and How We Got There* (New York: Pantheon, 1986).

29. Alfred Mechtersheimer, *Zeitbombe NATO: Auswirkungen der neuen Strategien* (Cologne: Diederichs, 1984).

30. William A. Schwartz and Charles Derber, *The Nuclear Seduction: Why the Arms Race Doesn't Matter—and What Does* (Berkeley: University of California Press, 1990).

31. Johnson, *Realism and Hope in a Nuclear Age*, p. 90.

32. George W. Rathjens, "First Thoughts About Problems Facing ExPro," The ExPro Papers, No. 5, 1986, pp. 19-20; cited in Johnson, *Realism and Hope in a Nuclear Age*, p. 85.

33. Quoted in Bess, *Realism, Utopia, and the Mushroom Cloud*, p. 92; see also E.P. Thompson, "The Soviet 'Peace Offensive,'" in his *The Heavy Dancers*.

34. Cited in Leif, *Die Strategische (Ohn-) Macht der Friedensbewegung*, p. 175.

35. "Die 'Friedensbewegung' über die Blockadefrage zerstritten," *Frankfurter Allgemeine Zeitung*, August 5, 1986, pp. 1-2.

36. Perhaps the earliest book to make this point is Thomas C. Schelling, *The Strategy of Conflict* (Cambridge: Harvard University Press, 1960).

37. Several of these strategic issues are discussed in depth in Leif, *Die Strategische (Ohn-) Macht der Friedensbewegung*.

38. For the American corollary of this problem, see Michael T. Klare, "Road Map for the Peace Movement," *The Nation*, June, 29, 1985.

39. On the peace movement during the fifties, see Hans Karl Rupp, *Ausserparlamentarische Opposition in der Ära Adenauer: Der Kampf gegen die Atombewaffnung in den fünfziger Jahre* (Cologne: Pahl-Rugenstein, 1970).

40. Gordon D. Drummond, *The German Social Democrats in Opposition, 1949-1960: The Case Against Rearmament* (Norman, OK: University of Oklahoma Press, 1982), chapter 8.

41. *Die Politische Meinung,* May 1957, pp. 55-60.

42. Mark Cioc, *Pax Atomica: The Nuclear Defense Debate in West Germany During the Adenauer Era* (New York: Columbia University Press, 1988), chapter 2.

7

Tactics

Never doubt that a small group of thoughtful, committed citizens can change the world. Indeed, it's the only thing that ever has.

—Margaret Mead

Tactics are the means used to realize strategic ends or goals. The means employed by the Federal German movement in pursuit of its ends were diverse and mutable. A comprehensive political sociology requires understanding movement action—organizations in motion—and the varying approaches the movement took to action.

The first section discusses William Gamson's theoretical work on the nature of tactics and their "targets;" it develops the concept of the "object" of movement action; and it analyzes eight of the factors that help determine movement choice of tactics. The point is to explain why movements adopt particular tactics. The second section discusses Charles Tilly's "action repertoire" concept and the reasons why repertoires change; it discusses the nature of the relationship between movement action and its audiences; it surveys the variety of action forms in theory and practice; it raises the question of tactical nonviolence; and it closes with an analysis of the affinity group as one tactical-organizational structure employed by the movement in its struggle against the missiles.

The Determinants of Tactical Choice

Movement organizations, in William Gamson's view, take aim at three distinct targets: (1) the target of influence (antagonistic or friendly); (2) the target of mobilization (constituency); (3) the target of benefits (beneficiary).[1] This framework is not satisfactory for peace groups (as Gamson recognized) as their targets of mobilization and benefits largely overlap. That is, the people peace movements try to mobilize (as much of the whole citizenry as possible) are the same people who will benefit from successful movement action: decreased risk of nuclear war, deepened détente, more money for nonmilitary expenditures; even people classified as antagonists would gain as many peace movement benefits are public goods (indivisible and nonexcludable). Solidary benefits—feelings of increased efficacy and solidarity—accrue only to active participants. Despite its limited usefulness, Gamson's target typology conveys the important point that tactics are designed to communicate with one or more audiences.

Within the ranks of an audience in a position of power—the one of particular interest here—are the myriad objects of movement action. Objects, the foci of movement action or influence, are not created equal. Fighting a specific, yet to be deployed missile system is not the same as campaigning against the same missiles once deployed. These tactical objects are different again from battling a doctrine (e.g., AirLand Battle), or educating the public—what the movement called Informationsarbeit—about the military-industrial complex and its need for an arms race. There are at least three variables external to movements that help determine the tactics employed against these various objects: hardness, mobility, and time. Each can be conceptualized as a continuum with, for example, "very hard" at one pole and "very soft" at the other.

Hardness refers to the tangibility of an object. The following objects are in order from most to least hard: a weapons system or military facility, training overflights or maneuvers, a doctrine or strategy. *Mobility* affects hardness; a weapons system that can and does range over large spaces, such as an aircraft, is less hard than a fixed installation like the aircraft's base. The harder and less mobile the object, the more readily it can be protested. This does not mean that movements cannot 'harden' soft objects. The intangible can be personalized and made concrete. The role of Pershing II missiles in the Pentagon's contingency plans for a decapitation strike against the Soviet leadership is an example of the connections between hard and soft objects. While protesting the missiles, activists can also protest the strategies they are designed to implement.

And they can demonstrate against individuals—Ronald Reagan, George Bush, Caspar Weinberger—who, although highly mobile, work or live in symbolically powerful buildings and personify both hard and soft objects.

Objects exist in one of three dimensions of *time* depending on the currentness of their deployment or of the threat they pose to movement values. In descending order of currentness the dimensions are: existing, pending, and possible. Foreign troops, conventional and chemical arms are examples of existing threats. The Euromissiles were the primary pending preoccupation of activists in the early eighties. And SDI was a possible threat. The tactics employed to protest an existing or pending system or facility (e.g., blockades, rallies near the site) may differ from those employed to protest one in the research and development stage (e.g., lobbying legislators). Accounting for the hardness, mobility and currentness of an object is central to the process by which peace movements choose tactics.

Heberle identified two additional and overlapping variables that blur the line between "internal" from "external" determinants of movement tactics.

> The choice of tactics . . . is in part dependent on the political system within which the movement operates and in part on the size of the movement and its influence within the political system. Therefore, the tactics of a social movement may change as it grows—they may become less revolutionary as the movement gains influence, or they may become more aggressive as the chances of success increase.[2]

An open *political system* discourages conspiratorial methods. Underground vanguardism is inappropriate to movement groups professing transparency and participatory democracy. And this is where the theoretical boundary between internal and external is most nebulous. Primarily an internal attribute, movement ideology as expressed in internal group decisionmaking processes and goals can thus condition the choice of tactics. The *size* and variable influence of German peace movement organizations did condition choice of action forms. Large and credible groups leaned toward legal, mass-oriented means to preserve their size and status. Miniscule and obscure collectives, like the affinity groups discussed below, had much less at risk in this regard. They more easily employed confrontational tactics. There were, however, several exceptions to this tendency in the 1980s West German peace movement. For example, several large organizations were open to civil disobedience, and a number of grouplets shied away from direct action.

Choice of tactics is determined as well by two other factors that cross the line between the internal politics of movement groups and the political environment in which they operate—*specialization* and *gravity*. The vagueness of the boundary is a result of the socially constructed nature of movement reality.[3] Shared group understandings about the evils to confront and the means to confront them—"collective action frames"— are products of negotiation among activists.[4] A collective action frame is an "interpretive schemata that simplifies and condenses the "world out there" by selectively punctuating and encoding objects, situations, events, experiences, and sequences of actions within one's present or past environments."[5] Framing processes situate "relevant sets of actors in time and space by attributing characteristics to them that suggest specifiable relationships and lines of action."[6]

Specialization refers to the inclinations and dispositions of activists that shape their action preferences (e.g., love of publicity or distaste for large crowds). Individuals inclined toward quiet, behind-the-scenes tactics will act with a group conducting letter-writing campaigns. Individuals preferring adrenaline-releasing experiences will align with a group engaged in direct action. Gravity refers to the perceived seriousness of a threat. The assessments of threats (regardless of their currentness) may vary from group to group within the same movement. Like hardness and time, gravity can be conceptualized as a continuum; it ranges from life-threatening to innocuous. Judging the gravity of an action object helps groups manage their scarce resources. The omnipresent need to prioritize, to (re)allocate time, money and activists, forces most organizations to both specialize and estimate gravity.

Expectations comprise the final factor shaping organizational choice of tactics. These are negotiated group understandings about the efficacy of particular action forms. Coming to consensus on expectations is a form of the frame alignment process. Frame alignment strategies are "micromobilization processes whereby SMO actors seek to affect various audiences' interpretations regarding the extent to which the SMO's ideology and goals are congruent with targeted individuals' interests, values, and beliefs."[7] Expectations are less a function of individual political efficacy or sense of personal power than of two other considerations: the intensity of group and individual commitment to goals, and the extent of group and individual experience with the political system. Expectations about the results of single actions or even for campaigns of linked actions can be lower for the deeply committed (and thus probably long-lived) group. Overly high expectations can lead to frustration and demoralization. Common sense perceptions—'you can't change the world in a day'—work to guard against naïvete about the possibility for systemic change in the short-run.

Movements act in order to communicate with targets or audiences.

Action centers on an object with specific characteristics that resides in a particular political context. Variation among object characteristics and contexts requires tactical adaptation and flexibility across movements. At least eight factors—hardness, time, mobility, type of political system, movement size, specialization, gravity, and expectations—are essential determinants of movement tactical choice. These include factors internal and external to groups, factors mainly outside the ability of movements to do anything about them, and factors requiring intra-group communication and creativity. From the choice process comes the action form.

Action Forms

Two features of tactical or action forms are immediately apparent: they are "learned, understood, sometimes planned and rehearsed by the participants;" and the means available to people are limited by time and space—not everyone has all means available at all times.[8] Charles Tilly called the set of means available to a movement its "action repertoire." He used the musical term because it underlines the "learned character of the performance and the limits to that learning, yet allows for variation and even continuous change from one performance to the next." It allows for "improvisation, innovation and unexpected endings." When change and innovation in repertoires cease, a movement is in trouble. The British peace movement wore out its repertoire by the early 1960s. Demobilization followed shortly thereafter.[9] The nineteenth century repertoire is by and large still with us today: strikes, demonstrations, protest meetings. Once refreshingly new, these are now well worn.[10]

Action Repertoires and Change

Tilly cited three ways in which repertoires can change: (1) the invention or adoption of new means "e.g., the deliberate creation of the 'sit-in' by American civil rights workers of the 1950s;" (2) the evolution and adaptation of means already available, "e.g., the way London radicals expanded the long-established custom of sending a delegation to accompany a petition into mass marches with thousands of supporters for a petition to Parliament;" and (3) the abandonment of means no longer effective or appropriate, "e.g., the Parisian crowd's abandonment of ritual execution, with the display of traitors' heads on pikes after the initial years of the Revolution."[11] And repertoire change may be just what is needed, for as Heberle wrote, "in political as in military action and in business, success comes to the innovator."[12] A movement's capacity for innovation is limited not only by time and space but also by imagination, by the nature of the object acted upon, and by the content of the communication conveyed. Consider the innovative case of the "satellite bridges" rigged between Moscow and various cities in the U.S. as an antidote to the enemy images constructed by governments and media. Masterminded by people like American peace activist Kim Spencer, the communications links allowed individuals and organizations to directly share views, sing songs, discuss nuclear winter, and dance to Soviet rock and roll. Here were elements of the peace movement (and the Soviet state) using sophisticated communications technology to outmaneuver the Reagan administration's public diplomacy during the darkest days of the 1980s.[13]

The tactical innovations of the German peace movement can be seen as variations on a theme. The movement's variations on the traditional social movement action repertoire surely rivaled those of the Berlin Philharmonic on the recognized classical musical repertoire. Performances from the movement's repertoire were directed toward two audiences: the target of influence, and the target of mobilization and benefits. Individual actions communicated messages to one audience or the other, or to both targets at once. The recipients of movement messages perceived them as either seductive or coercive. Actions are not inherently seductive or coercive, although movements may intend one or the other perception. Both qualities are determined by recipients of messages. Beholder's eyes have filters which sort messages on the basis of preconceived notions about the legitimacy of movement action and on the basis of the recipient's target status.[14]

Movements, like other collective actors and like the audiences for movement communications, prefer seductive to coercive messages. Seduction of antagonistic targets of influence, however, is rare; this audience usually perceives movement action, even that ostensibly directed at potential constituencies, as coercive. Sympathetic targets of influence may be seduced; the longer the seductive interplay, however, the more likely it will ultimately be perceived as coercive. Misperception of movement intentions is possible; an action intended as seductive may be perceived as coercive. Misperception stems from either ambiguity of the message or from interference by authorities with its transmission. Tactical success—the correlation of movement intentions and recipient perceptions—depends on the uninterrupted transmission of "seductive messages" to the sympathetic or uncommitted and on "coercive messages" to the hostile.

Movement action, performances from the repertoire, takes one or more of three forms: polite, protest, and violent.[15] As argued in the previous chapter, the movement's strategy and tactics were overwhelmingly nonviolent. Thus, only polite and protest actions are pertinent here. The assortment of polite actions can be grouped together under the heading Informationsarbeit. An integral component of the movement's overall repertoire, Informationsarbeit was of two types: public education and propaganda. These are narrow but perhaps useful distinctions. Education was primarily targeted at current or potential movement constituents. Propaganda was means both for communication with potential constituents and for countering the "public diplomacy" campaigns of the state. Educational action could be both direct and indirect. Direct educational techniques included seminars, lectures, teach-ins, community forums, speeches at rallies, and materials (pamphlets, magazines, books) published by the movement. Indirect education overlapped with propaganda. Movement propaganda consisted of letters to the editor of mainstream periodicals, guest appearances by movement notables or counterexperts on television programs and at the meeting of associations, regular and hastily called press briefings and releases, the publication of a steady stream of monographs and anthologies on NATO and U.S. weapons and strategies, and other vehicles for outreach and influence.

Noncooperation

Lofland identified four classes of protest action: symbolic, noncooperation, intervention, and alternative institutions. The use of the term "symbolic" connotes the theoretical presence of its polar opposite, the "real." As "reality" is a social construction—a set of more or less structured beliefs centered around agreed upon codes and understandings—this is not a very useful dichotomy. The other three classes show more promise as typological categories. Noncooperation is the most common form of nonviolent action; it comprised 103 of the 198 instances of direct action Gene Sharp examined in his famous study.[16] Noncooperation has a social, economic or political focus. Economic noncooperation includes the strike, work slowdown, and purchasing boycott. These economic tactics could be given a political spin as well. Millions of DGBmembers staged a several minute work pause during Action Week in October 1983 to show their support for disarmament. Some activists even hoped trade unions would conduct a general strike to help prevent the INF deployment.[17] Noncooperation took many forms: young male pacifists destroyed their draft cards, adherents of all ages took part in "fasts for peace" or "vigils against the arms race," some citizens declared their refusal to cooperate with the NATO decision during visits to town halls and state parliaments, and others participated in "anti-militaristic walks" to military bases and weapons depots. Rallies and demonstrations, parades and marches are all forms of active, collective noncooperation. Individual refusal to cooperate could be formally declared by organizing or signing one or more of the countless petitions and appeals circulating during the early eighties against the Euromissiles and the arms race, and for a just, peaceful world.

Interventions

Interventions are, following Lofland, of four sorts: harassment, system overloading, blockade, and occupation. The movement included all four in its repertoire. Harassment involves continually calling attention to the displeasing activities of an individual member of the elite. Heads of state and government as well as their defense ministers are regular targets of peace movement harassment. Never popular among those resistant to the new politics, some forms of harassment were especially controversial. Pundits were outraged when a West German activist splashed an American general with blood. Forms of harassment, like heckling at public engagements, may be limited by the movements of and guarded access to a powerful individual, but the content of the harassment is limited only by the imagination of the protester. Less personal, system overloading means making unworkable some social or political arrangement such as a telephone number, a post office box, an editorial response function, or a legislator-constituent meeting. Some activists hoped a campaign of massive income tax resistance (which never came about) would overload the capacity of federal and state governments to collect revenues and police compliance with the tax system.

Blockades temporarily impede access to public or private facilities. One of the movement's most dramatic tactical innovations was a variation on the blockade theme: creation of human chains. The two best-known targets were the U.S. Army's headquarters in Stuttgart and its Wiley Barracks in Neu-Ulm, one of four hosts for Pershing IIs. Each of these chains was over a hundred kilometers long and required tens of thousands of human links. Smaller scale blockades took place with increased frequency as deployment neared. Occupations involve unwelcome entrance and obstinate refusal to leave some public or private space. Offices, lobbies, and even sidewalks as in the case of the "die-in," were targets for occupation. If obnoxious from the point of view of the state, and they usually were, occupiers could be prosecuted for trespassing or more serious offenses.

Alternative Institutions

Alternative institutions are a form of "positive intervention:" the establishment of "new behavior patterns, policies, relationships, or institutions which are preferred."[18] This is perhaps the most serious and weighty movement action form, and involves processes of withdrawal, refusal and construction. The first step in alternative institution building is individual or group withdrawal from common associations, expectations and understandings. Moving to West Berlin to dodge military service or refusing to vote on strategic grounds are forms of withdrawal. Critical questions followed by rejection of the dominant defense paradigm formed the nucleus of peace movement withdrawal and refusal. The next step is construction of the alternative institution. It is here the three features of NSMs discussed in Chapter 2 are worth reviewing—action in new arenas of conflict; display of new forms of identity and consciousness; employment of new types of organization and action—as they provided the context for peace movement construction of alternative institutions.

The peace movement showed great concern for the ways in which social information was generated and meaning communicated. For example, the movement publicized grievances and anxieties about nuclear deterrence, a "fact" of everyday life. Activists contested the meaning assigned deterrence by the authorities. The ongoing shift in advanced capitalism from the management of economic resources to the production of social relations creates this new arena encompassing the generation of information and transmission of meaning. Information and meaning are the conditions or parameters of movement action; they are the raw materials for the production of movement relations with other social actors. New conflicts thus revolve around the skill of individuals and groups to control these conditions. Alternative institutions, like pirate radio transmitters, provide movements the potential for such control. The still unfolding contest over alternatives to deterrence and reliance on nuclear weapons is at the center of the new arena. Social defense or civilian-based defense would (depending on the version) explicitly replace traditional military units with networks of lightly armed or unarmed citizens bent on noncooperation with and (non)violent resistance to an invader. From Klein-Pampau in the Lauenburg to Eching in Bavaria, community-based activists led efforts to declare their localities NFZs. For intellectual support, they could draw on the expertise of the Nuclear-free Europe Work Group in Berlin which sponsored a congress in 1981 to press the idea of nuclear-free Europe, and a conference on alternative European peace policy in 1982. Such alternatives drastically change the meaning of defense. In the process, alternative institutions are born.

The creation of new collective identities, of new forms of consciousness, necessarily entails the construction of alternative institutions. These new identities stress both individuation and solidarity; they are formed in struggles against the "government of individualization."[19] Peace movement adherents make plain the global character of life in the era of postindustrialism. A planetary citizenship of diversity supplants nationalism and narrow parochialisms, but the principle of difference lives on. Fraternity yes, sameness no. The new consciousness surfaced in the production of cards, T-shirts, even trash bags with sayings such as: "Rearmament? Never fear, a small pile of ashes awaits you too." It became clear, too, in the public singing of altered Christmas carols. A sense of humor (sometimes dark) characterized movement identity; borrowing from the advertising for laundry detergent, grassroots groups emblazoned rented billboards with slogans like "New missiles kill faster, better, more effectively." Others painted walls with graffiti: "NATO: Kohl loves you."

The new consciousness moved activists to patronize politically correct service providers, e.g., switch family doctors if the current one was not a member of Physicians Against Nuclear War. It moved others to perform or attend street or "guerilla" theater. The Berliner Compagnie, 15 people whose pacifist metier was the stage, put on "Rearmament," a play about nuclear arms, enemy images, and modes of resistance. These dramatists' interest in making links to the peace movement in the U.S. led them to produce "The Trial of the Catonsville Nine," a play about the Berrigan brothers' opposition to the Vietnam War. The Compagnie also created widely-circulated posters with slogans such as "Book a trip to Europe! (while it's still here)," and "Europeans cry NO!" Less colorful manifestations of movement identity led to philosophical discussions with the police and military led by Christian groups like ASF. Similar discussions were conducted with parties. The Forum Frieden—organized by Peter Glotz and sponsored by the SPD—was an example of the old consciousness initiating contact with the new.

Peace movement organizations themselves can be seen as alternative institutions. Decentralized, sectioned, without strong leaders; they generally have but weak centers and simple, temporary divisions of labor.[20] Gerlach's SPINs—segmented, polycentric, ideologically integrated networks—are the conscious creations of their members.[21] Infused by the spirit of participatory democracy, deepened individualization, and broadened solidarity, grassroots groups stand as models for human organization. Remnants of the traditional urges to direct from the center and to professionalize were constant reminders of the difficulties of creating wholly new institutions or alternative structures for social action.

The movement's new institutions were created within the ideological and political context of nonviolence. But advocates of tactical nonviolent action, direct and otherwise, argue that one need not be an ideological pacifist or cheek-turner to use it.[22] They suggest this active—not passive—tactic is superior to violence because it can restrict authorities' opportunities for repression. The power of public opinion and social movements around the globe has removed machine-gunning unarmed crowds from virtually all states' repertoires of action. While "disappearances" and torture remain tools for a dwindling number of states, nonviolent action works by withdrawing the citizen consent and obedience states require to work their will.[23] It works in both democratic and authoritarian systems and has been effective to varying degrees in places as diverse as: China, the Philippines, Eastern Europe, Sudan, Bangladesh, Morocco, South Africa, Myanmar, and the West Bank and Gaza, as well as in the former Soviet Union and the United States. But "it wouldn't work against Hitler" goes the old refrain. And yet on numerous occasions nonviolent direct action was successfully used against the Nazis in Norway, Denmark, the Netherlands, and even in the German capital after the war's tide had turned. Sharp cited an example from "Berlin in 1943, [where] an around-the-clock, nine-day demonstration by non-Jewish wives and friends of arrested Jewish men saved about 1500 from the gas chambers."[24] Nonviolent action also helped save thousands of Jews in Hungary and Bulgaria. Again, direct action by the movement was nearly always nonviolent. Among the more interesting organizational vehicles for civil disobedience in the German (as well as other movements) is the affinity group.

Affinity Groups

Many grass roots movement units adopted and modified the affinity group system created by anarchists during the Spanish Civil War.[25] Affinity groups are small autonomous units of six to twenty people. The participants know each other and prepare well in advance of actions: many affinity groups are communes in action whose members eat, play and live together. Members take on assignments during actions: a separate representative each for meetings with other affinity groups, for meetings with police, for public relations, for observation but not participation (in order to bail people out of jail), for discussion facilitation, and other specialized tasks.

Each affinity group operates on the consensus principle, a simple and effective way to institutionalize participatory democracy. In one system, members have one of five options in deciding on an action: "full agreement" (everyone is of one opinion); "do not understand" (someone does not fully understand some facet of an action but has trust in the others and thus will take part); "have doubts or objections" (about the action but will participate nonetheless); "step to the side" (disagree with the action and will not take part, but will not hinder others' participation); and "veto" (someone has fundamental objections to the action). Hand signals are used to signal participation, nonparticipation, and veto in the midst of actions. Only in the case of a veto is the action blocked. When this happens the group has several options: it can either attempt to convert the hold-out; begin the discussion process anew; postpone the decision to act; vote (rarely done); or persevere in the face of dissensus.

Affinity groups actively practice the future in the present. They believe simply demonstrating against things is an inadequate social critique; they work to show alternative ways of living through their organization, decisionmaking, and action. They hold up nonviolent direct action as an exemplar of social defense; through it they mean to show what unarmed but well-trained people can do in the face of state power.

Two dilemmas face affinity groups (and peace movement organizations in general). Ought actions to be regional or extra-regional? Should they be plain or spectacular? Typically, actions large in terms of space (of the event itself or of the territory from which participants are drawn) are also those large in terms of spectacle, and the converse holds too. Ideally, of course, a movement should consist of groups that do both either together or separately, as did the West German peace movement. Each option, even the smallest, reaches particular constituencies and has its strengths. Those committed to the local path believe the words painted on a sandwich board during the campaign against the Euromissiles: "Many little people from many little places who do many little things can change the face of the world."[26] Small, local actions aim not to shut down bases or appear as the lead story on the television news. They take their strength in numbers and can have a cumulative effect if multiplied a thousandfold. And this they were in the Federal Republic of the early eighties.

Conclusion

Movements act in order to communicate messages to audiences. Messages are (mis)perceived by recipients as seductive or coercive. Tactics are the means by which movements transmit signals and achieve ends. They can be learned, practiced and adapted to the fluid field of political opportunities. Each movement organization has a collection of tactics, its action repertoire. Repertoires grow, shrink and change with the needs of the group and the response of the authorities. Varying from group to group, tactics evolve out of the complex interaction of eight factors: the nature of the object of action (hardness, mobility and currentness), the openness of the political system in which organizations act, the size and influence of movements, the inclinations of activists (specialization), the seriousness of the threat (gravity), and the hopes assigned to the outcome of action (expectations).

Movement action is polite or disruptive. Polite action involves Informationsarbeit: public education and propaganda. Disruptive or protest action takes one of three forms: noncooperation, intervention, or the construction of alternative institutions. Much of the most visible movement action was noncooperation. Interventions come in four types: harassment, system overloading, blockade, and occupation. Each type was a vehicle for the communication of movement messages. Building alternative institutions allows movements to leave a legacy, and provides positive models for the construction of a new society. Affinity groups are an organizational realization of the new society. Schools of nonviolence and interpersonal relations, these groups provide members the opportunity to protest existing or impending threats while at the same time setting an example for the wider society.

Notes

1. Gamson, *The Strategy of Social Protest*, pp. 14-15.
2. Heberle, "Types and Functions of Social Movements," p. 442.
3. Peter Berger and Thomas Luckmann, *The Social Construction of Reality* (Garden City, NY: Doubleday, 1967).
4. David A. Snow, E. Burke Rochford, Jr., Steven K. Worden, and Robert D. Benford, "Frame Alignment Processes, Micromobilization, and Movement Participation," *American Sociological Review*, vol. 51 (1986).
5. David A. Snow and Robert D. Benford, "Master Frames and Cycles of Protest," in Morris and Mueller, eds., *Frontiers in Social Movement Theory*, p.137.
6. Scott A. Hunt, Robert D. Benford, and David A. Snow, "Identity Fields: Framing Processes and the Social Construction of Movement Identities," in Laraña, et al., eds., *New Social Movements*, p. 185.
7. Hunt, Benford, and Snow, "Identity Fields," p. 191.
8. Tilly, "Social Movements and National Politics," p. 307.

9. Richard Taylor, *Against the Bomb: The British Peace Movement, 1958-1965* (Oxford: Clarendon, 1988).

10. Bernd Jürgen Warneken, ed., *Massenmedium Straße: Zur Kulturgeschichte der Demonstration* (Frankfurt: Campus, 1991).

11. Tilly, "Social Movements and National Politics," p. 307.

12. Heberle, "Types and Functions of Social Movements," p. 442.

13. Gary Thatcher, "Americans and Russians 'Dance to Each Other's Music' via Satellite," *Christian Science Monitor*, December 17, 1984, p. 1.

14. Barnes and Kaase, *Political Action*; Michael Lipsky, "Protest as a Political Resource," *American Political Science Review*, vol. 62 (1968); and Ralph H. Turner, "The Public Perception of Protest," *American Sociological Review*, vol. 34 (1969).

15. Lofland, *Protest*, chapter 12.

16. Gene Sharp, *The Politics of Nonviolent Action* (Boston: Sargent, 1973).

17. Gerosa, *Grosse Schritte*, p. 134.

18. Sharp, *The Politics of Nonviolent Action*, p. 357.

19. Foucault, "The Subject and Power," p. 212.

20. Gerlach and Hine, *People, Power, Change*.

21. Gerlach, "Protest Movements and the Construction of Risk."

22. Sharp, *The Politics of Nonviolent Action* .

23. Roger Rawlinson, "Three Nonviolent Campaigns—Larzac, Marckolsheim, Wyhl—A Comparison," in Chadwick Alger and Michael Stohl, eds., *A Just Peace Through Transformation: Cultural, Economic, and Political Foundations for Change* (Boulder, CO: Westview Press, 1988).

24. Gene Sharp, "The Power of Nonviolence," *Christian Science Monitor*, July 31, 1989, p. 19.

25. Herbert Erchinger, "Bezugsgruppensystem und Sprecherratsmodell," in Jürgen Tatz, ed., *Gewaltfreier Widerstand gegen Massenvernichtungsmittel: Die Friedensbewegung entscheidet sich* (Freiburg: Dreisam, 1984).

26. Erchinger, "Bezugsgruppensystem und Sprecherratsmodell," p. 163.

8

Mobilization

The movement of nations is not caused by power, nor by intellectual activity, nor even by a combination of the two, as historians have supposed, but by the activity of all the people who participate in the event.

—Tolstoy

Mobilization, to employ our military metaphor a final time, involves recruitment, training, and logistics. Through mobilization, movement organizations gather and invest resources—guided by strategy and acting tactically—for the pursuit of goals. Mobilization refers to the processes which provide movement groups the wherewithal for the realization of ends. Mobilization, like strategy, goals and tactics, is a social construction which itself constructs the visible movement that leaves footprints in the consciousness of observers. It is that dimension of the social movement experience concerned about the "with what?" of movement action.

Political scientist Max Kaase wrote that political mobilization "as a process through historical time is linked very much *in political terms* to nation building, *in ideological terms* to egalitarianism, and in *socio-structural terms* to the growth of market economy and to industrialization"[his italics].[1] With the achievement of complete suffrage rights by Swiss women in 1971, the political mobilization of Western democracies through political parties was complete. And yet this landmark event took place in the midst of increased challenges to parties as central political mobilizers. Parties traditionally performed the two primary functions of mobilization: interest articulation and legitimation.[2] Over time, social movements called into question the ability of parties to perform these functions.

Gamson defined social movement mobilization as "a process of increasing the readiness to act collectively by building the loyalty of a constituency to an organization or to a group of leaders;" it "is part of an organizing process that precedes specific efforts at influence."[3] For Tilly, mobilization refers to the process by which challengers gain collective control over resources that make collective action possible.[4] The definitions share three common features: an emphasis on organizations and their members or leaders; a view of mobilization as process; and agreement that the aim of mobilization is preparation for action. The definitions lack only two ingredients: clarification of what is meant by "resources"; and a specific reference to the phases through which the mobilization process passes. I define resources broadly to include all persons, entities and relationships which can help a movement (organization) negotiate dilemmas, solve problems and attain goals. Mobilization processes can be analyzed with the aid of concepts like stages or periods. Mobilization of the 1980s West German peace movement is widely recognized to have passed through several perceptible if overlapping phases.[5]

The mobilization process has two components: the creation of commitment and the activation of commitment.[6] Commitment is related to dedication, but includes as well the willingness to take risks or experience discomfort and deprivation. Commitment must be created before it can be activated. Each component is assigned its own section here. The first examines two interdependent processes: the mobilization of commitment, and the recruitment of activists and generation of other resources. The second analyzes the conditions and context for propelling adherents into action. While vigorous movements never cease simultaneously creating and activating commitment, more or less distinct stages in these processes are discernible. These stages come in for analysis in the third section which discusses the abstract concept of mobilization stages before moving on, in the fourth section, to determine the particular mobilization cycle experienced by the Federal German peace movement of the 1980s.

"A movement," wrote Herbert Blumer, "has to be constructed and has to carve out a career in what is practically always an opposed, resistant, or at least indifferent world."[7] Mobilization, the revolving step-by-step creation and activation of commitment, must overcome this opposition, resistance, and indifference. Failing that, a movement is sure to shrivel, and perhaps ultimately, to die.

Creation of Commitment

The creation of commitment involves "a change from a low . . . to a high generalized readiness to act collectively."[8] To transform the collective action potential of people requires preexisting organizations and political entrepreneurs to alert, recruit, supply and perhaps educate a constituency, a target of mobilization or benefits. Alerts and education are part of the "mobilization of consensus."[9] Consensus is mobilized through the public and private construction of meaning, through discourse contests with other claimants to the loyalty and resources potential constituents can provide. Consensus is not mobilized for its own sake but as a necessary step to the activation of commitment; it is a preface to action. Recruitment is a variable set of techniques by which organizers and groups get the uncommitted to enlist in the collective effort. It is a process both dependent on and essential for the mobilization of other resources besides people (e.g., money). The creation of commitment is thus a process with a dual character: the recruitment of activists and mobilization of other resources, and the mobilization of consensus. I begin by examining the latter.

As movements arise, they tend to generate public controversy. Uncommitted citizens may be polarized into partisan supporters or resistant opponents; movements ask of as many citizens as possible: "Which side are you on?" The civil rights movement in the United States transformed a relatively quiescent citizenry into advocates and resisters of black civil rights. Regardless of organizational affiliation, the public takes positions and adjusts behavior in response to new norms. Issues emerge where consensus once reigned.[10] And these new norms and issues—the building blocks for the construction of meaning—become the front in the battle over creation of a new consensus.

> SMOs engage in the construction of meaning by interpreting grievances and evaluating opportunities, and through interactions with an external environment with a specific opportunity structure. The construction of meaning is accomplished in part by deliberate attempts of social actors (SMOs, countermovement organizations, opponents) to mobilize consensus; in part, it comes about through unplanned consensus formation within friendship networks, primary bonds, and so on.[11]

By mobilizing consensus—on the dangers of deterrence or the desirability of disarmament—peace movements can create commitment.

The presence of grievances is, however, no guarantee of the formation and mobilization of consensus. Diffuse protest and discontent more often than not does not coalesce into structured demands for change. Witness the thousands of protests, riots and disturbances around the world every year which are inchoate, unchanneled, abandoned. Eric Hobsbawm called one type of these unstructured expressions of vexation "archaic movements." Sicilian social banditry, nourished by the general complaint of the peasantry against the rich and the "outsider," never developed an ideology, organization, or program.[12] But the German peace movement was extraordinarily successful at identifying and interpreting grievances. Its opposition to the Euromissiles resonated with and interpreted public grievances about life under the nuclear threat.

Consensus can be mobilized—commitment can emerge—from shared understandings about the wise use of scarce resources: how to husband them, when, where and why to invest them. Understandings at odds create not consensus but a tendency toward factionalism or demobilization. Resource-use issues are in part questions of strategy and tactics, questions about how to best grasp available opportunities and to create new ones. Contingencies beyond the control of a movement may alter the array of opposing and supporting forces and thus significantly affect the mobilization of consensus and thus the creation of commitment. The hyperinflation of the Weimar years contributed mightily to the development of Nazism among a petty bourgeoisie whose militant nationalism already made them likely adherents of National Socialism.[13] The contingencies of the Reagan years—Polish worker rebellion, arms build-up, belligerent rhetoric, official resistance to arms control, intervention in the Third World—stoked the fear upon which much of the German anti-missile movement's allure rested, upon which consensus could be mobilized.

While the nature of a political system (in league with Machiavelli's *fortuna*) largely structure opportunities, opportunity structures are not simply given. Movements create opportunities and commitment through the generation of resources. These resources are at the same time necessary for the creation of commitment and opportunities. Movements are thus faced with Yossarian's paradox: the resource mobilization Catch-22. Mobilizing resources—consensus and commitment—takes resources. Resources have specific origins and costs. There are three key sources of mobilizable resources: the beneficiary constituency, any conscience constituencies, and nonconstituency institutions.[14] The first consists of political beneficiaries of the movement who also supply resources, and the conscience constituencyof those sympathizers who provide resources but are not directly (materially) benefitted by the work of the movement. Institutional resources are those provided by legal codes, police protection, foundation grants, and the like.

But as with Gamson's target typology, this is a framework designed with materialist movements in mind. The direct outcome of peace movement challenges is not more public housing, better pay and working conditions, or expanded civil rights (though these may be some of the long-term benefits of economic conversion from military to socially useful investment and industry). Peace movements provide indivisible public goods. This does not mean that a movement able to get its way would not provide some private (albeit perceived by some as public) "bads": far fewer positions in the armed forces, far fewer contracts for arms manufacturers, temporary dislocation for communities dependent on the military-industrial complex, a far less imperious foreign policy.

A major factor affecting the costs of mobilizing resources is their density. Movements in opposition to nuclear power are able to reach many potential adherents near actual or planned nuclear power plants. Movements to save tropical rain forests are able to reach those who live in them, such as rubber tappers. Scattered groups are, conversely, much more difficult and costly to mobilize. The West German anti-missile movement faced the unenviable task of creating commitment in as much of the populace as possible. In this the movement was assisted greatly by the existence of activists already mobilized for other campaigns. What appeared a hopeless task was made feasible by the presence of dense pockets of able people who required only to be made willing. According to Jo Freeman,

> The reason many different movements tend to appear during the same historical period is not that different groups just happen to discover their grievances at the same time, or even that the example of one group alerts others to opportunities to alleviate their own grievances. Rather, it is that the resources one movement generates can be used for cognate movements. Organizing or publicizing skills gained in one movement are transferable.[15]

The constituencies of seemingly diverse postmaterialist movements overlap to a large degree. The peace movement was able to draw on tens of thousands of ecologists, feminists, human rights activists, and people working in solidarity with the Third World. In the German case, NSMs have a less broad sympathy base and mobilization potential than certain other West European countries. But German "activation rates" (the proportion of those actually engaged in social movement activities) are the highest. During the early nineties, the peace movement had the highest rates of sympathy, potential support, and activism in the country. Franz-Urban Pappi found the activist core of the German peace movement at 3.9 percent of the population (in comparison to 3.1 percent for the anti-nuclear power movement, and 0.9 percent among women and 0.6 percent among men for the women's movement).[16]

Resources come in two intertwined types: animate and inanimate. Animate resources are people, the sine qua non of a mass movement; inanimate resources include money, office space, and media attention. Movements are generally richer in people than established interest groups which tend to mobilize inanimate resources. People become the sympathizers, activists and leaders of movement organizations. The many different resources people can contribute may be divided into three categories: specialized resources (expertise, status, access to decisionmakers); time (to perform necessary labor, to sit through meetings, and attend demonstrations); and dedication.[17] Different people bring different resources with them. The expertise and status of professional groups, for example, made them valuable peace movement constituents. Students and other youths have more time than most to devote to collective action. And the dedication of militants, e.g., their willingness to take risks or spend time in jail, distinguishes them from casual activists. Animate and inanimate resources intersect when people with a newfound sense of commitment bring funds, media connections or real estate with them.

People are recruited through two primary channels: the public and the private. Recruiting new movement members can share features with religious proselytization and conversion.[18] Private channels include the networks of everyday life: family, friends, neighbors, co-workers, fellow congregants, service providers, fellow students, team mates, fellow fraternal club or association members; new activists may emerge wherever and whenever the committed and the uncommitted gather and interact. Public recruitment channels are found in the spheres of civic society. They are either direct (movement controlled) or indirect (incidental to movement action). Direct public channels include: canvassing (door-to-door and telephonic); publications of all sorts (church newsletters, movement communications, popular peace research books, letters to the editor, newspaper advertisements, opinion pieces); public service announcements on broadcast media; town or neighborhood meetings; information stuck to kiosks, lamp posts, store windows, and other visible places; and on-line computer news groups. The primary indirect public channel is broadcast and print media coverage: articles and programs about particular groups or events, profiles of leaders, interviews, editorials, talk shows, documentaries, movies, and newscasts.

Peace movements, unlike labor movements, are usually unable to supply "selective incentives" (material benefits) to new recruits or potential members. Apart from the occasional bumper sticker (e.g., "You can't hug with nuclear arms"), poster (e.g., text against background of children climbing on play ground equipment: "It will be a great day when the Air Force has to hold a bake sale to buy a bomber"), button (e.g., "Nuclear war: it's not the heat, it's the humidity"), and magazine, peace movement groups have no tangible goods to offer the uncommitted. They must rely instead on "solidary incentives" to overcome the famous freerider problem—the alleged tendency of rational actors to pursue personal rather than collective interests.[19] Solidary incentives include friendship, camaraderie, a sense of belonging and of working for a good cause, respect, prestige, and the chance to exercise unused or unknown talents. Inability to provide selective incentives did not prevent the creation of commitment in millions of peace activists on both sides of the Atlantic during the early eighties. There are, nonetheless, genuine obstacles in the path of those who would mobilize masses.

The barriers to the creation of commitment are two: inertia and social control. Inertia is a consequence of ignorance, apathy or fatigue. Ignorance and apathy are combatted through public education. The enormity of the problems of the arms race and disarmament—a source of resignation—must be reduced; problems must be seen as open to resolution by ordinary human beings. Militarism and threats to security must be named, given a face or shape. Social control—the processes by which elites persuade or coerce citizens to conform to expectations—is countered by propaganda. Social control options include force, law, suggestion, imitation, praise, blame, reward and concession. State claims to efficiently provide for the common defense, work for disarmament, reduce international tensions, and promote peace, must be challenged. Movement propaganda must critique existing security policies and suggest alternatives, deconstruct government declarations, and offer a vision of a demilitarized and more harmonious world.

"Established groups," wrote Gamson, "must maintain the loyalty and commitment of those from whom they draw their resources; challenging groups must create this loyalty."[20] The mobilization of consensus, the recruitment of activists, and the gathering of other resources helps create commitment. Its maintenance is a never-ending task that can only be accomplished through the second step in the mobilization process: the activation of commitment.

Activation of Commitment

The activation of commitment—the move from consciousness to action—takes place on a hypothetical scale from elite representation to mass mobilization. The West German peace movement acted everywhere along the scale from the elite representation of the Coordinating Committee to the largest human gatherings in non-Nazi German history. Sustained mass mobilizations have three preconditions: problems that encroach directly on people's lives; catalytic events; and education and propaganda. This section analyzes the requirements for and the context of the mass activation of commitment.

Tangible Evil

The huge mass mobilizations of anti-nuclear power and anti-nuclear weapons movements show the paramount importance of a tangible evil; there is no substitute for something hard and shiny like a missile or a nuclear power plant to rally people. A return to the determinants of tactical choice from Chapter 7 is instructive in this regard. Generally, the harder and less mobile an object and the graver the threat it poses, the greater the likelihood organizers can activate the commitment of masses of people in opposition to the evil. Anti-nuclear power movements oppose very hard and shiny fixed facilities posing potentially grave threats to localities. The threat is not abstract. It is directly before the protester: the famous cooling towers—a symbol high in the iconography of nuclear perfidy—belching steam into the local sky. All the calculations showing greater or smaller probabilities of a core reactor melt down are made surreal by the high chain link fence topped by concertina wire. The same can be said for the Pershing II base outside Neu-Ulm or the Cruise missile base at Greenham Common. Symbols of nuclear deterrence become real when situated near unassuming neighborhoods. On the edge of town: Guard dogs and guard shacks, warning signs amidst signs of danger.

The existing facilities slated to receive Cruise and Pershing, if unobtrusive prior to an awakening to the threat of the Euromissiles, became symbols of increased nuclear menace. The tangible and the slippery merged, the doctrine of deterrence was embodied by the impending intermediate-range rockets. Strategies like forward defense lose their softness when represented by the armored personnel carriers that patrolled the inner-German or Czech borders. The jellyfish of NATO doctrine calcified in a moment of recognition, it became a growth on the great coral reef of the nuclear age. But the reef lived in the ocean of superpower relations, a sea whose temperature rose from below. The icy surface, blown this way and that by the gales of elite rhetoric, was gradually displaced by a pacifist El Niño. An upwelling of water warmed by movement action endangered the reef.

Catalytic Events

Mass activation of commitment also requires one or more catalytic events or shockers.[21] Generally, the more shockers the better for the purposes of mobilization. Catalytic events are not such in and of themselves. They need to be interpreted, cast in a useful light by the movement. A mobilized consensus creates the context for movement interpretation of shockers. The more widely disseminated the consensus, the deeper its internalization by sympathetic media, the more likely the event will have the desired effect. Catalytic events are generally irregular, unscheduled political opportunities. But during the early eighties, President Reagan could be counted on to shock movement constituencies nearly every time he opened his mouth about arms control and defense policy. It perversely but just as certainly aided the German peace movement to have an American president suggest on separate occasions that Europe could be the battlefield of a limited nuclear war, that nuclear weapons would inevitably be used, and that the warheads of submarine-launched ballistic missiles (SLBMs) could be recalled after firing.[22] American ecology groups were helped in the same fashion at the same time by the incredible statements of Reagan and his Secretary of the Interior James Watt about the environment and natural resources. This was a rare case of a near sure thing, of the spontaneous become routinized. Regular shocks present a danger for the activation of commitment, however, as they numb. Desensitized, people could write off the President's statements as the ravings of a harmless old man or as just another blow to a weary body politic. The latter sort of numbing can take place even against the conscious and vigilant opposition of the committed individual. For the affordable housing activist, civil rights worker, environmentalist, feminist, or pacifist in the United States not to have suffered some numbing (at least in emotional and intellectual extremities) during the twelve years of the Reagan-Bush era was truly extraordinary.

The ominous proximity of nuclear war at the turn of the decade—made to seem all the closer by interpretations of events based on a mobilized movement consensus—was probably the most important blanket stimulus to action. In the context of the movement consensus and with the sharp dip in superpower relations, fear became concrete, perception of danger existential. But as Kermit Johnson reminded us, "fear has its limits as a motivator; eventually, fearful people simply give up because the burden is too great and the results too meager. After all, fear got us into this mess in the first place. Reinforcing fear, even for the purpose of moving people to action, is not apt to get us very far."[23] There was nothing essentially new about this mobilization context. It was similar to that underlying the commitment activation of the Struggle Against Atomic Death, CND, and SANE in the mid-late fifties. The Cuban missile crisis gave renewed impetus to efforts against nuclear testing in the early sixties. Regardless of novelty, a context of interpreted catalytic events is essential. The case could be made, however, that evolution in military technology (MIRVs, etc.) and the piling up of greater and greater numbers of nuclear weapons did distinguish—qualitatively and quantitatively—the early 1980s from previous periods in the postwar period. It would follow then that the anti-nuclear mobilization of the later years would be both larger and more intense than that of earlier decades.

Catalytic events come in several sizes (small, medium, large) and have varying spatial impacts (from local to global). President Reagan's joke over a live microphone about commencing the "bombing" of the Soviet Union in five minutes was reported to an outraged world and reinforced the impression of the former actor as an irresponsible and dangerous nincompoop. The news greeting German citizens returning from All Saints Day holidays in 1982 of several accidents with Pershing I transporters, resulting in the death of a father of three, in Wahlprechtsweier and Schwäbisch Gmünd, was small or medium rather than large in size, and of national rather than global impact. But here was shocking evidence, reported throughout the country, of the dangers inherent in mobile nuclear missiles. Barring a shocker, social movements find it nigh to impossible to climb out of the cyclical trough of an "elite-sustained stage" of mobilization, a low visibility period of their careers.[24] If safeguards against psychic numbing are in place, a continuous stream of catalytic events like that in the early eighties helps assure steady, even predictable, mass activation of commitment.

Education and Propaganda

The third requirement for the mass activation of commitment is education and propaganda; the tools used for creation of commitment thus overlap with those used for its activation. It is necessary to educate the public to rouse them. Some basic ideas about the nature and dimensions of a problem and some more-or-less-specific notions about cures are essential for effective and sustained citizen incitement. As we shall see, widespread public expertise on defense issues typically came after some citizens had already been mobilized by the threat of the impending Euromissile deployment. These tens of thousands of citizens knew intuitively that Cruise and Pershing contributed to the arms spiral; what they later learned about decapitation strikes, throw weight and hard target kill capability confirmed their fears and made many of them remarkably informed and thus more effective opponents of the double-track decision. They also became educators themselves and were responsible for the recruitment and activation of enormous numbers of their formerly uncommitted fellow citizens. Without the knowledge transmitted through education, the activation of commitment would prove simply impossible.[25]

Propaganda is necessary because if the movement did not counter social control attempts by the authorities, commitment created might not be activated. Eager new activists, itching to shout slogans or stuff envelopes, may doubt the value of these activities if the government is indeed right when it says progress is being made toward an INF agreement. A high level of trust in government is not a resource for peace movements. If trust in government is placed on a scale from complete alienation to blind obedience, then peace movements do best when citizens are suspicious, when they realize states lie and manipulate but are also capable of righteous action. Movement propaganda proceeds from the following premises: the state will not wither away in the foreseeable future; the state is the source of the security dilemma; the bloc system shapes the security dilemma in the atomic epoch. The state and its alliance responsibilities are thus the focus of movement publicity. Propaganda is a means for individuals and organizations to rally the committed against state policies. Taken together, tangible objects, catalytic events, education and propaganda provide the targets, the context and the methods for mass activation of commitment.

The components of the social movement mobilization model discussed in this section appear below in list form, and graphically in Figure 8.1.

Creation of commitment:
  • entrepreneurial/leadership activities
      * goal-setting
      * strategizing
  • recruitment
      * incentives
      * public channels
      * private channels
  • mobilization of consensus
      * meaning frame construction
      * grievance interpretation
      * political opportunity evaluation

- mobilization of other resources
  - * nature of constituency
  - * resource density

Activation of commitment:
- tangible problems
- catalytic events
- education and propaganda

Tactical action:
- determinants of tactical choice
  - * object hardness
  - * object mobility
  - * object temporality
  - * nature of political system
  - * group size
  - * group specialization
  - * group expectations
  - * gravity of issue
- action repertoire
- action

Mobilization Phases

Charles Tilly identified a "duality of perspectives" regarding social movement life-histories.[26] He distinguished between how movements look "from above" and "from below." The former is the perspective of the challenged, those in power. According to Tilly, social movements appear "sustained and coherent" from above while appearing like a "hasty, temporary and risky alliance" from below. This distinction does not hold for the West German peace movement. Helmut Schmidt, Helmut Kohl, Hans-Dietrich Genscher and other leading politicians had all lived through the popular campaigns of the fifties and sixties. The Struggle Against Atomic Death came and went. The student Extraparliamentary Opposition came and went. The powerful are generally aware of the fragility and limited life expectancy of social movement coalitions. Some number of their public and private statements and actions—their attempts at social control—throughout the struggle over the Euromissiles were aimed at preventing the creation and activation of commitment. They denigrated the movement as communist-inspired and contrary to parliamentary democracy. These "qualities" were perceived by authorities as weak spots to exploit to split and thus marginalize and demobilize the movement.

FIGURE 8.1 A Model of Social Movement Mobilization

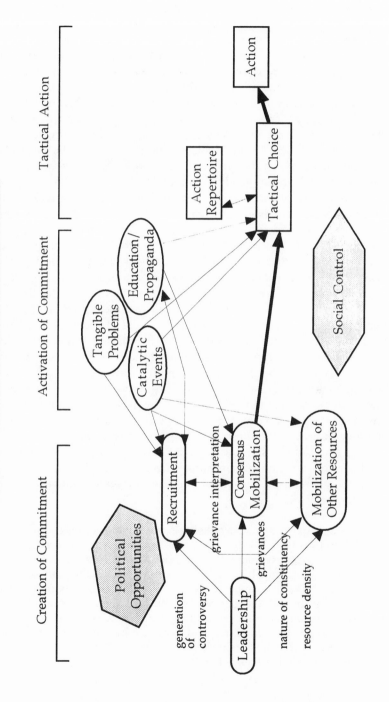

The chief variable here is the endurance of a mass movement. If a highly mobilized movement lasts long enough (at least for the better part of an electoral cycle), then the powerful must respond (through rhetorical or actual concessions, bargains, attempts at cooptation or repression) or face unknown electoral or other political dangers. Naturally, authorities hope to weather a challenge without making concessions; they hope a movement is no more than a flash in the pan. But when movements endure beyond the capacity of elites to ignore them or to respond only rhetorically to them (and this capacity varies depending on the temperament, party affiliation, ideology, and relative popularity or electoral strength of elites), as did the German anti-missile movement, then substantial concessions are likely to follow.

The duality of perspectives also accounts, according to Tilly, for the difficulty scholars have in studying social movements. It causes them to focus on cycles and life-histories. And the histories are those of groups. As discussed in Chapter 2, Tilly considered the "group image . . . a mystification." And yet the use of life-histories is common because of social science philosophy and not because of this problematic duality. Periodization and organizational analysis are trusty methods for the study of social movements. To separate an era or historical phenomenon like social movement mobilization into more or less logical and coherent periods or stages is useful and necessary for many studies, including this one. As long as analysts are cognizant of the artificiality of periodization and of its coercive character—forcefully ordering history about—the danger of inventing false patterns and conveying erroneous messages about phenomena is minimized. With this warning in mind, this section discusses the general concept of social movement phases as they relate to the specific case of the West German peace movement.

Tilly provided a standard account of the phases or stages movements pass through in "the contemporary United States." The account can, I think, be generalized (despite, of course, some variations) to postindustrial democracies.

> Small, scattered sets of people begin voicing a grievance or making a demand; more people join them; the separate sets of concerned individuals start to communicate and coordinate; activists, leaders, spokespersons, and formal associations become visible; the activists make claims to speak for larger constituencies (all blacks, all farmers, sometimes all citizens); the groups involved take action to dramatize their programs, demonstrate their strength and determination, enlist new support; power holders respond variously by means of concessions, bargains, co-optation, repression or alliances; the activists routinize and/or demobilize their action.[27]

Moving from this general scheme to the specific case of the 1980s West German peace movement, several observations are in order. First, the "small, scattered groups of people" were in many cases affiliates of long-lived peace organizations, including, for example: Reconciliation Action/Peace Service, Pax Christi, BUKO, and the German Peace Society. The eighties peace movement was not started from scratch; it drew support from the type of established organizations discussed by resource mobilization theory in Chapters 3 and 9. Second, "voicing a grievance or making a demand" for these established organizations and for the thousands of new ones mobilized during the struggle against the missiles means several things, some of them discussed in the Strategy and Goals section above. Existing groups had agendas prior to the threatened deployment of the neutron bomb. The bomb tended, however, to become a priority; it busied professional activists and brought into collective action thousands of other citizens. The movement began to grow beyond an elite-sustained stage. With Jimmy Carter's change of heart—the cancellation of the enhanced radiation warhead—these groups had but a short respite before the double-track decision. The Euromissiles became the new priority by the end of 1980. They were the movement's primary grievance; prevention of their deployment the main demand. But as we have seen, the movement was about more than fighting INF. Its demands encompassed alternatives to deterrence and the dangerous evolution in NATO and U.S. nuclear and conventional strategy, U.S. toleration of the Sandinistas and disengagement from the neofascist regimes in Guatemala and El Salvador, restrictions on the arms trade, genuine efforts to stem nuclear proliferation and to promote disarmament, and more.

Third, the subsequent steps—communication and coordination, sweeping claims making, action and elite response—began in earnest in 1981. The next two years witnessed the "routinization" of this pattern. The concept routinization, however, fails to explain the phenomenal growth of the visible movement. It also does not allow for social learning. Movement organizations and leaders became more adept over time at communication and coordination, at making claims, and at eliciting responses from the authorities. Elites too refined their social control techniques during the movement's mobilization. "Demobilization" began rapidly after the onset of deployment at the end of 1983, the climax of movement action. The next year saw failed if vigorous efforts to sustain the level of mass mobilization of the previous couple years. The rest of the decade can by and large be described as a slide down from the peak of the mobilization cycle. Routinization also does not well describe the movement's uneven but steady return to an elite-sustained stage.

The Stages of West German Peace Movement Mobilization

Joyce Mushaben identified three distinct mobilization stages for the German anti-Euromissile movement. Her periodization provides a solid basis for my own.

> Insecurity based on rising unemployment figures and outbursts of youth unrest set the stage for initial surges of peace protest in June, 1981, when some 150,000 uninvited youth descended upon the 19th annual Congress of the German Evangelical Church in Hamburg. Grounded in a growing, albeit amorphous sense of existential *Angst*, this wave peaked in a nonviolent demonstration of 300,000 church and ecology group activists in Bonn on October 10, 1981.[28]

The fear underlying peace protest was rational rather than "amorphous." It was based on more or less sober reflections on the superpower problematic. The "initial surges" of protest were more a result of the stirrings of renewed cold war, the readiness of the professional peace lobby in the Federal Republic to move out of the elite-sustained ghetto, the mobilization potential stimulated by opposition to the neutron bomb, and the organizing surrounding the Krefeld Appeal than of economic and emotional insecurity. The Church convention was the stimulus for the formation of the Breakfast Club which planned the huge demonstration for the following October. This was the movement's second stage rather than its first; to periodize otherwise misses the importance of preexisting organizations, the stirrings against enhanced radiation weapons in the late-seventies, and the important initial steps toward mass mobilization in 1980.

> Statements attributed to Ronald Reagan concerning the prospects for a conceivably "winnable," limited nuclear war later that month gave rise to a second phase, during which nuclear *Angst* acquired a concrete foundation as Central European residents discerned how "flexible response" would affect them. Additional ecological, political and professional groups began to ally themselves publicly with the peace cause; their efforts culminated in the June, 1982 anti-Reagan demonstrations in Bonn and Berlin.[29]

In the discussion of shockers we saw the importance for mass movement mobilization played by the slipping clutch between the gearshift of the President's mind and the transmission of his lips. The protest occasioned by the June 1982 NATO Summit was a product of the organizing efforts of the first Coordinating Committee. This phase is not distinctive for providing fear a "concrete foundation." Again, fear was a logical response to developments prior to October 1981.

Instead, this phase is marked by a tightening of the movement center's coordination and communication capacities. And by the explosion of creative strategic and tactical thinking within the movement: alternative security proposals, clever innovations in action forms, concern for alliances and coalitions. This third phase was also marked by the increased volume of media attention directed toward the movement, its actions, and its prescriptions; and by the growing anxiety of the authorities. Movement grievances about the nature of deterrence and about the arms race were translated into claims and demands far exceeding the minimum consensus and intentionally incompatible with the security policy status quo. Political opportunities multiplied with the movement's higher public profile, the steady deterioration of superpower relations, and the Schmidt government's uneasy efforts at social control. Mushaben was right to describe this as a distinct phase of mobilization, but it is the third rather than the second.

> An ex officio national Coordinating Committee dominated the third stage, when Helmut Kohl's election to the Chancellorship in March, 1983 cleared the path for the initial Pershing II deployments at the end of the year. This stage—saying "No" to a specific NATO decision—climaxed with a nation-wide "Action Week," October 15-22, 1983 that rallied 2-4 million direct participants. The Coordinating Committee which began to experience splits along traditional lines (e.g., church groups backing away from hard-core communists and violence-prone "autonomous" groups, ecology groups who feared cooptation by Social-Democratic elements), disbanded in November, 1984. Local and regional mobilization efforts continued on both the religious and ecological/alternative fronts, often overlapping.[30]

The CC developed in response to the centripetal and centrifugal tendencies within the movement. Tensions within the CC were more or less intense depending on how urgent was the need for definite decisions. The emphasis on consensus decisionmaking tended to paper over differences. Issues not commanding a consensus were postponed in the hope agreement would later surface. If it did not, dissension within and without the Committee was at its fiercest. The climactic events of October 1983 focused almost solely on preventing deployment, but the movement busied itself with numerous other issues during the rest of this fourth phase. Indeed, the movement's agenda grew in 1983 to include opposition to Star Wars and the invasion of Grenada.

The public and private faces of the Schmidt and Kohl governments differed somewhat on the necessity and dangers of the Euromissiles.

Publicly, both leaders and their lieutenants defended NATO's case for the missiles. Privately, and especially in consultation with the Americans over progress at the negotiations in Geneva, both Social Democrats and Christian Democrats expressed deep concerns over the domestic political price of deployment, and sincere hopes that a superpower bargain could be struck eliminating the need for the missiles. There was a crucial difference, however, in the amount of support the public face of each Chancellor received from his respective party. Rank-and-file Social Democrats were both more likely than Christian Democrats to have doubts about the wisdom of the double-track decision and more willing to voice them. It was far harder for Schmidt to publicly demonize the movement when it directly or indirectly included as activists or sympathizers prominent members of his party, men like Erhard Eppler and Oskar Lafontaine, and a million or more SPD voters.

Changes in action forms can signal transitions in mobilization. The adoption of new means, such as civil disobedience, may signal a move from protest to resistance. Some activists (especially the Autonomen) argued that this was precisely what the movement needed to do in 1983: escalate its opposition to the missiles beyond protest to active resistance. The Greens' Marieluise Beck-Oberdorf denied the German peace movement, during the fall of 1983 or at any other time, became a resistance movement.[31] For her the wide-ranging discussion and controversy within and without the movement over the resistance question remained just that, discussion. The practice of the movement remained fixed primarily on the level of legal protest. The actions "were above all demonstrative, more enlightenment, more symbol, and more sign of spiritual strength" than the display of power necessary to pressure the government.[32]

There is no doubt that the vast bulk of movement actions with the vast majority of participants were of the legal sort. The question whether truly massive resistance would have won the day for the movement by making the country ungovernable is problematic. There is a romantic quality to direct action that makes it attractive to many pacifists. But large-scale resistance may have backfired. Timid sympathizers may have turned away from the movement. And it surely would have given the government the opening for repression: police riots, conspiracy trials, stiff sentences. The anti-abortion movement in the United States experienced a certain degree of alienation from less militant followers after its well-publicized attempts to "rescue the preborn" (by shutting down abortion clinics) in Wichita, Buffalo and Milwaukee in 1991-1992. The uncommitted appeared to respond negatively to the inconvenience (e.g., redirected traffic), incorporation of children willing to break the law in the actions, pressure put on police (people complained of being unable to summon a squad car during protests), and the expense incurred by municipalities to arrest, jail and prosecute trespassers, blockaders, and disturbers of the peace. These were actions clearly designed not to create commitment in the uncommitted but to activate commitment in the already committed.

The demobilization of the mass anti-missile movement following the onset of emplacement should be considered a separate and fifth stage, 1984-1986.[33] The failure to prevent deployment led to a decline in the visible movement as sharp as its rise. But the movement pursued several major campaigns in 1984: an abortive "Besiege the Bundestag" protest organized by the Independents, a consultative referendum on the missiles in conjunction with European Parliament elections in June, and the annual fall actions (this time including interference with military maneuvers in the "Fulda Gap," three regional human chain/demonstrations, and a demonstration in solidarity with Nicaragua). The first fizzled; only some 3000 Independents took part in the penetration of the one-kilometer "no protest zone" encircling the Bundestag building. The referendum, although controversial—some leading Greens and Independents opposed it as demobilizing—allowed over five million voters to directly express their opposition to the Cruise and Pershing missiles then still arriving from the United States. The interference with maneuvers was also controversial; some thought it thoughtless "actionism," action for the sake of action. The Christian groups refused to take part.

The gravest financial crisis of the Coordinating Committee and the most serious disagreements ever about its functions marked the end of 1984. A group of eight organizations led by the Protestant groups recommended a dissolution of the Committee and its replacement by a simple deliberative body without the power to pass binding resolutions. This group organized the Peace Cooperative (Friedenskooperative) as a less conflictual and actionistic alternative to the CC. It met from the end of 1984 to the middle of 1986. The new organization was to meet concern that the apparent growth of militancy within the CC damaged the movement's image. Independents and others accused the eight organizations of a "decapitation strategy" and of engineering a movement split. Others suggested that the eight were doing the bidding of the SPD, with which they were sympathetic or allied. With the CC out of the way, thought Independents and other groups not connected to the Peace Cooperative, the SPD could finally take over the movement. A compromise was worked out whereby the movement would enter a "deliberation phase" during which it would discuss future goals but abstain from organizing actions. The compromise also included a new decisionmaking technique to employ when the Committee could not achieve consensus. Called the "15 percent veto," it blocked resolutions opposed by more than 15 percent of the membership. I do not consider the deliberation phase a separate stage of movement mobilization as it was brief and did not signal a notable shift in mobilization.

The "deliberation phase" lasted until the middle of 1985. Several concerns stood out for discussion during the interregnum including the state of the INF negotiations, and the fortieth anniversary of the end of the Second World War on May 8. The Coordinating Committee issued a paper on the negotiations that held out little hope for positive results in Geneva. Instead, thought the movement's leading organizations, the likely result was a new round in the arms race. On the question of how to commemorate May 8, the movement produced a paper that linked fascism to war, and reminded readers that another outbreak of war from German soil was still possible. The apparent rejuvenation of the Western European Union (WEU)—spurred by European government concern over the course of the Reagan administration—was also a subject for study and condemnation.

Planning for a demonstration to counter the Western economic summit in May 1985 went ahead without the CC, as did an anti-NATO conference sponsored by the Independents, and an alternative nuclear test ban conference. The Committee was torn over how to respond to SDI. It issued a press declaration warning against German participation, but was unable to do much more. Individual organizations published their own analyses, and physicists and other specialists weighed in with several popular books. The movement's first ever Strategy Conference was held—without much fanfare—in June. The goal—the development of a long-term perspective for the movement—was not achieved. Poor preparation prevented the development of a new minimum consensus. An "Information Week" was held in place of more vigorous fall action in November.

At the end of 1985, the Committee devised an action plan for the following year. There would be only one mass action in 1986, in October. It would center around the U.S. base in Hasselbach yet to receive its contingent of Cruise missiles (a large minority of CC groups wanted to return to the Pershing II base in Mutlangen). The seventh Action Conference took place in February outside Bonn. Attended by some 650 representatives, it was the first regular Action Conference since May 1984. In a highly unusual move, Gerd Greune (DFG-VK) opened the conference with a speech critical of the less than democratic relations between the Coordinating Committee and the movement grassroots. A proposal by the Greens to work for a federal constitutional change to allow for plebiscites on individual questions usually the preserve of the Bundestag passed overwhelmingly. The AC's final resolution included for the first time an explicit call for civil disobedience. This was the least well prepared Action Conference yet, a testimony to the fatigue and waning motivation of the functionaries. None of the controversial issues troubling the CC—what position to take on Gorbachev's initiatives, how central a theme to make SDI, what relationship the movement ought to have toward the upcoming elections—were discussed at any length.

The sixth stage in movement (de)mobilization was the post-INF Treaty phase, 1987-1990. Signed in December 1987 and ratified by the U.S. Senate the following June, the INF Treaty finally brought the Euromissile episode, nearly a decade old, to a close. The movement greeted the Treaty, but was naturally unhappy with the long delay in its negotiation and its small quantitative impact on superpower arsenals. German pacifists could nonetheless take much credit for creating an atmosphere in which disarmament could proceed. The threat of another nuclear missile deployment, the SNF issue, worried the movement throughout 1987-1989. The opposition of Chancellor Kohl and Foreign Minister Genscher to new nuclear weapons on German soil prevented NATO (urged on by Reagan and Thatcher, and later Bush) from having its way. Here the shadow of the movement was all-important. Genscher knew yet another double-track decision would have brought hundreds of thousands back out on the streets, this time more angry than afraid. The Coordinating Committee voted itself out of existence in September 1989 and most of its members simultaneously came together in a new organization, the Peace Cooperative (now called Peace Cooperative Network). This new organization was designed with the defects of the old in mind. Discussion of fundamental questions, information exchange, and social learning were to be paramount activities. In this the new organization mirrored its experimental predecessor of the same name.

Shortly thereafter, the extraordinary changes wrought by the peoples of Central and Eastern Europe, the Soviet Union, and two individuals—Mikhail Gorbachev and Boris Yeltsin—put an end to the Berlin Wall and the Iron Curtain, the hegemony of Communist parties and planned economies, (most) secret police and press censors. German unification put an end to movement concern about the fate of its sister movement in the GDR but raised new worries inside and outside the country about a "Fourth Reich" (or at least a regional power able to confidently have its way economically and politically). Startling success in strategic nuclear arms control (START), in conventional arms control and confidence-building in Europe (CFE and CSCE), on a chemical weapons ban and all the rest seemed to do away with much of the peace movement's reason for being.

Then came the August 1990 Iraqi invasion of Kuwait and Operations Desert Shield and Desert Storm, and the seventh stage of movement mobilization. The movement quickly remobilized in opposition to an armed response to Saddam's aggression and any role for the Bundeswehr in the coalition put together by George Bush and James Baker. The experience gained and the structures remaining from the previous decade's anti-missile struggle allowed for a remarkably rapid response. Two large and noisy demonstrations (organized around the same slogan—"Kein Blut für Öl"—heard at anti-war rallies in the U.S.) and actions directed against German arms manufacturers followed in November 1990 and January 1991. A demonstration in support of Kurdistan took place in April 1991. Most of the organizations that took the lead during the 1980s were in front once again.

After the Gulf war, the movement returned to several long-term campaigns, and moved into its eighth stage. Two stand out: "Federal Republic Without an Army" (Bundesrepublik Ohne Armee or BOA) and restrictions on German exports of dangerous materials to sensitive regions. Both can be seen as elements of a vision of an alternative new world order. The first campaign aimed at abolition of the German armed forces and its replacement by civilian-based social defense. This seemed the logical next step from one movement perspective, and was pressed in opposition to intensified Franco-German military cooperation and German participation in UN or EU peacekeeping forces, "out-of-area" (Bosnia) or otherwise. The second campaign pursued the long-running goal of an economy cleansed of merchants of death. The conscience of the ethical and religious pacifist was troubled greatly by the thought of South African police riding in Mercedes trucks on their way to shoot-up a township. The anti-arms export campaign was stimulated by several shockers: revelations about a German role in an alleged poison gas factory in the Libyan desert (which American columnist William Safire called "Auschwitz in the sand"), admissions of deals with Saddam Hussein, and the discovery of a shipment of former East German military vehicles to Israel (which led to the resignation of a few top officials).

This periodization of mobilization phases reflects interactive changes in time, movement size, and political opportunity. The movement began the decade in an elite-sustained stage and returned to one. See Figure 8.2 (which covers most of the period in question). In between the elite-sustained stages, the movement passed through three mass mobilization phases: 1981, 1982, 1983. Two demobilization stages followed: 1984-1986 and 1987-1990. The movement returned briefly to a relatively high state of mobilization at the end of 1990 through the early part of 1991, and returned to a state of lower visibility by the middle of the year. A list of the eight stages looks thus:

1) elite-sustained (pre-late seventies)/germination (late seventies);
2) sprout/growth (1980-1981);
3) coordination/growth (1982);

FIGURE 8.2   Number of West German Social Movement Protests by Year, 1965-1989

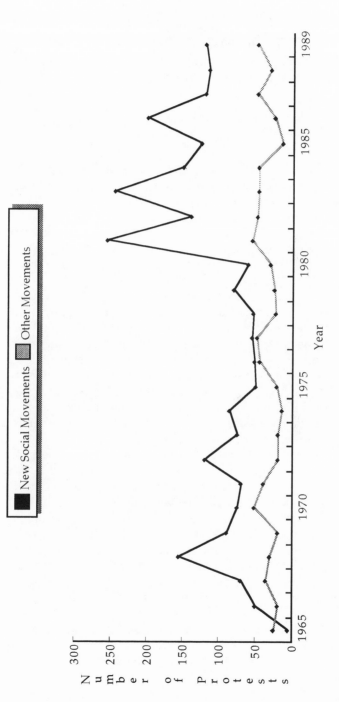

Source: Adapted from Ruud Koopmans, "The Dynamics of Protest Waves: West Germany, 1965-1989," *American Sociological Review,* vol.58 (1993), p. 639. Used by permission.

4) blossom/peak (1983);
5) wilt/post-deployment (1984-end 1987);
6) shrivel/post-INF Treaty (end 1987-end 1990);
7) rapid response/anti-Gulf War (end 1990-mid 1991);
8) elite-sustained (mid-1991-present).

Conclusion

One of the outstanding characteristics of the life-cycle of the 1980s West German peace movement was its tendency to mobilize people previously estranged from politics or only nominally politicized.[34] Mobilization has both microstructural and macrostructural roots. The former are in the activities of pacifist elites and political entrepreneurs who started the movement up out of the mobilization trough. The latter are in the changed institutional framework—party failure and the rise of alternative organizations—and in the larger sense of crisis surrounding the emergence of Cold War II and the weak global economy. Efforts at structuring and mobilizing discontent—the mobilization of consensus—aid in the development of new perspectives toward the established order and give meaning to the social and political changes underlying disquiet. The mobilization of unhappiness—the development of leadership, coherent actions and ideology—can give rise to new avenues owing to an initial explosion of energy. So it was that the Hungarian uprising of 1956, whose opening urban riots were hardly revolutionary in origin, took on an insurrectionary hue as the movement for a new regime mobilized support through a formal structure.[35]

The West German peace movement has proved to be a hardy plant, a perennial. Rarely in bloom, but never without signs of life, it has showed itself able to return from an elite-sustained stage on a moment's notice, to be a sort of political movement Minuteman. Movement strategy, goals and tactics shifted over the course of these phases. Opposition to the missiles never faded despite their successful deployment. Informationsarbeit, protest and resistance (education and propaganda, noncooperation, intervention and alternative institutions) were more or less important action forms depending on the goal, context and mobilization phase. The movement both created and activated commitment, manufactured and responded to grievances, made and reacted to political opportunities. While certainly a tale of imperfect resource mobilization and identity formation, this is an unprecedented postwar German mobilization story. Never before had so many fought so long for so much.

Notes

1. Max Kaase, "The Challenge of the 'Participatory Revolution' in Pluralist Democracies," *International Political Science Review*, vol. 5, no. 3 (1984), p. 301. The modern history of political mobilization has been well-studied. See, for example, the classic works of Karl W. Deutsch "Social Mobilization and Political Development," *American Political Science Review*, vol. 75 (1961); and Seymour Martin Lipset and Stein Rokkan, eds., *Party Systems and Voter Alignments* (New York: Free Press, 1967).

2. J.P. Nettl, *Political Mobilization: A Sociological Analysis of Methods and Concepts* (New York: Basic Books, 1976).

3. Gamson, *The Strategy of Social Protest*, p. 15.

4. Tilly, *From Mobilization to Revolution*, p. 54.

5. Ulrike C. Wasmuht, "Zur Analyse der Friedensbewegungen in der Bundesrepublik Deutschland," *Wissenschaft und Frieden*, vol. 1, no. 2 (1985).

6. Gamson, *The Strategy of Social Protest*, pp. 14-15.

7. Herbert Blumer, "Collective Behavior," in Joseph B. Gittler, ed., *Review of Sociology: Analysis of a Decade* (New York: Wiley, 1957), p. 147.

8. Gamson, *The Strategy of Social Protest*, p. 15.

9. Klandermans, *Organizing for Change*.

10. Herbert H. Hyman and Paul B. Sheatsley, "Attitudes Toward Desegregation," *Scientific American*, no. 211 (1964).

11. Klandermans, "Introducion," in *Organizing for Change*, p. 11.

12. Eric Hobsbawm, *Primitive Rebels: Studies in Archaic Forms of Social Movement in the 19th and 20th Centuries*, 2nd ed. (New York: Praeger Press, 1963).

13. See Erich Fromm, *Escape From Freedom* (New York: Holt, 1960); and Seymour Martin Lipset, *Political Man* (New York: Doubleday, 1960).

14. Jo Freeman, "Resource Mobilization and Strategy: A Model for Analyzing Social Movement Organization Actions," in Mayer N. Zald and John D. McCarthy, eds., *The Dynamics of Social Movements* (Cambridge, MA: Winthrop, 1979).

15. Freeman, "Resource Mobilization and Strategy," p. 176.

16. Pappi, "Neue soziale Bewegungen und Wahlverhalten in der Bundesrepublik," in Kaase and Klingemann, eds., *Wahlen und Wähler*.

17. Freeman, "Resource Mobilization and Strategy," p. 176.

18. Lofland draws the parallel in *Protest*.

19. On the freerider problem, see Olson, *The Logic of Collective Action*.

20. Gamson, *The Strategy of Social Protest*, p. 140.

21. Roderick Frazier Nash brought the term "shocker" to my attention.

22. For a partial collection of Reaganite wit and wisdom catalytic for the German (and other) peace movements, see Robert Scheer, *With Enough Shovels: Reagan, Bush & Nuclear War* (New York: Random House, 1982).

23. Johnson, *Realism and Hope in a Nuclear Age*, p. 105.

24. Verta Taylor, "The Continuity of the American Women's Movement: An Elite-Sustained Stage," in West and Blumberg, eds., *Women and Social Protest*.

25. For more about the role of knowledge in movement mobilization, see Breyman, "Knowledge as Power."

26. Tilly, "Social Movements and National Politics," p. 311.

27. Tilly, "Social Movements and National Politics," p. 311.

28. Joyce Marie Mushaben, "Innocence Lost: Environmental Images and Political Experiences Among the West German Greens," *New Political Science*, vol. 14 (1985-86), p. 44.

29. Mushaben, "Innocence Lost," p. 45.

30. Mushaben, "Innocence Lost," p. 45.

31. Marieluise Beck-Oberdorf, "Friedensbewegung und Widerstand," in Tatz, ed., *Gewaltfreier Widerstand*.

32. Beck-Oberdorf, "Friedensbewegung und Widerstand," p. 71.

33. This discussion draws on Leif, *Die Strategische (Ohn-) Macht der Friedensbewegung*, pp. 106-116.

34. See the similar tendency of Solidarity analyzed in Jerzy J. Wiatr, "Mobilization of Non-Participants During the Political Crisis in Poland, 1980-1981," *International Political Science Review*, vol. 5, no. 3 (1984).

35. Feliks Gross, *The Seizure of Political Power in a Century of Revolutions* (New York: Philosophical Library, 1958).

9

Theory Revisited:
Novelty and Origins

Giving in social ideas is like planting seeds. One wants to see the fruit of one's efforts. One wants to behold if only a little flower from all the labor one has had in digging in the soil.

—Emma Goldman

This chapter has a dual purpose. The first is to return to the discussion begun in Chapter 2 about what is new about new social movements, and to address the claims for new movement novelty in light of what we now know about the nature and mobilization of the 1980s West German peace movement. My second aim is to search the clusters of social movement theory first presented in Chapter 3 for concepts to help explain the origins of the West German peace movement. A solid foundation upon which to address the usefulness of the six theories emerged between the initial theoretical presentation in Chapter 3 and this chapter. Because they are not fully reiterated here, I urge the reader to return to the pertinent sections of Chapters 2 and 3 for a refresher on the arguments for NSM newness and for the main points of the six theories.

New Social Movements?

New Arenas of Conflict?

The stress on NSMs as symbolic actors struggling over signs and messages in new arenas of conflict, common to the work of Michel Foucault and Alberto Melucci, while instructive, uncovers only part of the peace movement challenge to contemporary societies. While there is much symbolic power in nuclear weapons, they are at the same time frighteningly tangible. The challenge to security policymaking elites has a symbolic dimension, but becomes concrete in the sense that a real authority, a real power to decide on weapons systems, arms control, and the determinants of deterrence, is directly challenged by the peace movement. Government officials, elected and otherwise, are most resentful of what they consider illegitimate, upstart defiance toward their control over national defense. This resentment, much concerned with symbols and codes, also reflects the reduced decisionmaking room, the narrowed field for elite operations, that is one product of peace movement mobilization.

Someone intending to rescue the traditional Marxist view of social movements as parties to material struggle could plausibly do so by conceptualizing information and its communication as "postmaterial goods and services." The stress in this reconfiguration is on change in the objects, not the subjects of the classic struggle over the means of existence. An even more traditional view might marvel at how the targets of NSM action—states and corporations bent on economic and military "development"—more clearly comprehend the class and economic challenge posed by movements than do academic observers. Bush administration budget director Richard Darman, when asked by reporters whether with the decline in superpower competition a "peace dividend" of resources might be redirected from military spending to environmental protection responded: "Americans did not fight and win the wars of the twentieth century to make the world safe for green vegetables."[1] In this view, claims for pollution prevention, conversion of defense industries to social uses, wholesale cuts in defense spending, and comparable worth, are salvos in the class struggle. Though (mostly) new, these (only partially postmaterialist) claims remain centered on questions about the control of corporations, the economy, and the state. David Plotke believed this view, an inversion and restatement of Marxist orthodoxy with the working class replaced by the new movements, a distortion of the novelty of the NSM.[2]

But even granting the novelty of conflict areas and the increased importance of knowledge and information in the postmodern world, information is sought not for its own sake (regardless of a general preference for the right to know). Rather, the struggle over information is instrumental. Peace movements seek and disseminate information on deployment sites so the sites can be blockaded. The raison d'être of NSMs in this regard remains that of old social movements: the struggle for power. This is true, I think, whether power be sought for offensive purposes (to extend rights or status) or defensive purposes (to protect or preserve rights or status). Whether a struggle over pension plans or the interpretation of signs (e.g., sexist advertising), movement-antagonist conflicts are still about power. Whatever the extent of change in the nature of power with the arrival of postindustrial society, the fundamental fact of movement-authority struggles as contests between established power and challengers has not changed.

The grievance-airing activity and transnational scope of the new movements noted by newness proponents are not in themselves novel. Giving transnational voice to social complaints and recruiting adherents across borders were practices of leftist parties and trade unions in the nineteenth century. Nor is publicizing the bankruptcy of national security policy peculiar to the latter half of the twentieth century. Bertha von Suttner, daughter of an Austrian field marshal, published her best selling and widely translated anti-war novel *Lay Down Your Arms!* in 1889. She swiftly became a leading figure in the international peace movement working to prevent what became the First World War. NSM gripes, however, do have social and cultural dimensions foreign to past collective action. The bourgeois European peace movement did not produce new cultural codes within submerged networks. Comparing movements across time as unified empirical entities obscures the different systemic location, and thus different significance, of the new conflicts.

New Collective Identities?

New movements are said to be deeply embroiled in the construction of new collective identities. Jean Cohen's claim that this new identity is, above all, a "self-limiting radicalism" is itself self-limiting. The choice is not between reform and revolution, but between action and inaction. And even if we retain the classic categories Cohen employs, the notion of self-limiting radicalism does not capture the revolutionary character of NSM challenges to advanced societies. Upon their founding, the Greens were symbolically and programmatically revolutionary. Their vision of postcapitalist and postindustrial society was as far-reaching in its overhaul of the existing order as any anarcho-syndicalist or communist blue-print from an earlier era. What confuses observers is the lack of a plan among NSM thinkers of how to get from here to there. Absent are the Leninist organizations and insurrectionary methods. Cohen was careful, however, to qualify the breadth or scope of novel identities: "The old patterns of collective action certainly continue to exist. In some movements they may even be statistically preponderant."

One old pattern of collective action that continues to exist is the instrumental focus of many movement campaigns. Melucci granted this continuity on some occasions and rejected it on others. To describe the new movements as more than instrumental is valid, but it is a mistake to go so far as to call them "no longer a means to an end," or purely "ends in themselves," as does Melucci. Recent peace movements consider their identities, goals, and modes of association as new and improved over the class-based, formally organized Old Left and the revolutionary rhetoric and totalizing character of the New Left. Yet, neo-romantic myths of a community free of all power and all forms of inequality have not completely dissipated. To call peace activists self-limiting on account of their conscious exclusion of Leninist strategies and general abhorrence of violence is to miss the deeply radical quality of a nonviolent, nonconspiratorial identity *and* approach to politics.

The new movements do indeed see themselves as issue-raisers, as claimed, even though all issues raised may not be addressed by existing interest aggregation and mediation processes. To call NSMs "homeless," however, is an exaggeration, at least in relation to the 1980s West German peace movement. The Greens and radical Social Democrats served as its voice in the Bundestag and other legislative bodies. Peace movement frustrations with the contradictions and limitations of liberal democracy did not deter members from making constitutional arguments against missile deployment. Missile foes emerged in parties, churches, offices, trade unions, professional associations, garden clubs, and hiking groups. Rather than socially homeless, peace activists and sympathizers were by and large well-integrated members of society. Older movements also acted as issue- and consciousness-raisers. One can find early parallels to the recent peace movement's global awareness in the writings of pacifist intellectuals before and after the Great War.[3] Yet many of the issues raised, the content of the current consciousness, and the contours of peace movement identity are distinctive. Alfred Fried, major spokesman of the German Peace Society before the First World War, was reluctant to criticize those in power. He was a virulent nationalist, Social Darwinist, and neomercantilist. His views and values were with few exceptions foreign to those of his successors (especially the postmaterialists) in the German peace movement of the 1980s. Peter Merkl compared the values and attitudes of Federal German NSMs to their forerunners throughout modern German history.[4] He employed a qualified generational analysis that attributed identity to the formative experiences of late adolescence and early adulthood. Merkl found very few similarities between the 1980s and previous peace (or other) movements due to the widely diverging life experiences of adherents.

Unlike the green consumers L.A. Kauffman profiled, the vast majority of anti-Euromissile movement members were not at risk of substituting individualization for politics. Personal transformation, such as a commitment to nonviolence, was for many a central task, and widely respected accomplishment, of the movement. But this new collective identity as nonviolent human being did not induce quietism, instead it realized the potential of consciousness-raising: it empowered individuals and prefaced the movement's collective action.

New Organizations and Action?

New movements are said to have developed new organizational structures characterized by consensus decisionmaking, anti-authoritarianism, and decentralized structures. Through these organizations, adherents are said to invent new experiences and ways of life, and to challenge dominant codes of societal routine. It is on this question of organization and action that the claims of NSM novelty, at least in the case of the German peace movement, are least vague and assailable. Many peace groups neatly fit Luther Gerlach's SPIN model and Melucci's conception of submerged networks. And there can be little doubt that these forms are new, that they differ in significant ways from German peace groups of past decades. But viewing the peace movement as a sign, again, stresses only one aspect of its challenge to society, that directed (mostly) toward civil society. It ignores the largely state-directed dimension of the challenge. The movement did not just symbolically communicate with the state. It directly challenged state power. Peace movement organizations spend much time preparing for these challenges; this is why they are not always publicly visible.

As we have seen, the peripheries and interstices of political institutions are not the only breeding grounds for new movements. We watched peace movement groups sprout within established institutions: labor unions, parties and their youth organizations, churches, and professional associations. The invisibility of most peace movement action and organization, and the conscious practice of new group dynamics, does not exempt pacifists confronting the state from determining their own level of commitment to the cause. Richard Flacks was right: incorporating family and friends into movement networks does not fully obviate the necessity for choice between public and private life. Sacrifice has yet to become an obsolete concept.

Theory and Movement Origins

Party Failure

While Kay Lawson and Peter Merkl assigned the peace movement to the environmentalist grouping of alternative organizations said to arise from the failure of parties (due to its new politics, participatory, action-oriented profile), peace organizations also share certain characteristics found in what they called supplementary organizations.

> What characterizes [supplementary] groups is not their conviction that the issues they address are new, nor that they themselves constitute a community sharply distinct from all others . . . but simply their belief that at the present time there is no way to compel the existing parties to pay attention to them. They seek supplementary representation, and in order to acquire it they create their own new organizations.[5]

The broad cluster of concerns the word "peace" connotes are among th oldest confronting citizens and leaders. Nuclear weapons first arrived in Germany in the 1950s; the 108 Pershing II and 96 ground-launched Cruise missiles threatened by NATO in the double-track decision were, however, new. Peace movement identity was both singular and undistinctive. On one hand, adherents considered themselves liberated from "old" security policy thinking.[6] They shucked off the blinders of the peace through strength defense philosophy for one situated in pacifism, disarmament, and freedom from the Cold War. On the other hand, activists saw themselves as more or less ordinary citizens doing their bit in the face of what they took to be a growing nuclear threat. Movement dissatisfaction with the SPD, the traditional German "peace party" and accomplice in the NATO decision, was acute and undoubtedly a taproot of the movement. And yet to describe "the movement" as despairing of influencing "the existing parties" directly contradicts one of its central, instrumental focuses.

Anti-authoritarianism, another of Lawson and Merkl's alternative organization types, is not unique to citizens of repressive regimes.[7] Peace movement organizations too were directed toward "the masses," and activists certainly considered security policymaking the domain of a narrow elite with questionable aims. Policymaking as a species of political activity can be distinguished from the legitimacy of elected officials and bureaucrats; electoral legitimacy need not rule out technocratic or selfish officials. And, of course, the German polity is characterized by remarkably low levels of trust in government, a measure of legitimacy, especially among movement members.[8] The upshot here is that peace movement organizations overlapped the boundaries of three of Lawson and Merkl's four alternative group types. They constituted a wide-ranging challenge to the West German party system. The broad-gauged nature of peace movement defiance confronted parties, especially the SPD, with a difficult quandary. Whereas satisfying the demands of even a single alternative organization type could prove trying, the SPD leadership faced a three-pronged assault from the peace movement in the 1980s. The breadth of the movement challenge improved its prospects for influencing Social Democratic security policy.

Federal German party failure from the sixties through the eighties took several forms:

- steady loss of voter support;
- difficulty in addressing issues like budgets, pensions, unemployment, and the environment;
- loss of power in legislatures and coalitions;
- problems recruiting young and first-time voters;
- trouble integrating dissident members;
- loss of control of the political agenda;
- loss of legitimacy as a result of scandals.[9]

Not all parties failed in all these ways nor to the same extent, but as it is of primary concern, my very brief examination centers on the SPD.

Suzanne Berger's analysis of the then "current phase of West European politics" (decay of parties during a period of growing politicization of everyday life) coincided with Gene Frankland's historical account of the five phases of the West German party system.[10] The first phase saw the emergence of the "Bonn System" comprised of the three main parties: CDU/CSU, FDP, and SPD. In the second phase, during the 1950s, the two major parties adopted catch-all strategies designed to embrace voters outside of traditional class-based constituencies. Third, after the Grand Coalition between the Union parties and the Social Democrats in the mid-late 1960s, the Federal Republic moved from a center-right to a center-left coalition. The fourth phase took place in the early and mid-1970s when the citizen's initiatives focused on "new" problems (particularly environmental) neglected by the major parties. It is in this fourth phase that significant roots of the peace movement can be found.

In his study of West German civil disobedience since the late 1960s, Theodor Ebert tallied examples from campaigns against rent increases and urban renewal, battles over conditions at universities, and over nuclear power.[11] In the latter instance, he cited figures from a 1975 poll commissioned by the Federal Ministry for Research and Technology to probe citizen opposition to a nuclear plant in a rural area, Wyhl, and a plant in an industrial area, Ludwigshafen. A representative sample of citizens from Ludwigshafen, Freiburg and Landkreis Emmendingen (in the immediate vicinity of the plant near Wyhl) were asked for their reaction to two opinions: (1) "We do not need citizen initiatives. Our opinion can be represented in the elections or also in a party;" and (2) "The government and the parties do not listen to us. Therefore we must represent our interests ourselves in a citizens initiative." Only 16 percent of respondents in Ludwigshafen agreed with the first opinion, whereas 47 percent agreed with the second. Thirty-two percent agreed to some extent with both opinions. In Emmendingen, 63 percent of respondents agreed with the second opinion, and 72 percent agreed with it in Freiburg. A mere 9 percent of Freiburgers, residents of what Ebert described as "this once conservative, Catholic, bishopric," agreed with the first statement. Predictably, Freiburg would later become a stronghold of the Greens, and the state of Baden-Württemberg (site of Pershing II bases) host to intense peace movement activity.

Many peace activists had experience in the citizen initiatives of the 1970s. Survey data indicates that more people were actively involved in the various civic action groups than were members of all the parties combined.[12] The relative attractiveness of citizens initiatives as compared to parties can be explained by such factors as the simplicity of their programs, the ease and informality of membership and participation, and differences in organizational structure and decisionmaking principles.[13] The proliferation of these grassroots networks is among the clearest signs of party decline and failure. By the late 1970s, increased public discontent with the established parties led to the fifth stage in the development of the West German party system, the beginnings of Green and Alternative electoral activity at the local and state levels (and the first rumblings of the nascent peace movement in the scattered efforts against the neutron bomb). Green electoral activity at the federal level, reunification, and the rise of far right populist parties in the 1980s and early 1990s present opportunities for further periodization.

Since its peak federal electoral performance in 1972 (45.8 percent), the SPD has more or less steadily declined: 1976 (42.6 percent), 1980 (42.9 percent), 1983 (38.2 percent), 1987 (37.0 percent), 1990 (33.5 percent), 1994 (36.4 percent).[14] The party's slide is more dramatic when assessing its ability to attract young and first-time voters. Looking just at the 1980s,

Social Democratic voters in the 18-24 age bracket decreased from 48.9 percent in 1980, to 39 percent in 1983, to 38.1 percent in 1987. In the 25-34 age bracket, SPD support slipped from 47.1 percent in 1980, to 39.4 percent in 1983, to 39 percent in 1987.[15] According to former Social Democrat Petra Kelly of the Greens, "the SPD is worn out, finished. It had the chance and lost it. It lost the young voters, it lost the women, it lost the movement."[16] For Peter Glotz, former SPD business manager, "The SPD awakened false hopes that parties could change lives and alter the relationships among human beings."[17] The SPD was wracked by several embarrassing scandals: the Guillaime spy incident, the pretext for Willy Brandt's resignation, to name the best-known scandal from the 1970s, and the Flick Affair, and Neue Heimat dealings, to name two from the 1980s. The 1990s witnessed several scandals regarding war materiel sales and deals with Libya and Iraq, and revelations about former East Germans' relationships with the secret police. Some leading Social Democrats, Helmut Schmidt in particular, ignored the ascent of the new social movements, considering them mere blips on the political radar, and thus not worthy of serious attention from the party. This is especially clear in the case of the anti-nuclear power movement, which found little sympathy, and much outright hostility, in the leading ranks of the SPD. The inhospitable attitude of the ruling SPD-FDP coalition toward environmentalists combined with limitations on direct democracy at the federal level enshrined in the Basic Law to constrict mainstream participatory opportunities for dissenters.[18] It seems clear in the case of the SPD, that the chicken of party failure laid the egg of peace movement emergence.

The "participation explosion" engendered by the Socialist German Student League (SDS), the Extraparliamentary Opposition, and the Jusos during the sixties, was extended by the citizen initiatives during the seventies. Young voters' massively increased political participation elicited little positive response from the centralized state and institutionalized parties at which it was aimed. The SPD remained wed to its pro-nuclear power and pro-economic growth philosophies in direct opposition to citizen groups. The adaptability of parties when faced with grassroots demands for peace and ecological integrity is problematic. For Samuel Huntington,

> The core participant institution, the political party, appears to be verging on a state of institutional and political decay. . . . Unless there is a clear-cut reversal of current trends . . . parties do not appear to be likely mechanisms for structuring the higher levels of participation which should characterize postindustrial society.[19]

There has yet to be a clear-cut reversal of the trends Huntington observed in the early 1970s. And yet, the SPD has not disappeared from the political scene. The fact of SPD adaptation to the peace movement and other challenges is important. It raises the possibility that the party did not fail after all. But adaptation is not the antithesis of failure. Adaptation is the recognition of failure.

The anti-nuclear weapons movement, a polyglot formation of several types of alternative organizations, constituted a broad challenge to the West German party system. This was a party system unable to stem the loss of voter support and unable to solve difficult problems. The peace movement proved adept at cultivating disaffected Social Democrats and the young; it was able to wrest control of the security policy agenda away from the government and the parties. Peace movements develop from, among other sources, the failure of parties to connect citizens and policymakers. The less capable parties are of forging and maintaining linkage, the more likely the appearance of alternative organizations like those of peace movements. The German party system since the late-1960s proved progressively less able to perform its customary functions: mediating group interests, structuring elections, managing the state, and devising public policy. The mediation and problem-solving functions of German parties, especially the SPD, were those most sorely missed by citizens; these were the gaps which alternative organizations like citizen initiatives filled during the 1970s. Large numbers of future peace activists labored in grassroots groups fighting nuclear power and ecologically harmful economic development. The movement was able to restore failed connections and construct fresh ones for those new to politics. Linkage repair and building took place within a domestic political context of the proliferation of "new" public issues and the founding of new politics and postmaterialist parties. A growing number of progressive citizens recoiled from a Social Democratic leadership not just reconciled to but content with NATO, nuclear weapons and power, Cold War and compromise. The failure of the SPD to keep postindustrial discontents in the fold led directly to the rise of the 1980s West German peace movement. The double-track decision engineered by Schmidt and reluctantly agreed to by the SPD was tantamount to security policy (and thus party) failure from the perspective of peace-minded citizens. The flowering of new groups and the extraordinary growth of existing peace organizations must be seen in the light of weak or failed linkages between citizen and state.

Fear of War

Numerous observers, not all unsympathetic, have pointed to the importance of the fear of (especially nuclear) war in the emergence and rise of the West German peace movement. Some hostile explanations of peace movement origins that focused on fear of war are close cousins of Gustave Le Bon's classic *The Crowd*, and William Kornhauser's influential *The Politics of Mass Society*.[20] The latter underlies the mass society approach to the study of social movements, and the former is the original work in the crowd psychology approach. These approaches generally presume an excited and irrational emotionalism or alienated atomism on the part of participants, and emphasize violent outbursts, panics, and anomie. They are of little use in ferreting out the roots of peace movements, and are not discussed here. A fear-oriented explanation that is a distant and estranged cousin of the classical tradition is preferred.

Many unfriendly critics, including most notably Richard Perle, attributed the rise of the movement to "Protestant Angst," or some other relative of Straub, Werbick, and Zitterbarth's war fear types two and four. Ironically, many in the movement accused governments of reacting to neurotic fears about external threats in the formulation of their security policies. The work of Alice Miller found strong resonance among many peace activists looking for an explanation of the dangerous paradox they considered official security policy.[21] Her development of Freudian understandings about the behavior of adults mistreated as children provided one possible psychoanalytic path to making sense of decisions about nuclear weapons. Another path was through Freud's revised concept of Thanatos, the individual death instinct, which when thwarted by Eros, the individual life instinct, leads to interpersonal or intergroup aggression; the repression of Thanatos by civilization (and its agents: family, school, religion) necessarily produces neurosis. Apparently self-destructive security policies can be symptomatic of this neurosis.[22]

Clay Clemens cited the influence attributed to angst throughout modern German history by Karl Dietrich Bracher and Fritz Stern, and described it as both of "particular significance" for a discussion of peace movement origins, and as "peculiarly German." Defined variously by Clemens and his sources as "deep-rooted cosmic despair," and "fear of the future . . . related to forms of archaic superstition," this is an angst with little explanatory power in the peace movement case.[23] People in a state of cosmic despair are unlikely organizers and activists. Peace movement participants do not fit the profile of unattached marginals, and movement action is neither spontaneous nor disorganized. Concern about the ultimate consequences of a runaway superpower arms race could be described as other than superstitious. This does not discount the importance of war fear shared by many movement adherents. But this fear displays little resemblance to existential angst; it is instead fear with a small "f," a sort most closely resembling Straub, Werbick, and Zitterbarth's type one. While nowhere near as intense in most cases, peace movement fear of war is related to the fear one feels when confronted by muggers in a dark alley. It is a natural, instinctual response to a threatening situation. Fear in this situation is functional for survival; it is according to Sheryl Breyman, a "logical emotion." Not to feel fear when bodily threatened suggests an overconsumption of Bruce Lee or Chuck Norris movies, a preternatural sense of inner peace, or the need for psychiatric observation. Providing no assurance of emerging unscathed from the encounter, fear is a necessary first step toward coping in an environment of insecurity.

Jeffrey Herf dismissed the possibility that "there is a greater danger of war now [early eighties] than before, to which the movement is a sensible response."[24] Exploitation of popular fears of war nonetheless played a central role in movement mobilization. Movement entrepreneurs like Helen Caldicott incubated and nurtured such fears through graphic descriptions of the medical consequences of nuclear explosions. Peace movement entrepreneurs were not alone in exploiting constituent fears. Hope and action in the face of fear also figures prominently in some ecology movements and in SMOs—like ACT UP!—struggling to make the fight against AIDS a high public priority. Following her "bombing run" presentation, Caldicott challenged the assembled to act through a movement organization to prevent nuclear apocalypse, skillfully manipulating their newfound or concretized fears. I heard Caldicott's famous presentation at a nuclear freeze and anti-Euromissile gathering in Los Angeles in 1983. Her recruitment technique was controversial. It was possible, claimed some friendly critics, that rather than stimulate an audience to action, Caldicott's approach would frighten it into passivity. A demobilizing rather than inspirational fear might be planted or exacerbated. But Caldicott's frightening presentations had numerous defenders. Anecdotal evidence suggests it was an effective bridge to constituencies with well developed senses of political efficacy. What is important in the context of movement origins is the fact that fear of (nuclear) war was common to movement adherents and a conscious, articulated source of their motivation to participate.

It is uncontroversial, contrary to the claims of Herf and others, to assert that in the late 1970s-early 1980s there existed in Western Europe an increased fear of impending world war.[25] According to two Soviet analysts,

> It is becoming increasingly clear to West Europeans of different political views that the United States would like to deflect nuclear retaliation away from its own continent and to direct it to Europe instead. This awareness is at the root of the . . . movement.[26]

Fear of war was not the exclusive province of any narrowly defined social or political group. Helmut Schmidt likened the world situation during the Euromissile years to 1914.[27] In 1982, Richard Pipes estimated the probability of nuclear war at 40 percent.[28] Some 32 percent of German respondents to a October 1981 poll agreed with the statement that a new world war was "probable within the next ten years."[29] A German peace movement pamphlet with the title *We Have But a Few Months Time* appeared shortly before deployment of the Euromissiles.[30] There were myriad objective (type one) reasons for this ubiquitous perception:

- superpower sparring over Angola and the Horn of Africa;
- the U.S. Senate's refusal to ratify SALT II;
- the brutal Soviet subjugation of Afghanistan, and resultant American grain embargo and (partial) Western Olympic boycott;
- the psychodrama of the Iranian hostage crisis;
- the risks of superpower involvement in the Iran-Iraq war;
- the rise and suppression of the Solidarity movement in Poland;
- the bellicosity, arms racing and lack of interest in arms control of the Reagan administration;
- Reaganite plans for victory in limited and protracted nuclear wars;
- the ignorance of Reagan himself on military-strategic matters;
- U.S. intervention on behalf of neo-fascist forces and regimes in Central America.

The fear felt by most peace movement activists was an informed fear, a mobilizing fear, one that stemmed from a reasoned analysis of the state of the world. The nuclear anxieties produced by the loose talk and rhetoric of leaders and by rampaging military-industrial complexes contributed much to both the willingness of people to construct and participate in the movement and to the intensity of their commitment. For many people, the thought of fiddling prior to the burning of the planet was intolerable. They simply had to do something and this impetus led to the initiation of myriad new groups and the swelling of long-lived professional organizations. Again, this impetus was perhaps accentuated in the German case because of the burden of the past. Empowering fear stemmed from concern across the span of the temporal continuum: concern that the past not be repeated (that there be no "Euroshima"); concern about the real and present danger that some incident lead to a crisis that could spin wildly out of control; and concern for future generations, for the long-run survival of the planet. Without fear—stoked by the remarkable statements of President Reagan, by huge military build-ups, and by superpower intervention in the Third World—far fewer people would have been drawn to the movement.

Collective Behavior

Neil Smelser's model signaled an advance in the field of social movement study as it included, although did not fully develop, structural conduciveness, mobilization, and social control as central variables for an understanding of the emergence and rise of movements. His distinction between norm-oriented and value-oriented movements works, perhaps, to distinguish between the goals of some movements. The anti-abortion movement could be seen as norm-oriented, and the Bolsheviks as value-oriented. But not too many important movements and certainly not many NSMs can easily fit into one category or the other, including the radical faction of the Russian Social Democrats or the pro-life movement. The German peace movement could be characterized as desiring changes in both norms (e.g., the formulation and implementation of security policy) and values (e.g., the centrality of confrontation with the East).

How might the movement be explained in Smelser's terms? The failure of the parties, especially the SPD, and the rise of the citizen initiatives from which the anti-missile movement drew succor might be seen in terms of strain. An SPD that was willing to ally with the CDU/CSU in the Grand Coalition, but was unwilling to adapt to dissident forces (radical students) and grassroots demands for policy changes (citizen initiatives) caused a rupture in the social order of traditional party members or would-be members (youth). In their efforts at repairing the rent, these citizens helped construct or turned to the peace movement through generalized beliefs about a bloc-free world, the removal of nuclear weapons from the Federal Republic, or the overthrow of the security dilemma. The clash between the postmaterialism of the postwar generations and the consumerism and anti-communism of their elders could be considered a form of "value strain." "Normative," "mobilization," and "facilities" strains arose when these postmaterialists were confronted with a dearth of career and lifestyle opportunities that provided constructive outlets for their distinctive energies.

Ralph Turner and Lewis Killian's concept of emergent norms also sheds some light on the origins of the movement. The belief, shared nearly universally within the movement, about the inherent badness of nuclear weapons, and the urgent need for their reduction or abolition, could be characterized as a norm that emerged in opposition to the official idea that nuclear deterrence kept the peace. The norm "structured meaning" for adherents and served as an ideational basis for peace movement mobilization. Turner and Killian's concept allows for the essential rationality of movement actors working on behalf of a principle deemed superior to the reigning norm. To contend that rumor was the mode of communication for this new norm, however, overlooks the vast output of the media, peace research institutes, and movement organizations and peace information clearinghouses. Public debates, town meetings, rallies, neighborhood gatherings, teach-ins, lecture series, sermons, television and radio specials, and countless publications (leaflets, handbills, signs, posters, books, magazines, journals) helped to propagate, refine, criticize, support and defend the emergent norm.

One problem with Smelser's approach is its definition of collective behavior as noninstitutionalized. In what terms, if not institutional, can we portray the Greens' vigorous (if impolite) use of parliamentary procedures to prevent the deployment of the Euromissiles? Here was an unconventional political party, newly seated in the Bundestag, that utilized all institutional means at its disposal (in addition to noninstitutionalized, unconventional means in the streets). Collective behavior, said Smelser, is that sort "formed or forged to meet undefined or unstructured situations."[31] The political context of the rise of the peace movement was, however, highly structured and very well defined. The main precipitating factor, in Smelser's language, was NATO's dual-track decision of December 1979. The decision evolved over the course of several years of intra-alliance consultation and assessment of the regional military balance and geopolitical situation. It was a more or less routine and ordinary decision to modernize nuclear weapons on the Continent. The unprecedented public response it sparked can not be satisfactorily attributed to strain, disorganization or malintegration left in its wake.

Peace movement adherents were not primarily immigrants, the unemployed, dislocated peasants or others whose worlds had been upended. They were many for whom the missile decision was not a scrambling agent at all: it did not lead to any cultural or structural breakdown. Rather, it was seen by much of the movement as one more development in the highly structured system of deterrence, NATO politics, and nuclear weapons policy. The argument can be made that the Euromissiles did shake individual world views, that once contacted by a movement organizer citizens' meaning frames were shaken and needed to be shored up or replaced. But Smelser focused on structural rather than individual strain. It is important to note the continued normal functioning, not breakdown, of the system that produced the double-track decision. From the perspective of NATO governments, the movements' challenge was direct and clearly defined. From the perspective of the transnational movements confronting those governments, official stubbornness on the question of the missiles and general security policy left no doubts about the definition of the situation.

Apart from the disparaging character assigned to social movement participants and action, the primary flaw in the collective behavior paradigm is its separation of standard political participants from movement actors. A distinction is drawn between the politics and practioners of social movements (clumped together in the paradigm with rioters and faddists) and the politics and practioners of mainstream, respectable groups: parties, lobbies, and interest groups. It is as if, in the words of William Gamson, the "actors who engage in these two types of behavior are seen as different species."[32] The implicit assumption is that conventional old politics is preferable to (and safer than) noninstitutionalized or unconventional new politics. The side-by-side development of social movements and political parties in parallel streams during the nineteenth century is ignored. Social movements have long been an ordinary way of conducting political business. That their twentieth century business was sometimes totalitarian partly explains the bias against them in collective behavior theory.

The collective behavior paradigm is unable to adequately account for the emergence of postmaterialist, new politics movements. Smelser's primary emphasis is on strain, a structural breakdown of the components of social action. The Chicago School theorists emphasize spontaneity, and the creation of meaning frames. What both collective behavior schools miss is the importance of the structural creations of movement entrepreneurs: organizations. But Smelser's notions of strain, precipitating factors, and generalized beliefs, when modified, add key pieces to the puzzle of movement origins. "Grievances" better captures the nature of the pacifist lament than does "strain." There were sharp value and norm conflicts between authorities and challengers, as predicted by Smelser's model, and these colored the movement's interpretation of the political environment and the construction of grievances. But peace movement grievances stemmed from the regular functioning of the national security state, not from the breakdown of Parsonian stability. I use the phrase "mobilization of consensus" to refer to the processes Smelser included in the growth and spread of generalized beliefs and Turner and Killian included in their emergent norm notion. I differ strongly, however, with what I take to be the Chicago School and Smelser's stress on short-circuiting, contagion, rumor, and the magical character of generalized beliefs. Movements certainly need to share interpretations and meanings to be able to act collectively. But this new consensus is a product not of gullibility, mysticism, or sleight of hand, but of a conscious effort on the part of movement organizers to recruit and educate adherents. Each modified collective behavior concept describes a crucial component of peace movement formation and mobilization. Modified collective behavior concepts can be integrated into my mobilization model: grievances are connected to fear of war and party failure, catalytic events include the statements and actions of President Reagan and others, and consensus mobilization processes enable movements to interpret events, policies, and trends, and to act on the basis of such interpretations.

Resource Mobilization

The emphasis on the fundamental importance of preexisting organizations and the availability of resources makes RMT better suited to explain "how" rather than "why" people engage in social movement collective action. Although the organizational-entrepreneurial model seems to adequately explain the emergence and operation of economic interest groups, it is less helpful when examining the peace movement. Peace movement members and constituencies were not oppressed groups similar to the working class, the poor, or African-Americans. The "oppressed group" in the struggle against nuclear weapons, the direct constituency, was not a particular racial or ethnic group, class or economic interest group, but the entire human race and the whole planet. The very essence of the targeted evil—the indiscriminate nature of nuclear explosives and the all-encompassing (if hypothetical) character of nuclear winter—sets anti-nuclear weapons movements apart from most other movements, old and new. Peace movements have few, if any, competitors for the breadth and expansiveness of their self-proclaimed constituency. Recent competitors may include those ecology movements which have moved a basis of their critique of nuclear power plants, toxic waste dumps, or destructive development from NIMBY (not-in-my-backyard) to NOPE (not-on-planet-earth). Nongovernmental human rights organizations such as Amnesty International also work on behalf of universal aims.

RMT tends to restrict the menu of resources available to movement groups to external ones like "money, access to the media, and support from powerful organizations."[33] The conscience constituency concept used by John McCarthy and Mayer Zald does not accurately characterize the mass base of the German anti-missile movement. While many members were affluent, with discretionary time and income to devote to the cause, active adherents themselves provided resources. The rich but detached angels found indispensable by McCarthy and Zald run up against many German peace movement groups' ideological preference for principles of participation and grassroots democracy. "Checkbook activism" (financial contributions to the cause in lieu of active participation) and professional cadre control contradicted movement ideology. Indeed, the movement suffered from constant tension over the question of central control by professional organizers. There was never grassroots acquiescence in elite direction. But there was far more to the movement than a handful of full-time organizers. The organizational-entrepreneurial approach exaggerates the importance of affluent conscience constituencies and directorial cadres in the case of the West German anti-Euromissile campaign.

The concept and practice of sacrifice are not provided for by the organizational-entrepreneurial model. It is as if supporters as envisioned by McCarthy and Zald are merely looking for a feel-good tax write-off or something to do in their spare time. The high level of emotional and ideological commitment common to peace movement participants is lost in this economistic approach. Commitment is left out of game theoretic approaches as well.[34] Affluence is a necessary but not sufficient condition for peace movement emergence. Professional organizations and entrepreneurs too are undoubtedly important. But they are only part of the story. Again, German peace movement organizations included more than just a handful of professionals. Without the energies and direct participation of hundreds of thousands of other citizens, the effort to block Euromissile deployment would not have gone beyond the interest group level to become one of the largest and most vocal mass movements in all-German history.

The rational actionists' assumption of movement adherent rationality is a refreshing departure from the psychopathological explanations of the crowd psychologists and some of the collective behaviorists. But, argued Bert Klandermans, RMT "went too far in nearly abandoning the social-psychological analyses" of classical movement theories.[35] Myra Marx Ferree faulted the rational actionists' "neglect of value differences and conflicts . . . misplaced emphasis on the free-rider problem . . . and . . . presupposition of a pseudo-universal human actor without either a personal history or a gender, race, or class position within a societal history."[36] After all, among the other problems of the perspective, how calculable are costs and benefits? Is it even possible for movement participants to know what rewards and sanctions accrue to particular action choices? Might challengers avoid narrowly defined economic rational choice while at the same time engaging in sober and reasonable collective action? A study of Boston anti-busing activists found:

> very few people who protest do so because they believe it will end busing. In fact, the overwhelming majority are convinced that this goal will never be achieved. Those who join in anti-busing protest do so because they believe it is likely to result in a nonspecifiable but positive gain, in an indefinite but reasonable length of time.[37]

The claim that protesters do not conduct narrow economic cost-benefit analyses prior to participation seems sound. Decisions made with incomplete information are an inescapable fact of everyday life. Certainly some rough arithmetic about time available for collective action is necessary. Whether this time is spent "economically" is for the individual to decide. Anthony Oberschall's concept of "selfish interests" seems out of place for peace activists. Peace protest can not be characterized as narrowly selfish; it requires a redefinition of selfishness away from the conventional notion of material aggrandizement toward a concept of psychic or solidary benefits.[38] Outwardly, selfishness becomes selflessness. Inwardly, to paraphrase Nietzsche, selflessness appears as selfishness. The idea of nonspecifiable gains seems plausible; as for those opposed to busing, many opposed to the Euromissiles thought a revoked deployment decision unlikely. Yet people protest even if unable to articulate a precise notion of gain. To protest a wrong is simply the right thing to do. One economist called such practices "irrational behavior without regret."[39] Sociologists stress the concepts of principle and solidarity and have found that when people see their fates bound together with those of others with whom they strongly identify, they are not likely to base their decision to participate on utilitarian calculations.[40]

Taken together, RM approaches provide three insights useful for an understanding of movement emergence: the assumption of collective action rationality, the importance of entrepreneurs, organization and social control in forming and sustaining movements, and the view of movements as resource mobilizers. Rational calculations do not, in most cases, approach the formality assumed by neo-classical economists. Instead, the expectation of positive but unspecified gain is useful in explaining the propensity of citizens to participate in peace movements. Peace protest provides psychic or solidary benefits rather than material benefits. Established institutions, informal and professional networks, and more or less formal SMOs were all crucial to the genesis of the peace movement. Preexisting organizations gave structure to the movement. Veteran activists and their extant organizations built and coordinated the anti-missile movement's central decisionmaking body. An organizational-entrepreneurial perspective on the rise of 1980s German peace movement sees political entrepreneurs organizing around grievances linked to the double-track decision and the larger geopolitical problematic. It took political entrepreneurs, professional organizations and thousands of ad hoc groups to rouse a mass public, to bring them out of their nuclear sleep and to show them that something could be done.

Political Process

The political process model developed on the basis of claims about organization, consciousness, and the structure of political opportunities. Extraordinary organization—beyond parties and interest groups—was deemed necessary for movements in the making. This is so, it is said, because sprouting movements do not have the ear of those in power. Some version of the distinction between actors inside the polity (members) who have routine access to decisions that affect them and those outside the polity (challengers) who do not is crucial for political process theorists.[41] The collective attempts of challengers to move inside the polity and to be treated as members are what, it is thought, give rise to movements. This etiological corollary of the distinction does not work well for peace movements. Only a miniscule fraction of the polity has what could be considered routine access to governmental decisions about nuclear security policy. To demand such access can be seen as more than an attempt to gain membership in the polity. Whereas citizens have more or less access to the decisions of school boards, or legislatures at all levels, decisions about the deployment of nuclear weapons are on another plane. This is not to suggest that other public policy issue-areas conform to some textbook type of pluralism. While in some sense made by the same class of legislators, executives and lobbyists as is policy regarding dairy price supports or social security, nuclear weapons policy is unique. The stakes are higher and the traditional decisionmaking circles are considerably smaller. Secrecy pervades the process and limits access. A narrow technical expertise is thought necessary for admission. These characteristics work to keep out the uninitiated. Nuclear weapons deployment decisions, especially for emplacements on foreign soil, require consultation with overseas allies. And security policy is that rare type of public policy which directly affects all citizens, whether members or challengers, virtually equally and virtually everywhere in a society.

Movements and their adherents can be both inside *and* outside the polity simultaneously depending on the issue pressed. Recall the experience of European and North American labor movements, or the case of West European ecology parties which have representatives in legislatures at all levels, from city councils to national legislatures to the European Parliament. At the same time these groups find themselves seated in august assemblies, they are struggling, less politely, within and from an alternative context. It might be more fruitful to see *issues* rather than people as inside or outside the polity, as on or not yet on the public agenda. It is mostly the legitimacy and the moderation of demands on the part of mainstream groups that permits them membership in the day-to-day workings of the polity. Should they make a radical demand such as the banning of legal abortions, and should they not have the patience to wait for legislative or judicial satisfaction of their demand, they will find themselves in front of abortion clinics as part of Operation Rescue. The distinction drawn by political process theorists assumes challengers would accept membership in the polity were it offered them. This may be true for some social movement sectors such as certain African-American civil rights organizations during the 1950s and 1960s. But others, including revolutionaries like Emiliano Zapata and many German peace activists, may agree with Woody Allen's quip and never be a member of a club that would have them.

The peace movement critique of security policy went beyond questions of substance to those of form. The nature of power in postindustrial societies, the imperfect practice of representative democracy, the pivotal role of inscrutable bureaucracies, the hegemony of executive prerogatives, secrecy, and other factors conspire to make membership in an actually existing security policy polity a nightmare for rather than an aspiration of many grassroots peace activists. This obviously does not rule out the desirability of standard polity-type goals such as the prevention of nuclear weapons deployments. But it does limit the analytical power of the distinction between challengers and authorities. Groups like the German Greens were divided as to the costs and benefits of membership in the "system" (defined as parliamentary democracy and coalition government at the state and local level). This was a real source of tension for the Greens, and gave rise to factionalism and splintering. Those in favor of polity membership believed their's would be a very different sort from that of established elites, and that wholesale social change required work on the inside as well as the outside. Supporters of nonmembership, of "fundamental opposition," saw membership in the system as synonymous with corruption, decay and a betrayal of basic values.

One consequence of the radical peace movement critique is, still using William Gamson's language, the need for a new, restructured polity rather than for membership in the polity that gave rise to the very circumstances the movement mobilized against. This qualification of the political process approach in the case of peace movements does not contradict its basic validity regarding the centrality of the political process to movement action. Peace movements were pursuing political interests in a political struggle with other interested contenders for power. Wolfgang Abendroth made the interesting point that during the first six years of SPD-FDP rule, between its onset and the completion of the Helsinki Accords in 1975, the peace movement was the least visible it had ever been in West German history.[42] This was so because the government was vigorously pursuing part of the movement's program through its Ostpolitik. But as soon as Genscher and Schmidt uncoupled their government from this path (in line with shifts in Jimmy Carter's foreign policy), the movement reappeared. This happened between about 1976 and 1979. Tens of thousands hit the streets, and intense discussions about security policy began within the SPD. Without the movement activity of these years, thought Abendroth, there would have been no internal wrangling in the SPD.

Process theorists are not clear about what sparks the consciousness change they claim necessary to spawn movements. When does "the system lose legitimacy"? When does fatalism give way to bold assertions of rights? The assumption of cost-benefit calculations on the part of protestors does not explain the apparent shift in the outcome of these calculations. That is, no clear answer is given for the transition from a perception of prohibitive costs to a perception of reasonable risks. People must be convinced that a situation is not hopeless but holds the promise for change in order for them to get involved. This requires strong organizations with clear agendas and messages. Not to protest would be a betrayal of values and one's friends. This protest imperative was strong for many middle-age and younger Germans whose personal civic culture was overcast by the ominous clouds of Nazism and the Holocaust.

Doug McAdam's use of the political opportunity structure concept is overly broad. Its analytical value is reduced because it is undiscriminating about its contents. When any event or trend that contributes to movement mobilization is part of its POS, we are unable to determine whether one event was more important than another. In the same way grievances are ubiquitous, so are political opportunities. Many grievances do not spark concerted action, at least not at the level of a mass movement. The same must be said for political opportunities. Most—even when recognized—do not act as an ingredient in the formation of a social movement. What determines whether a political opportunity is acted upon or not? The level of organization and the level of consciousness (and other concrete strategic considerations) determine whether an event is catalytic or whether it is just another lost chance for action.

In his POS conception, Sidney Tarrow's first point about the openness of the polity requires specification. If it includes variation across regimes (Weimar republic versus Nazi dictatorship), then it perhaps encompasses longer periods of time than the POS concept should to be most useful as a tool of fine grained political analysis. If it includes variation between successive governments within the same regime (Schmidt versus Kohl) it takes on the shorter time frame necessary to analyze movement mobilization. This is not to say that "decades" do not matter for the formation of movements. Of course they do. But "years" and even "months" and "weeks" may sometimes be the temporal units of greater use for uncovering movement roots (recall the British statesman's remark that "a day can be a long time in politics"). Tarrow's second, third and fourth points about the stability of political alignments, the presence of allies, and the toleration of protest, respectively, are useful within the shorter periods sometimes necessary for political analysis of movement mobilization.

Noninstitutionalized political action fits neatly within the political process model; there is no need for the special theories required by some collective behaviorists' to explain protest action. The political process is central to movement action. Tarrow's insight about the political origins of the NSM is useful. But the power of Inglehart's theory of postmaterialism to explain the protest potential drawn on by the peace movement must be retained. Surely the movements of the sixties had much to do with the spread of postmaterialist values, and peace movement mobilization in the eighties needs to be better described and explained than as an ideological and tactical residue of the previous cycle of mobilization. The distinction drawn by political process theorists between polity members and outsiders misses the extent to which the movement was able to cull support from established institutions, and the extent to which this support from polity members legitimized the movement and its demands. The West German peace movement critique of security policy questioned the very operation of power in society; membership in the traditional nuclear policymaking elite was not a goal. Instead, a polity transformed by grassroots democracy would make possible the abolition of the nuclear priesthood, and the adoption of alternative strategy proposals.

New Social Movement Theory

Ideally, in his attempt to overcome the old views of movements as unified actors on the stage of history, Alberto Melucci would have devised some new term that better reflected the phenomenology of contemporary collective action than "social movement." The substitutes he used—collective action, mobilization—are also "old" terms which do not automatically reflect the specific meaning Melucci imputed to them. But the term "social movement" need not be abandoned. Despite the horrific crimes committed in the names of totalitarian and kindred movements, the term itself can be rehabilitated. Most NSM evince neither certainty about the course of history nor desire to force feed society their vision of utopia. Melucci's critique does not completely end the allure of the old views. Empirical and ontological notions of social movements as unitary actors make macropolitical analysis possible. It is at least partly as actors on the stage of history—as players in policymaking and political processes—that recent peace movements are so interesting to so many. No, the peace movement was not a unified empirical entity. At the same time, an assessment of its political character requires one to assume some cohesiveness, even during less visible phases of the movement. The 1980s West German peace movement was without a doubt a social construction. But for the purposes of this study, it was first and foremost a political actor. Melucci's project is in this regard less useful than it might be otherwise.

In their analyses of conflicts in complex societies, NSM theorists provided valuable insights into the deep structure of peace protest. Identifying as sites of movement emergence areas where pressure for social conformity is high is appropriate for peace movements as there is, of course, significant pressure to fall in line on security issues. Anticommunism helped limit dissent in the West from the fall of Czar Nicholas to the fall of Mikhail Gorbachev. Appeals to patriotism and nationalism have been highly effective methods of minimizing defense dissent. Fears about the health of German democracy and over German responsibilities to NATO worked to pressure and discredit security policy nonconformists. Incantations such as "democracy has spoken, now obey," or "we can't let some marginal, outspoken (and perhaps manipulated) minority dictate policy to the majority (or their elected representatives)," have long worked to pressure and discredit security policy dissidents. Invocations of alliance requirements—"we're part of NATO, thus we must do our part"—and songs in praise of NATO were sung in order to make "our part" more palatable. These various pressures were especially onerous for the Federal Republic because of the German past.

Shifts in the loci of power within postindustrial societies observed by NSM theorists are perhaps less relevant for the mobilization of peace movements than for other recent social developments. While power relations may have become less clear and overbearing in postindustrial society as compared to industrial society, this shift has had little direct impact on the appearance of peace movements. The state executive remains the primary holder of security policy power. However, legislatures and even judiciaries, political parties, unions, churches, professional associations, academic and other institutions were increasingly important both as movement targets of action and as constituencies, as "fields" of collective action, and as allied producers of meaning and signs. But the executive remains the chief antagonist of peace movements. It is vital not to lose sight of the continued preeminence of the *state* vis-à-vis the whole gamut of peace movement activities: identity construction, goal-setting, direct action, and so on.

Melucci made three points regarding the rise and occasional coherence of peace protest during the 1980s. It was first of all a reaction to changed military policies, thus a defensive movement. The question arises as to the extent to which the deployment was a *change* in policy rather than business-as-usual (a modernization, a response to a Soviet build-up, a shoring up of extended deterrence) as claimed by NATO. Should the latter be the case, the movement reacted not to a policy change but to new means for old ends. The other view, put forward by the movement at various times, saw PD-59 and Reagan-era NSDDs (expanding nuclear warfighting doctrine), the new single integrated operational plan (SIOP 7), AirLand Battle 2000 and other threatening doctrinal developments courtesy of Presidents Carter and Reagan as necessitating vigorous citizen responses. As the views are not easily reconciled, the type-one fear of war explanation perhaps better captures the defensive character of the peace movement. But regardless of whether the stimulus for peace protest was innovative or not, Melucci had it right, activists responded to stimulus from the state.

Melucci claimed in his second point that "the contemporary international conjuncture provides a social and cultural opportunity for a form of collective action which has only casual links with the precipitating military situation."[43] Social and cultural opportunities are not dependent on the contemporary world situation or the state of superpower relations as were political opportunities grasped by the peace movement. The links between movement action and the "precipitating military situation" were considerably stronger than casual. He correctly rejected a historical materialist interpretation of peace protest. Marxist categories, as noted earlier, must be stretched perhaps too far to apply to the origins and nature of peace movements.[44] Roberta Ash Garner employed a sweeping Marxism:

> All movements are ultimately produced by transformations of the base.
> ... First, and most obviously, changes in the base put new pressures on
> classes. A second way in which the base generates movements is by the
> expansion of a system of production to new groups. ... The base can
> generate movements in a third and more complicated way by inducing
> inaccurate and irrational belief systems.[45]

While essentially unobjectionable, the level of abstraction prevents finer-grained analysis such as specification of the relationship of economic change to actual movement origins.

What is clear is that an explanation of peace movement emergence must be primarily political. To liken the "moral utopianism" of the peace movement to the claims of small sects and heretical circles, as did Melucci, ignores the powerful theory of postmaterialism put forward by Ronald Inglehart. And it echoes the portrayal of peace protest by conservative critics and the general depiction of collective action by some collective behaviorists. The moral claims brandished by peace activists turned their movement away from merely defending the status quo ante, and can be seen as other than utopian. Was it "moral utopianism" to demand that Earth and humanity be spared nuclear incineration? That providing for the common defense need not involve threats of and preparations for nuclear apocalypse? That economic resources, personnel and expertise devoted to vast military-industrial complexes might be better invested elsewhere? These claims, and the other expectations of the peace movement, can and have been cast in economic or political language (and in the simple wisdom of the average citizen). Morality was but one facet of the peace movement critique of NATO security policy. The unabashedly moral dimension of peace protest is miscast as heretical or marginal. Peace movement complaints about the dubious morality of nuclear deterrence were picked up and extended by moral philosophers, Jewish rabbis, Catholic and Protestant bishops, Buddhist monks. These claims were at the very center of theological debate about war and peace during the 1980s, and not the province of marginalized "circles." Peace movement prescriptions may be characterized as heretical not in Melucci's sense, but in the sense the Reformation was heresy from the perspective of Rome.

In his third point about the rise of peace protest, Melucci seemed to contradict his earlier reliance on mobilization of political actors and collective fear as determinants of movement action. He denied a leading role for institutional processes, social interests and the psychological preferences of participants in movement formation. There are at least three responses to this point. First, his claim that political actors were marginal to the movement is puzzling. Presumably by "political actor" Melucci meant parties, unions, and interest associations. But the movement both drew support from political actors and was in itself a political actor. His claim is less puzzling when factoring in Melucci's deemphasis of the political aspects of NSM collective action. The fear of the bomb may not explain the "how" of pacifist collective action, but it surely helps explain its "why." Stress on the nonpolitical nature of movements is instructive. But politics—instrumental political goals, strategies and tactics—rather than culture was the primary context of the movement. These factors were not controlling for Melucci because they are essentially political: "my argument is that peace mobilizations also express [deeper] conflicts peculiar to complex societies."[46] It is these conflicts that were Melucci's real interest and an analysis of which his means to transcend political explanations.

Second, Melucci claimed the movement's offensive character was one of "moral utopianism." Moral utopianism was for him a general expectation of happiness rather than a focused critique. But, again, this clearly missed the movement's wide-ranging ethical critique of nuclear deterrence, a center piece of its attraction to citizens and its challenge to authorities. His denial of a close connection between the military situation and peace movement mobilization is, I think, simply wrong. Third, Melucci qualified his identification of a deteriorating geopolitical climate, fear of war, and moral utopianism as roots of the movement. The patterns of solidarity, organization and identity of pacifist action, he contended, originated elsewhere. This qualification also stems from his deemphasis on the political aspects of peace movement action. But as we have seen, fear of war is very helpful in explaining the origins of the German peace movement. Instead, Melucci would have us look to "conflicts peculiar to complex societies."

Melucci argued that the "planetary system" and centrality of information in complex societies were important for an understanding of the "nuclear situation." Access to information and the ability to manipulate it—the new source of power—makes life faster and unexaminable. Peace movements would slow life down in complex societies. The paramount issue for peace mobilizations, he said, is the "*the self-production of the human species* at the individual and collective level." If control over individual and collective destiny within this system was a root of the peace movement plant, then the political decisions over the deployment and fate of the Euromissiles were the plant's seeds. Nuclear war presents humanity with a unique time-space conjuncture: instantaneous and global destruction. Global society's inability to close the Pandora's Box of nuclear information gave rise to national security states and the tiny decisionmaking elites that manage them. The policy decisions of this handful of men have, at times, sparked public resistance. But here we need to have it both ways. The global context of peace movements he outlined is convincing. But we can not shunt aside, as he did, the military situation and specific catalytic events leading to the movement. The global *and* the proximate causes of peace movement mobilization must be explained.

In his paradox about expertism and general effects of nuclear war (nuclear war is the domain of experts but has consequences for all), Melucci missed a crucial aim of peace movements: to break down the barriers of nuclear expertise and to resolve the contradiction. Activists breached the walls surrounding the arcane world of "circular error probable", "hard target kill capability," C^3I, and the rest of the sanitized jargon insulating atomic witch doctors from public scrutiny. Peace movement "counter-experts" despoiled the church of the nuclear priesthood. War has always been a universal social concern, but since 1945 it has been a preeminently German concern as well. Below the surface of the paradox lies a nuclear version of the struggle over social constructions of national security and power that has varied only with the inclusiveness of the polity and the ability of citizens to take part in these struggles. The related but more relevant paradox is instead Einstein's: with the coming of the atomic bomb, everything has changed save our way of thinking. And it was the way of thinking of nuclear experts and decisionmakers (as well as that of the general public) that the movement aimed to change.

The decline of the state system was, for Melucci, "perhaps the fundamental message of contemporary pacifism." He was right to stress the decreased capacity of states to manage the trajectory of nuclear development and confrontation. Peace movements are both cause and effect of this diminished capacity. The withering of the international system stems from the erosion of state authority both from above (multinational corporations and international nongovernmental organizations) and from below in a more powerful civil society. The political means for global system survival, and for the continued viability of states, lie in the social transformation of the state system, a crucial focus of peace mobilizations. Perhaps more radical even than the transformation of the state system that Melucci noted, was the peace movement message that issues of life and death need not remain in the hands of the few, that ordinary citizens can make their own history.

Melucci's emphasis on the symbolic dimension of nuclear weapons and doctrine while necessary was not sufficient. Confrontation short of war, argued Melucci, is now a symbolic battle for the control of information. Deterrence "intervenes in the information and representations of opponents by creating a mirror game in which every player tries to influence the other and to take advantage of the enemy's misperception." This view obscures the very real and obvious manifestations of the preparations for nuclear war that were crucial for movement mobilization. A Pershing II missile was more than a symbol. Neutron bombs have features besides the symbolic. Deterrence required "credibility" that had tangible consequences. Defense spending, war games, and military bases all served as reminders of the concrete side of security policy. This recounting stresses what was a prerequisite for German peace movement mobilization: a hard threat. Obtrusive preparations for nuclear war acted as a powerful fertilizer on the roots of the peace movement. The Euromissiles were undoubtedly powerful symbols of an endless arms race and increased nuclear danger. But real people lived in Mutlangen near the Pershing base.

A Synthetic Explanation of Movement Origins

Each of the six theoretical perspectives sheds some light on the origins of the Federal German peace movement. An amalgam of insights provides an empirically-based theoretical account of the roots of the movement (see Figure 9.1). These propositions form the basis of a hybrid explanation that addresses the sources of social action: personal and political, cultural and psychological, structural and technological. The amalgamated theory, lean but comprehensive, tries to explain movement origins at each level of social causation: individual, organizational, communal, societal, transnational, global. Designed with the Federal German peace movement in mind, the theoretical account might also explain the roots of other Western anti-nuclear weapons movements in the 1980s.

The roots of the 1980s West German peace movement are found in: the rational and strategic responses of individuals, entrepreneurs and preexisting organizations to NATO's 1979 double-track decision. Responses emerged as part of the political process, and within an evolving political opportunity structure. The political process unfolded within an environment of changing culture, pressure to conform to dominant codes and signs, symbolic conflicts unique to complex societies, the centrality of information, and the decreased capacity of states to provide security. Activists were motivated partly by the reasonable fear of nuclear war sparked by the deterioration of U.S.-Soviet relations, the loose talk and rhetoric of (especially American) political leaders, and by the accelerating nuclear arms race. Increased risk of war was one of a number of grievances adherents had about the making and substance of defense policy. Acting on these grievances, individuals and organizations were dissatisfied by the inability of political parties, especially the SPD, to mediate their interests, provide genuine electoral and policy alternatives, and shield the populace from the fall out of superpower conflict. The organizations activists formed or grew in response to party failure bypassed or complemented the party system, mobilized consensus about the nature of the problem and what could be done about it, and capitalized on catalytic events that aided recruitment, education and propaganda efforts.

Conclusion

Erhard Eppler summarized the three propositions about NSMs examined in this chapter: that they act in new arenas of conflict; that they

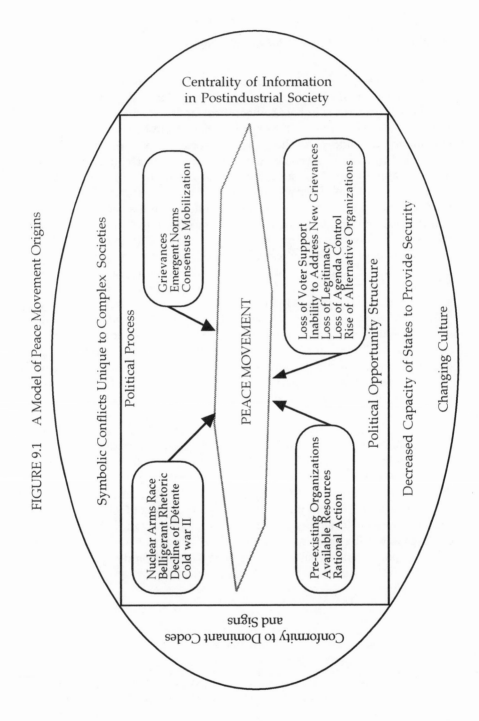

FIGURE 9.1   A Model of Peace Movement Origins

display new forms of identity and consciousness; and that they employ new types of organization and action.

> The new [character of social movements] does not make its appearance as a comprehensive program, as a winged utopia, as an irresistible wave; rather, it manifests itself as an expression of doubt with respect to current conditions, as an apprehensive search for a more fulfilling way of life, as new forms of human communication, as citizen initiatives against large-scale technocratic insanity, as an argument involving [those developments] that have not yet been argued against, as a new map [for society] upon which no final destination has yet been drawn, one that indicates in any event the very next stopping point and the township after that.[47]

Social movement theory has much to say about the origins of movements. The main propositions of six theory clusters were examined for what they could tell us about the roots of the Federal German anti-missile movement. We found that by careful sorting and modification, a satisfactory theoretical account of movement origins was possible. The 1980s German peace movement was a construction of diverse, rational individuals and organizations acting within the polity in response to a policy decision. The decision emerged against a domestic background of legitimacy crisis, party failure, postmaterial value change, and an ample supply of experienced activists. The decline of détente, several economic and political crises, and the complex forces of globalization provided the international background to the decision. Citizens grew afraid, organized and looked for alternative parties and policies. They gathered resources, mobilized consensus, and acted in pursuit of goals.

Notes

1. Quoted in "The Talk of the Town," *The New Yorker*, June 18, 1990, p. 25.
2. Plotke, "What's So New?," pp. 87-88.
3. See Alfred H. Fried's *Handbuch der Friedensbewegung* (New York: Garland, 1972), originally published in 1904; and Walter Fabian and Kurt Lenz, eds., *Die Friedensbewegung: Ein Handbuch der Weltfriedensströmungen der Gegenwart* (Cologne: Bund-Verlag, 1985), which first appeared in 1922.
4. Peter Merkl, "How New the Brave New World: New Social Movements in West Germany," *German Studies Review*, vol. 10, no. 1 (1987).
5. Lawson and Merkl, eds., *When Parties Fail*, p. 7.
6. On the stubbornness of old thinking among security policy elites in the United States, see Kull, *Minds at War*.

7. Herbert Kitschelt and Staf Hellemans, *Beyond the European Left: Ideology and Political Action in the Belgian Ecology Parties* (Durham: Duke University Press, 1990).

8. Barnes and Kaase, *Political Action*; and Baker, Dalton and Hildebrandt, *Germany Transformed*.

9. Donald Schoonmaker, "The Challenge of the Greens to the West German Party System," in Lawson and Merkl, eds., *When Parties Fail*.

10. E. Gene Frankland, "Interpreting the Green Phenomenon in West German Politics, 1977-83," unpublished manuscript, September 1983.

11. Ebert, *Ziviler Ungehorsam*, chapter 5.

12. Helm, "Citizen Lobbies in West Germany;" and Udo Bermbach, "On Civic Initiative Groups," in Max Kaase and Klaus von Beyme, eds., *Elections and Parties* (Beverly Hills, CA: Sage Publications, 1978).

13. Ebert, *Ziviler Ungehorsam*, p. 106.

14. Data for 1972-1987 from Table A.1 of Richard M. Scammon and Alice V. McGillivray, Appendix A, in Karl H. Cerny, ed., *Germany at the Polls: The Bundestag Elections of the 1980s* (Durham, NC: Duke University Press, 1990), p. 266. Figure for 1990 from *Statistisches Jahrbuch* (Wiesbaden: Statistisches Bundesamt, 1991). Figure for 1994 from Forschungsgruppe Wahlen data via the German Information Center in New York.

15. Data from David P. Conradt and Russell J. Dalton, "The West German Electorate and the Party System: Continuity and Change in the 1980s," *Review of Politics*, vol. 50 (1988), p. 9.

16. Quoted in Jörg R. Mettke, ed., *Die Grünen: Regierungspartner von Morgen?* (Hamburg: Spiegel, 1982).

17. Quoted in Reimar Oltmanns, *Du Hast Keine Chance, Aber Nutze Sie—Eine Jugend Steigt Aus* (Reinbek: Rowohlt, 1980), p. 114.

18. Peter H. Merkl, "The Challengers and the Party Systems," in *When Parties Fail*, pp. 582-84. The possibilities for democratic renewal through direct mechanisms are the subject of Thomas E. Cronin, *Direct Democracy: The Politics of Initiative, Referendum, and Recall* (Cambridge: Harvard University Press, 1989); and David S. Schmidt, *Citizen Lawmakers: The Ballot Initiative Revolution* (Philadelphia: Temple University Press, 1989).

19. Samuel Huntington, "Post-Industrial Politics: How Benign Will it Be?" *Comparative Politics* (1974), p. 175.

20. Gustave Le Bon, *The Crowd* (London: Benn, 1896); and William Kornhauser, *The Politics of Mass Society* (New York: Free Press, 1959).

21. Alice Miller, *For Your Own Good* (New York: Farrar, Strauss & Giroux, 1984).

22. For a critical assessment of these analyses, see Gerhard Wettig, *Psychoanalyse, Friedensbewegung und Sicherheitspolitik* (Bonn: Bundesinstituts für ostwissenschaftliche und internationale Studien, 1983).

23. Clay Clemens, "The Antinuclear Movement in West Germany: Angst and Isms, Old and New," in James E. Dougherty and Robert L. Pfaltzgraff, Jr., eds., *Shattering Europe's Defense Consensus: The Antinuclear Protest Movement and the Future of NATO* (Washington: Pergamon-Brassey's, 1985), pp. 62-63.

24. Jeffrey Herf, "War, Peace, and the Intellectuals," p. 172.

25. Bruce Russett and Donald R. Deluca, "Theater Nuclear Forces: Public Opinion in Western Europe," *Political Science Quarterly*, vol. 98, no. 2 (1983), pp. 180-83; Straub, Werbick and Zitterbarth, "Friedensbewegung und Kriegsängste," pp. 93-95; and Manfred Efinger, Thomas Nielebock, and Volker Rittberger, "Was Muß Uns Ängstigen? Zur Kriegsgefahrenwahrnehmung der Friedensbewegung und Kriegsgefahrenanalyse der Friedens- und Konfliktforschung," in Horn and Rittberger, eds., *Mit Kriegsgefahren Leben*.

26. Anatoly Grishchenko and Vladimir Semenoy, *Danger: NATO*, (Moscow: Progress Publishers, 1985), p. 158.

27. Cited in Karsten D. Voigt, "Nuclear Weapons in Europe: A German Social Democrat's Perspective," in Pierre, ed., p. 100.

28. See the interview with him in the *Washington Post*, April 11, 1982.

29. *Euro-Barometer*, No. 21-22, December 1984; cited in Wilfried von Bredow and Rudolf H. Brocke, "Ost-West Konflikt, Krisenbewusstsein und Protestbewegung in Westeuropa," *Aus Politik und Zeitgeschichte*, vol. 5 (1986), p. 41.

30. For an extraordinary personal account of one woman's type-one fears about nuclear war, see Kutte, *Angst vor dem Atomkrieg*.

31. Smelser, *Theory of Collective Behavior*, pp. 8-9.

32. Gamson, *The Strategy of Social Protest*, p. 132.

33. Turner and Killian, *Collective Behavior*, p. 235.

34. Dennis Chong, *Collective Action and the Civil Rights Movement* (Chicago: University of Chicago Press, 1991).

35. Bert Klandermans, "Mobilization and Participation: Social-Psychological Explanations of Resource Mobilization Theory," *American Sociological Review*, vol. 49 (1984), p. 584.

36. Myra Marx Ferree, "The Political Context of Rationality: Rational Choice Theory and Resource Mobilization," in Morris and Mueller, eds., *Frontiers in Social Movement Theory*, p. 31.

37. D. Garth Taylor, *Public Opinion and Collective Action* (Chicago: The University of Chicago Press, 1986), p. 9.

38. Steve Breyman, "The Rationality of Class Action," unpublished manuscript, 1982.

39. Robert H. Frank, *Passions Within Reason: The Strategic Role of the Emotions* (New York: Norton, 1988).

40. Bruce Fireman and William Gamson, "Utilitarian Logic in the Resource Mobilization Perspective," in Zald and McCarthy, eds., *The Dynamics of Social Movements*.

41. See, for example, Gamson, *The Strategy of Social Protest*, p. 140.

42. Quoted in Deppe, et al., eds., *Friedensbewegung und Arbeiterbewegung*, p. 76.

43. Melucci, *Nomads of the Present*, p. 82.

44. For an analysis of the NSM with frequent critical references to Marxism, see Carl Boggs, *Social Movements and Political Power: Emerging Forms of Radicalism in the West* (Philadelphia: Temple University Press, 1986). For a survey and rejection of class analysis of NSM, see Jan Paluski, "Mass Movements and Social Class," *International Sociology*, vol. 8, no. 2 (1993).

45. Ash Garner, *Social Movements in America*, pp. 8,10.
46. Melucci, *Nomads of the Present*, p. 83.
47. Quoted in Mushaben, "Innocence Lost," p. 39.

Appendix

The Coordinating Committee of the West German
Peace Movement (1983-84)

Typology of Structure and Composition
(30 Member Organizations)

Parties and Working Groups
- Greens
- Liberal Democrats
- Democratic Socialists
- Social Democratic Women's Working Group

Political Youth Organizations
- Young Socialists (Jusos)
- Young Democrats
- Socialist Youth of Germany (SJD-*die Falken*)
- Socialist German Worker Youth (SDAJ)

Party-Affiliated Organizations
- Initiative for Peace, International Compromise and Security (IFIAS)
- Committee for Peace, Disarmament and Cooperation (KOFAZ)

Youth Associations
- DGB-Youth
- Conference of State Pupils' Representations (KdLSV)/[after March 1984]: Federal Pupils' Representation (BSV)
- United German Student Bodies (VDS)

Coordination Groups and Associations
- Civil Disobedience Coordination Office
- Federal Congress of Autonomous Peace Initiatives (BUF)/[later]: Federal Conference of Independent Peace Groups (BUKO)
- Federation of Nonviolent Action Groups (FÖGA)

Women
- Women's Incitement for Peace
- Women in the Bundeswehr?—We Say No!

Conscientious Objectors
- German Peace Society/United War Service Opponents (DFG/VK)

Antifascists
- Union of Nazi Regime Persecutees/League of Antifascists (VVN-/BdA)

Third World Groups
- Federal Conference of Development Policy Action Groups (BUKO)

Ecology Groups
- Federal Association of Environmental Protection Citizen Initiatives (BBU)

Christian Groups
- Reconciliation Action/Peace Service (ASF)
- Service for Peace Action Community (AGDF)
- Protestant Student Associations (ESG)
- Initiative for a Church from Below (IKVU)
- Live Without Arms (ORL)
- Pax Christi

Personal Alliances/Associations
- Gustav-Heinemann-Initiative (GHI)
- Committee for Constitutional Rights and Democracy

Bibliography

Albrecht, Ulrich, "Zur politischen Bedeutung der neueren Friedensbewegungen in der Bundesrepublik Deutschland," *Osterreichische Zeitschrift für Politikwissenschaft*, vol. 2 (1983).

Aglietta, Michel, *A Theory of Capitalist Regulation: The US Experience* (London: Lowe and Brydone, 1979).

Aktion Sühnezeichen/Friedensdienste, "Ein Vorschlag zur Auseinandersetzung—Keine neuen Atomwaffen in der Bundesrepublik," in Lutz Plümer, ed., *Positionen der Friedensbewegung: die Auseinandersetzung um den US-Mittelstreckenraketenbeschluss—Dokumente, Appelle, Beiträge* (Frankfurt: Sendler, 1981).

Aktion Sühnezeichen/Friedensdienste and Aktionsgemeinschaft Dienst für den Frieden, eds., *Bonn 10. 10. 81.: Friedensdemonstration für Abrüstung und Entspannung in Europa* (Bornheim: Lamuv Verlag, 1981).

Aldridge, Robert C., *First Strike! The Pentagon's Strategy for Nuclear War* (Boston: South End Press, 1983).

"'Alles oder nicht—egal, aber storno.' Die Autonomen—der militante Ableger der Friedensbewegung," *Der Spiegel*, no. 39 (1983).

Arbeitsgruppe Friedensforschung Tübingen, ed. *Atomwaffen-Freiheit und Europäische Sicherheit: Möglichkeiten und Probleme einer anderen Sicherheitspolitik* (Tübingen: Verein für Friedenspädagogik, 1983).

Ash, Roberta, *Social Movements in America* (Chicago: Markham, 1972).

Bahro, Rudolf, *Wahnsinn mit Methode: Über die Logik der Blockkonfrontation, die Friedensbewegung, die Sowjetunion und die DKP* (Berlin: Olle & Wolter, 1982).

Baker, Kendall, Russell J. Dalton and Kai Hildebrandt, *Germany Transformed: Political Culture and the New Politics* (Cambridge, MA: Harvard University Press, 1981).

Barnes, Samuel H., Max Kaase, et al. *Political Action: Mass Participation in Five Western Democracies* (Beverly Hills, CA: Sage, 1979).

Barth, Karl, *Church Dogmatics*, 4 vols. (Edinburgh: T. and T. Clark, 1961).

Bastian, Gert, *Atomtod oder europäische Sicherheitsgemeinschaft: Abrüstung statt Abschreckung* (Cologne: Pahl-Rugenstein, 1982).

Bell, Daniel J., *The Coming of Post-Industrial Society: A Venture in Social Forecasting* (New York: Basic, 1973).

Bellah, Robert, "Populism and Individualism," *Social Policy* (Fall 1985).

Benedict, H.J., "Auf dem Weg zur Friedenskirche: Entstehung und Erscheinungsformen der neuen Friedensbewegung in der evangelischen Kirche," *Friedensanalysen*, vol. 16 (1982).

_____ . "Das Selbstverständnis der kirchlichen Friedensbewegung—Einheit und Vielfalt," *Jahrbuch für Friedens-und Konfliktforschung*, vol. 10 (1982).

Berger, Suzanne, "Politics and Antipolitics in Western Europe in the Seventies," *Daedalus*, vol. 108, no. 1 (1979).

Bergmann, W., "Was bewegt die soziale Bewegung? Überlegungen zur Selbstkonstitution der 'neuen' sozialen Bewegungen," in D. Bäcker, ed., *Theorie als Passion* (Frankfurt: Suhrkamp, 1987).

Bermbach, Udo, "On Civic Initiative Groups," in Max Kaase and Klaus von Beyme, eds., *Elections and Parties* (Beverly Hills, CA: Sage Publications, 1978).

Bess, Michael, *Realism, Utopia, and the Mushroom Cloud: Four Activist Intellectuals and Their Strategies for Peace, 1945-1989* (Chicago: University of Chicago Press, 1993).

Biehle, Alfred, ed., *Alternative Strategien: Das Hearing im Verteidigungsausschuss des Deutschen Bundetages* (Koblenz: Bernard & Graefe Verlag, 1986).

Birch, Anthony H., "Overload, Ungovernability and Delegitimation: The Theories and the British Case," *British Journal of Political Science*, vol. 14 (1984).

Birchard, Bruce and Rob Leavitt, "A New Agenda: Common Security is the First Step on the Road to Disarmament," *Nuclear Times*, November-December 1987.

Blumer, Herbert, "Collective Behavior," in Joseph B. Gittler, ed., *Review of Sociology: Analysis of a Decade* (New York: Wiley, 1957).

Boggs, Carl, *Social Movements and Political Power: Emerging Forms of Radicalism in the West* (Philadelphia: Temple University Press, 1986).

Booth, Ken, "Nonnuclear Defense for Britain" *Alternative Defense Working Paper*, no. 1 (May 1988).

Boserup, Anders, and Andrew Mack, *War Without Weapons* (New York: Schocken, 1975).

Boutwell, Jeffrey, "Politics and the Peace Movement in West Germany," *International Security*, vol. 7, no. 4 (1983).

Bowles, Samuel, David M. Gordon, and Thomas E. Weisskopf, *Beyond the Wasteland: A Democratic Alternative to Economic Decline* (New York: Anchor, 1983).

Bowles, Samuel, and Herbert Gintis, *Democracy and Capitalism: Property, Community, and the Contradictions of Modern Social Thought* (New York: Basic Books, 1986).

Brand, Karl-Werner, *Neue soziale Bewegungen: Entstehung, Funktion und Perspektive neuer Protestpotentiale—Eine Zwischenbilanz* (Opladen: Westdeutscher Verlag, 1982).

Brand, Karl-Werner, ed., *Neue soziale Bewegungen in Westeuropa und den USA: Ein internationaler Vergleich* (Frankfurt: Campus Verlag, 1985).

Brand, Karl-Werner, et al., *Aufbruch in ein andere Gesellschaft* (Frankfurt: Campus Verlag, 1983).

Braunthal, Gerard, *The German Social Democrats Since 1969: A Party in Power and Opposition* 2nd ed. (Boulder: Westview Press, 1994).

Breyman, Steve, "The Rationality of Class Action," unpublished manuscript, 1982.

_____ . "Social Movement Theory, the New Social Movements, and the Greens," paper delivered at the Annual Meeting of the American Political Science Association, New Orleans, August 1985.

_____ . "Knowledge as Power: Ecology Movements and Global Environmental Problems," in Ronnie D. Lipschutz and Ken Conca, eds., *The State and Social Power in Global Environmental Politics* (New York: Columbia University Press, 1993).

Bright, Charles and Susan Harding, eds., *Statemaking and Social Movements* (Ann Arbor: University of Michigan Press, 1984).

Brzezinski, Zbigniew, *Between Two Ages: America's Role in the Technotronic Age* (New York: Viking, 1970).

_____ . *Power and Principle: Memoirs of the National Security Adviser, 1977-1981* (New York: Farrar, Straus, Giroux, 1983).

Bundy, McGeorge, "'No First Use' Needs Careful Study," *Bulletin of the Atomic Scientists*, vol. 36, no. 6 (1982).

Bundy, McGeorge, George F. Kennan, Robert S. McNamara, and Gerard Smith, "Nuclear Weapons and the Atlantic Alliance," *Foreign Affairs*, vol. 60, no. 4 (1982).

Bürklin, Wilhelm, "The Greens: Ecology and the New Left," in H.G. Peter Wallach and George K. Romoser, eds., *West German Politics in the Mid-Eighties: Crisis and Continuity* (New York: Praeger, 1985).

Buro, Andreas, "Die Entstehung der Ostermarschbewegung als Beispiel für die Entfaltung von Massenlernprozessen," *Friedensanalysen*, vol. 4 (1977).

Butterwegge, Christoph, ed., *Friedensbewegung—Was nun? Probleme und Perspektiven nach der Raketenstationierung* (Hamburg: VSA, 1983).

Butterwegge, Christoph and Bernhard Docke, eds., *Kriminalisierung der Friedensbewegung: Abschreckung* (Cologne: Theurer, 1985).

Butterwegge, Christoph, and M. Ossenbeck "SPD und Friedensfrage: Positionen fortschrittlicher Sozialdemokraten zur Friedenssicherung," *Marxistische Studien*, no. 6 (1983).

Canby, Steven and Ingemar Dörfer, "More Troops, Fewer Misslies," *Foreign Policy*, no. 53 (1983-4).

Cartwright, John and Julian Critchley, *Cruise, Pershing and SS-20* (Washington: Pergamon-Brassey's, 1985).

Chalmers, Douglas, *The Social Democratic Party of Germany* (New Haven: Yale University Press, 1964).

Charles, Daniel, *Nuclear Planning in NATO: Pitfalls of First Use* (Cambridge, MA: Ballinger, 1987).

Chatfield, Charles, and Peter van den Dungen, eds., *Peace Movements and Political Cultures* (Knoxville, TN: University of Tennesee Press,1988).

Chong, Dennis, *Collective Action and the Civil Rights Movement* (Chicago: University of Chicago Press, 1991).

Cioc, Mark, *Pax Atomica: The Nuclear Defense Debate in West Germany During the Adenauer Era* (New York: Columbia University Press, 1988).

Clemens, Clay, "The Antinuclear Movement in West Germany in West Germany: *Angst* and Isms, Old and New," in James E. Dougherty and Robert L. Pfaltzgraff, Jr., eds., *Shattering Europe's Defense Consensus: The Antinuclear*

Protest Movement and the Future of NATO (Washington, DC: Pergamon-Brassey's, 1985).

Cohen, Jean, "Strategy or Identity: New Theoretical Paradigms and Contemporary Social Movements," *Social Research*, vol. 52, no. 4 (1985).

Cohen, Sam T., "Enhanced Radiation Warheads: Setting the Record Straight," *Strategic Review*, vol. 6 (1978).

Conradt, David P., and Russell J. Dalton, "The West German Electorate and the Party System: Continuity and Change in the 1980s," *Review of Politics*, vol. 50 (1988).

Cooper, Alice Holmes, *The West German Peace Movement of the 1980s: Historical and Institutional Influences* (Ann Arbor: University Microfilms, 1988).

Conradt, David P., and Russell J. Dalton, "The West German Electorate and the Party System: Continuity and Change in the 1980s," *Review of Politics*, vol. 50 (1988).

Coram, Bruce T., "Why political parties should make unbelievable promises: A theoretical note," *Public Choice*, no. 69 (1991).

Cronin, Thomas E., *Direct Democracy: The Politics of Initiative, Referendum, and Recall* (Cambridge, MA: Harvard University Press, 1989).

Cuthbertson, Ian M., and Robertson, David, *Enhancing European Security: Living in a Less Nuclear World* (New York: St. martin's Press, 1990).

Cutnell, John D., and Kenneth W. Johnson, *Physics*, 2nd ed. (New York: Wiley, 1992).

Czempiel, Ernst-Otto, "Friedensbewegung—wohin?," *Die Neue Gesellschaft/Frankfurter Hefte*, no. 1 (1984).

Dahrendorf, Ralf, *Class and Class Conflict in Industrial Society* (Stanford: Stanford University Press, 1959).

Dalton, Russell J., "Political Parties and Political Representation: Party Supporters and Party Elites in Nine Nations," *Comparative Political Studies*, vol. 18 (1985).

_____ . *Citizen Politics in Western Democracies: Public Opinion and Political Parties in the United States, Great Britain, West Germany, and France* (Chatham, NJ: Chatham House Publishers, 1988).

Dalton, Russell J., and Kendall L. Baker, "The Contours of West German Opinion," in H.G. Peter Wallach and George K. Romoser, eds., *West German Politics in the Mid-Eighties: Crisis and Continuity* (New York: Praeger, 1985).

Dalton, Russell J., Scott Flanagan, and Paul A. Beck, eds., *Electoral Change in Advanced Industrial Democracies* (Princeton: Princeton University Press, 1984).

Dalton, Russell J., and Küchler, Manfred, eds., *Challenging the Political Order: New Social and Political Movements in Western Democracies* (Oxford: Oxford University Press, 1990).

Dankbaar, Ben, "Alternative Defense Politics and the Peace Movement," *Journal of Peace Research*, no. 2 (1984).

Das Komitee für Grundrechte und Demokratie, *Frieden mit anderen Waffen—Fünf Vorschläge zu einer Alternativen Sicherheitspolitik* (Reinbek: Rowohlt, 1981).

de Perrot, Michel, ed., *European Security: Nuclear or Conventional Defence?* (Oxford: Pergamon, 1985).

Deppe, Frank, ed., *Friedensbewegung und Arbeiterbewegung: Wolfgang Abendroth im Gespräch* (Marburg: Arbeiterbewegung und Gesellschaftswissenschaft, 1982).

Deutsch, Karl W., "Social Mobilization and Political Development," *American Political Science Review*, vol. 75 (1961).

"Die 'Friedensbewegung' über die Blockadefrage zerstritten," *Frankfurter Allgemeine Zeitung*, August 5, 1986.

"Dieses Getto hat der Kirche nie gutgetan," *Der Spiegel*, September 15, 1986.

Donat, Helmut, and Karl Holl, eds., *Die Friedensbewegung: Organisierter Pazifismus in Deutschland, Österreich und in der Schweiz* (Düsseldorf: Econ Taschenbuch, 1983).

Dougherty, James E. and Robert L. Pfaltzgraff, Jr., eds., *Shattering Europe's Defense Consensus: The Antinuclear Protest Movement and the Future of NATO* (Washington: Pergamon-Brassey's, 1985).

Douglass, James, "Judges Must Speak Out For Peace: An Interview With West German Judge Ulf Panzer," in Arthur J. Laffin and Anne Montgomery, eds., *Swords into Plowshares: Nonviolent Direct Action for Disarmament* (San Francisco: Harper & Row, 1987).

Drummond, Gordon D., *The German Social Democrats in Opposition, 1949-1960: The Case Against Rearmament* (Norman, OK: University of Oklahoma Press, 1982).

Ebert, Theodor, "Vorüberlegungen zum Widerstand," in Jürgen Tatz, ed., *Gewaltfreier Widerstand gegen Massenvernichtungsmittel: Die Friedensbewegung entscheidet sich* (Freiburg: Dreisam, 1984)

———. *Ziviler Ungehorsam: Von der APO zur Friedensbewegung* (Waldkirch: Waldkircher, 1984).

Efinger, Manfred, Thomas Nielebock, and Volker Rittberger, "Was Muß Uns Ängstigen? Zur Kriegsgefahrenwahrnehmung der Friedensbewegung und Kriegsgefahrenanalyse der Friedens- und Konfliktforschung," in Klaus Horn and Volker Rittberger, eds., *Mit Kriegsgefahren Leben: Bedrohtsein, Bedrohungsgefühle, und Friedenspolitisches Engagement* (Opladen: Westdeutscher Verlag, 1987).

Eisenbeiss, Wilfried, *Die bürgerliche Friedensbewegung in Deutschland während des Ersten Weltkrieges: Organisation, Selbstverständnis und politische Praxis, 1913/14-1919* (Frankfurt: Lang, 1980).

Enzensberger, Hans Magnus, *Political Crumbs* (London: Verso, 1990).

Epstein, Barbara, "Rethinking Social Movement Theory," *Socialist Review*, vol. 20, no. 1 (1990).

Erchinger, Herbert, "Bezugsgruppensystem und Sprecherratsmodell," in Jürgen Tatz, ed., *Gewaltfreier Widerstand gegen Massenvernichtungsmittel: Die Friedensbewegung entscheidet sich* (Freiburg: Dreisam, 1984).

Evangelische Kirche in Deutschland, ed., *Deutscher Evangelischer Kirchentag Hamburg 1981: Dokumente* (Stuttgart: Kreuz, 1981).

———. *Frieden Wahren, Fördern und Erneuern: Eine Denkschrift der EKD* (Gütersloh: Gütersloher Verlagshaus Gerd Mohn, 1981).

Evans, Peter, Dietrich Rueschemeyer, and Theda Skocpol, eds., *Bringing the State Back In* (New York: Cambridge University Press, 1985).

Everett, Melissa, *Breaking Ranks* (Philadelphia: New Society Publishers, 1989).

Fabian, Walter and Kurt Lenz, eds., *Die Friedensbewegung: Ein Handbuch der Weltfriedensströmungen der Gegenwart* (Cologne: Bund, 1985).

Ferree, Myra Marx, "The Political Context of Rationality: Rational Choice Theory and Resource Mobilization," in Aldon D. Morris and Carol McClurg Mueller, eds., *Frontiers in Social Movement Theory* (New Haven: Yale University Press, 1992).

Feyerabend, Paul, *Philosophical Papers* (New York: Cambridge University Press, 1981).

_____. *Wissenschaft als Kunst* (Frankfurt: Suhrkamp, 1981).

_____. *Farewell to Reason* (London: Verso, 1987).

Fireman, Bruce, and William A. Gamson, "Utilitarian Logic in the Resource Mobilization Perspective," in Mayer N. Zald and John D. McCarthy, eds., *The Dynamics of Social Movements* (Cambridge: Winthrop, 1979).

Flacks, Richard W., "The Liberated Generation: An Exploration of the Roots of Student Protest," *Journal of Social Issues*, vol. 23 (1967).

_____. "Making History vs. Making Life: Dilemmas of an American Left," *Social Inquiry*, vol. 46, no. 3-4 (1976).

Flacks, Richard, *Making History: The American Left and the American Mind* (New York: Columbia University Press, 1988).

Ford, Daniel, *The Button: The Pentagon's Command and Control System—Does It Work?* (New York: Simon and Schuster, 1985).

Forsberg, Randall, "Defensive Defense: A US View, *Bulletin of Atomic Scientists*, September 1988.

Foucault, Michel, "The Subject and Power," in Hubert L. Dreyfus and Paul Rabinow, eds., *Michel Foucault: Beyond Structuralism and Hermeneutics* (Chicago: University of Chicago Press, 1983).

Frank, Robert H., *Passions Within Reason: The Strategic Role of the Emotions* (New York: Norton, 1988).

Frankel, Boris, *The Post-Industrial Utopians* (Madison: University of Wisconsin Press, 1987).

Frankland, E. Gene, "Interpreting the Green Phenomenon in West German Politics, 1977-83," unpublished manuscript, September 1983.

_____. "The Greens: Parliamentary Challenges and Responses," paper delivered at the Annual Meeting of the American Political Science Association, New Orleans, August 1985.

Frankland, E. Gene and Donald Schoonmaker, *Between Protest and Power: The Green Party in Germany* (Boulder: Westview Press, 1992).

Freeman, Jo, "Resource Mobilization and Strategy: A Model for Analyzing Social Movement Organization Actions," in Mayer Zald and John McCarthy, eds., *Dynamics of Social Movements* (Cambridge, MA: Winthrop, 1979).

Fried, Alfred H., *Handbuch der Friedensbewegung* (New York: Garland, 1972).

Fromm, Erich, *Escape From Freedom* (New York: Holt, 1960).

Galtung, Johan, "Die Chancen der Friedensbewegung," in Anselm Skuhra and Hannes Wimmer, eds., *Friedensforschung und Friedensbewegung* (Vienna: VWGÖ, 1985).

_____ . "Twenty-Five Years of Peace Research: Ten Challenges and Responses," *Journal of Peace Research*, vol. 22 (1985).

_____ . "The Green Movement: A Socio-Historical Explanation," *International Sociology*, vol. 1, no. (1986).

Gamson, William A., *The Strategy of Social Protest* (Homewood, IL: Dorsey, 1975).

Gamson, William A., Bruce Fireman, and Steven Rytina, *Encounters with Unjust Authority* (Homewood, IL: Dorsey, 1982).

Garner, Roberta Ash, *Social Movements in America* 2nd ed. (Chicago: Rand McNally, 1977).

Generals for Peace and Disarmament, *Generals for Peace and Disarmament: A Challenge to US/NATO Strategy* (New York: Universe, 1984).

Gerhards, Jürgen, and Dieter Rucht, "Mesomobilization: Organizing and Framing in Two Protest Campaigns in West Germany," *American Journal of Sociology*, vol. 93, no. 3 (November 1992).

Gerlach, Luther P., "Protest Movements and the Construction of Risk," in B.B. Johnson and Vincent T. Costello, eds., *The Social and Cultural Construction of Risk* (Amsterdam: Reidel, 1987).

_____ . "Territorial and Cultural Borders and the Role of New Stakeholders in the Management of Global Resources," unpublished manuscript, March 1990.

Gerlach, Luther P., and Virginia H. Hine, *People, Power, Change: Movements of Social Transformation* (Indianapolis: Bobbs-Merrill, 1970).

Gerosa, Klaus, ed., *Grosse Schritte Wagen: Über die Zukunft der Friedensbewegung* (Munich: List, 1984).

Giddens, Anthony, *The Constitution of Society* (Berkeley: University of California Press, 1984).

Glatzel, Norbert, and Ernst Josef Nagel, eds., *Frieden in Sicherheit: Zur Weiterentwicklung der Katholischen Friedensethik* (Freiburg: Herder, 1981).

Gottfried, Kurt, Henry W. Kendall, and John M. Lee, "'No First Use' of Nuclear Weapons," *Scientific American*, vol. 250, no. 3 (1984).

Grishchenko, Anatoly, and Vladimir Semenoy, *Danger: NATO* (Moscow: Progress Publishers, 1985).

Gross, Feliks, *The Seizure of Political Power in a Century of Revolutions* (New York: Philosophical Library, 1958).

Gugel, Günther and Rainer A. Roth, *Herausforderung Frieden: Modelle zur Friedenspädagogik für die ausserschulische Jugendarbeit* (Waldkirch: Waldkircher Verlag, 1976).

Gurr, Ted, *Why Men Rebel* (Princeton: Princeton University Press, 1970).

Gusfield, Joseph R., "The Study of Social Movements," in David L. Sills, ed., *International Encyclopedia of the Social Sciences*, vol. 14 (New York: Free Press, 1968).

_____ . "The Reflexivity of Social Movements: Collective Behavior and Mass Society Theory Revisited," in Enrique Laraña, Hank Johnston, and Joseph R. Gusfield, eds., *New Social Movements: From Ideology to Identity* (Philadelphia: Temple University Press, 1994).

Gusfield, Joseph R., ed., *Protest, Reform and Revolt: A Reader in Social Movements* (New York: Wiley, 1970).

Habermas, Jürgen, *Legitimation Crisis* (Boston: Beacon, 1975).

Hassner, Pierre, "Arms Control and the Politics of Pacifism in Protestant Europe," in Uwe Nerlich, ed., *Soviet Power and Western Negotiating Policies* (Cambridge, MA: Ballinger, 1983).

Heberle, Rudolf, "Types and Functions of Social Movements," in David L. Sills, ed., *International Encyclopedia of the Social Sciences*, vol. 14 (New York: Free Press, 1968).

Hegedus, Zsuzsa, "Social Movements and Social Change in Self-Creative Society: New Civil Initiatives in the International Arena," in Martin Albrow and Elizabeth King, eds., *Globalization, Knowledge and Society: Readings from International Sociology* (London: Sage, 1990).

Heirich, Max, *The Spiral of Conflict: Berkeley, 1964* (New York: Columbia University Press, 1968).

Helm, Jutta, "Citizen Lobbies in West Germany," in Peter H. Merkl, ed., *West European Party Systems* (New York: The Free Press, 1979).

Herf, Jeffrey, "War, Peace and the Intellectuals: The West German Peace Movement," *International Security*, vol. 10, no. 4 (1986).

Hertel, Peter, and Alfred Paffenholz, eds., *Für eine politische Kirche: Schwerter zu Pflugscharen—Politische Theologie und basiskirchliche Initiativen* (Hannover: Schmidt-Kuster, 1982).

Hildebrandt, Kai, and Russell J. Dalton, "The New Politics: Political Change or Sunshine Politics," in Max Kaase and Klaus von Beyme, eds., *German Political Studies*, vol. 3 (1978).

Hobsbawm, Eric, *Primitive Rebels: Studies in Archaic Forms of Social Movement in the 19th and 20th Centuries* 2nd ed. (New York: Praeger, 1963).

Hodges, Donald, "Old and New Working Classes," *Radical America*, vol. 5, no. 1 (1971).

Hoffman, Eric, *The True Believer* (New York: Harper & Row, 1951).

Höfling, Beate, *Katholische Friedensbewegung Zwischen Zwei Kriegen: Der "Friedensbund Deutscher Katholiken," 1917-1933* (Waldkirch: Waldkircher Verlag, 1979).

Holzkamp, K., "Nur wer Angst hat, kann vernünftig sein: Gefühl und Rationalität in der Friedensbewegung," *Psychosozial Heute*, vol. 20 (1983).

Horn, Klaus, and Volker Rittberger, eds., *Mit Kriegsgefahren Leben: Bedrohtsein, Bedrohungsgefühle, und Friedenspolitisches Engagement* (Opladen: Westdeutscher Verlag, 1987).

Horn, Klaus, and Eva Senghaas-Knobloch, eds., *Friedensbewegung—Persönliches und Politisches* (Frankfurt: Fischer, 1983).

Huber, W., "Die Kirchen und der Frieden: Folgerungen aus einem Vergleich," *Frankfurter Hefte*, no. 4 (1982).

Hunt, Scott A., Robert D. Benford, and David A. Snow, "Identity Fields: Framing Processes and the Social Construction of Movement Identities," in Enrique Laraña, Hank Johnston, and Joseph R. Gusfield, eds., *New Social Movements: From Ideology to Identity* (Philadelphia: Temple University Press, 1994).

Huntington, Samuel P., *Political Order in Changing Societies* (New Haven: Yale University Press, 1968).

_____ . "Post-Industrial Politics: How Benign Will it Be?" *Comparative Politics* (1974).

Huntington, Samuel P., Michel Crozier, and Joji Watanuki, *The Crisis of Democracy: Report on the Governability of Democracies to the Trilateral Commission* (New York: New York University Press, 1975).

Hyman, Herbert H., and Paul B. Sheatsley, "Attitudes Toward Desegregation," *Scientific American*, vol. 211 (1964).

Inglehart, Ronald, "The Silent Revolution in Europe: Inter-generational Change in Post-industrial Societies," *American Political Science Review*, vol. 65 (1971).

_____ . *The Silent Revolution: Political Styles Among Western Publics* (Princeton: Princeton University Press, 1977).

_____ . "Generational Change and the Future of the Atlantic Alliance," *PS*, vol. 17, no. 3 (1984).

_____ . *Culture Shift in Advanced Industrial Society* (Princeton: Princeton University Press, 1990).

"Ist die Friedensbewegung tot?" *S & F Vierteljahresschrift für Sicherheit und Frieden*, vol. 3, no. 3 (1985).

"Ist die Spaltung perfekt? Der Graben zwischen Autonomen und Gewaltfreien wird grösser," *taz*, July 12, 1983.

Jäger, Uli, and Michael Schmid-Vöhringer, eds., "*Wir werden nicht Ruhe geben. . .*": *Die Friedensbewegung in der Bundesrepublik Deutschland 1945-1982, Geschichte, Dokumente, Perspektiven* (Tübingen: Verein für Friedenspädagogik, 1982).

Jahn, Egbert, "Friedensforschung und Friedensbewegung," *Friedensanalysen*, vol. 16 (1982).

_____ . "Aussichten und Sackgassen der neuen Friedensbewegung: Teil 1," *Die Neue Gesellschaft/Frankfurter Hefte*, no. 1 (1984).

_____ . "Aussichten und Sackgassen der neuen Friedensbewegung: Teil 2," *Die Neue Gesellschaft/Frankfurter Hefte*, no. 2 (1984).

Janning, Josef, Hans-Josef Legrand, Helmut Zander, and Ulrich Albrecht, eds., *Friedensbewegung: Entwicklung und Folgen in der Bundesrepublik Deutschland, Europa und den USA*, (Cologne: Verlag Wissenschaft und Politik, 1987).

Jansen, Mechthild, "Rundbrief zur Vorbereitung des Frauentages im Rahmen der Aktionswoche der Friedensbewegung," unpublished manuscript, September 1983.

Japp, Karl P., "Selbsterzeugung oder Fremdverschulden: Thesen zum Rationalismus in den Theorien sozialer Bewegungen," *Soziale Welt*, vol. 25 (1984).

Jenkins, J. Craig, "Resource Mobilization Theory and the Study of Social Movements," *Annual Review of Sociology*, vol. 9 (1983).

_____ . "Social Movements, Political Representation, and the State: An Agenda and Comparative Framework," in J. Craig Jenkins and Bert Klandermans, eds., *The Politics of Social Protest: Comparative Perspectives on States and Social Movements* (Minneapolis: University of Minnesota Press, 1995).

Jenkins, J. Craig, and Craig M. Eckert, "Channelling Black Insurgency," *American Sociological Review*, vol. 51 (1986).

Jenkins, J. Craig, and Bert Klandermans, eds., *The Politics of Social Protest: Comparative Perspectives on States and Social Movements* (Minneapolis: University of Minnesota Press, 1995).

Johnson, Kermit D., *Realism and Hope in a Nuclear Age* (Atlanta: John Knox, 1988).

Johnston, Hank, and Bert Klandermans, eds., *Social Movements and Culture* (Minneapolis: University of Minnesota Press, 1995).

Johnstone, Diana, *The Politics of Euromissiles: Europe's Role in America's World* (London: Verso, 1984).

Joppke, Christian, "Explaining Cross-National Variations of Two Anti-Nuclear Movements: A Political Process Perspective," *Sociology*, vol. 26, no. 2 (May 1992).

JW-Dienst, April 28, 1982.

Kaase, Max, "The Challenge of the 'Participatory Revolution' in Pluralist Democracies," *International Political Science Review*, vol. 5, no. 3 (1984).

Kaase, Max and Hans-Dieter Klingemann, *Wahlen und Wähler: Analysen aus Anlass der Bundestagswahl 1987* (Opladen: Westdeutscher, 1990).

Kaiser, Karl, Georg Leber, Alois Mertes, and Franz-Josef Schulze, "Nuclear Weapons and the Preservation of Peace," *Foreign Affairs*, vol. 60, no. 5 (1982).

Kauffman, L.A., "The Anti-Politics of Identity," *Socialist Review*, vol. 20, no. 1 (1990).

_____ . "Tofu Politics in Berkeley," *The Nation* , September 16, 1991.

Kayden, Xandra, and Eddie Mahe, Jr., *The Party Goes On: The Persistence of the Two-Party System in the United States* (New York: Basic, 1985).

Kennedy, Paul, *The Rise and Fall of the Great Powers: Economic Change and Military Conflict From 1500 to 2000* (New York: Random House, 1987).

Kern, P. and H.-G. Wittig, "Die Friedensbewegung—zu radikal oder gar nicht radikal genug?" *aus politik und zeitgeschichte*, vol. 17 (1983).

King, Roger, *The State in Modern Society: New Directions in Political Sociology* (Chatham, NJ: Chatham House, 1986).

Kitschelt, Herbert, "Political Opportunity Structures and Political Protest: Anti-Nuclear Movements in Four Democracies," *British Journal of Political Science*, vol. 16 (1986).

_____ . "New Social Movements and Resource Mobilization: The European and the American Approach," *International Journal of Mass Emergencies and Disasters*, vol. 4 (1986).

Kitschelt, Herbert, and Staf Hellemans, *Beyond the European Left: Ideology and Political Action in the Belgian Ecology Parties* (Durham, NC: Duke University Press, 1990).

Klandermans, Bert, Hanspeter Kriesi, and Sidney Tarrow, eds., *From Structure to Action: Comparing Social Movement Research Across Cultures* (Greenwich, CT: JAI, 1988).

Klandermans, Bert, "Mobilization and Participation: Social-Psychological Explanations of Resource Mobilization Theory," *American Sociological Review*, vol. 49 (1984).

_____ . "The Peace Movement and Social Movement Theory,"*International Social Movement Research*, vol. 3 (1991).

_____ . "The Social Construction of Protest and Multiorganizational·Fields," in Aldon D. Morris and Carol McClurg Mueller, eds., *Frontiers in Social Movement Theory* (New Haven: Yale University Press, 1992).

_____ . "Transient Identities? Membership Patterns in the Dutch Peace Movement," in Enrique Laraña, Hank Johnston, and Joseph R. Gusfield, eds., *New Social Movements: From Ideology to Identity* (Philadelphia: Temple University Press, 1994).

Klandermans, Bert, ed., *Organizing for Change: Social Movement Organizations in Europe and the United States* (Greenwich, CT: JAI, 1989).

Klare, Michael T., "Road Map for the Peace Movement," *The Nation*, June, 29, 1985.

Kleidman, Robert, *Organizing for Peace: Neutrality, the Test Ban, and the Freeze* (Syracuse: Syracuse University Press, 1993).

Knoke, David, "Resource Acquisition and Allocation in U.S. National Associations," *International Social Movement Research*, vol. 2 (1989),

Knorr, Lorenz, *Geschichte der Friedensbewegung in der Bundesrepublik* 2nd ed. (Cologne: Pahl-Rugenstein, 1984).

Kodama, Katsuya, and Unto Vesa, eds., *Towards a Comparative Analysis of Peace Movements* (Hants, UK: Dartmouth, 1991).

Komitee für Grundrechte und Demokratie, ed., *Frieden mit anderen Waffen—Fünf Vorschläge zu einer Alternativen Sicherheitspolitik* (Reinbek: Rowohlt, 1981).

Koopmans, Ruud, "The Dynamics of Protest Waves: West Germany, 1965-1989," *American Sociological Review*, vol. 58 (1993).

Koordinierungsausschuß der Friedensorganisationen, ed., *Aufstehn! Für den Frieden: Friedensdemonstration anläßlich der NATO-Gipfelkonferenz in Bonn am 10. 6. 1982* (Bornheim-Merten: Lamuv Verlag, 1982).

Kornhauser, William, *The Politics of Mass Society* (New York: Free Press, 1959).

Krassin, Juri and Otto Reinhold, eds., *Internationale Friedensbewegung vor neuen Anforderungen* (Berlin: Dietz Verlag, 1989).

Krell, Gert, Thomas Risse-Kappen, and Hans-Joachim Schmidt, "The No-First-Use Question in West Germany," in John D. Steinbruner and Leon V. Sigal, eds., *Alliance Security: NATO and the No-First-Use Question* (Washington: Brookings Institution, 1983).

Kriesi, Hanspeter, "The Political Opportunity Structure of New Social Movements: Its Impact on Their Mobilization," in J. Craig Jenkins and Bert Klandermans, eds., *The Politics of Social Protest: Comparative Perspectives on States and Social Movements* (Minneapolis: University of Minnesota Press, 1995).

Kriesi, Hanspeter, Ruud Koopmans, Jan Willem Duyvendak, and Marco G. Giugni, "New Social Movements and Political Opportunities in Western Europe," *European Journal of Political Research*, vol. 22 (1992).

_____ . *New Social Movements in Western Europe: A Comparative Analysis* (Minneapolis: University of Minnesota Press, 1995).

Kriesi, Hanspeter, R. Levy, G. Ganguillet, and H. Zwicky, *Politische Aktivierung in der Schweiz, 1945-1978* (Diessenhoffen: Ruëgger, 1981).

Küchler, Manfred, "Die Anhänger der Friedensbewegung in der BRD: Einstellungsmuster, Wertorientierung und Sozialdemographische Verankerung," in Anselm Skuhra and Hannes Wimmer, eds., *Friedensforschung und Friedensbewegung* (Vienna: VWGÖ, 1985).

Kull, Steven, *Minds at War: Nuclear Reality and the Inner Conflict of Defense Policymakers* (New York: Basic, 1988).

Kutte, Waldemar, *Angst vor dem Atomkrieg: Hoffnung durch die Friedens-Bewegung* (Hamburg: Kutte, 1981).

Lafontaine, Oskar, "Gegen die Enthauptungsstrategie der USA," *Der Spiegel*, no. 16, (1983).

Lang, Kurt, and Gladys Lang, *Collective Dynamics* (New York: Crowell, 1961).

Laquer, Walter and Robert Hunter, eds., *European Peace Movements and the Future of the Western Alliance* (New Brunswick, NJ: Transaction,1985).

Laraña, Enrique, Hank Johnston, and Joseph R. Gusfield, eds., *New Social Movements: From Ideology to Identity* (Philadelphia: Temple University Press, 1994).

Lauber, Volkmar, "From Growth Consensus to Fragmentation in Western Europe—Political Polarization over Redistribution and Ecology," *Comparative Politics*, vol. 15, no. 3 (1983).

Lawson, Kay, and Peter H. Merkl, eds., *When Parties Fail: Emerging Alternative Organizations* (Princeton: Princeton University Press, 1988).

Leahy, Peter, and Allen Mazur, "A Comparison of Movements Opposed to Nuclear Power, Fluoridation, and Abortion," *Research in Social Movements: Conflicts and Change*, vol. 1 (1978).

Le Bon, Gustave, *The Crowd* (London: Benn, 1896).

Leif, Thomas *Die Strategische (Ohn-) Macht der Friedensbewegung: Kommunications- und Entscheidungsstrukturen in den Achtziger Jahren* (Opladen: Westdeutscher Verlag, 1990).

———. *Die Professionelle Bewegung: Friedensbewegung von Innen* (Bonn: Forum Europa, 1985).

Lipset, Seymour Martin, *Political Man* (New York: Doubleday, 1960).

Lipsky, Michael, "Protest as a Political Resource," *American Political Science Review*, vol. 62 (1968).

Lofland, John, *Protest: Studies of Collective Behavior and Social Movements* (New Brunswick, NJ: Transaction, 1985).

Lösche, Peter, ed., *Parteien in der Krise: Das Parteinesystem der Bundesrepublik und der Aufstand des Bürgerwillens* (Munich: Beck, 1986).

Lowi, Theodore, *The Politics of Disorder* (New York: Basic Books, 1971).

Lukes, Steven J., *Essays in Social Theory* (New York: Columbia University Press, 1977).

Luxemburg, Rosa, *Gesammelte Werke* 2nd ed. (Berlin: Dietz, 1972).

Markovits, Andrei S., and Philip S. Gorski, *The German Left: Red, Green and Beyond* (New York: Oxford University Press, 1993).

Massarat, Mohssen, *Kriegsgefahr und Friedensbewegung* (Kassel: Weber, Zucht, 1984).

Mayer, Milton, *They Thought They Were Free* (Chicago: University of Chicago Press, 1955).

McAdam, Doug, *Political Process and the Development of Black Insurgency* (Chicago: University of Chicago Press, 1982).

_____ . "Tactical Innovation and the Pace of Insurgency," *American Sociological Review*, vol. 48 (1983).

_____ . "Culture and Social Movements," in Enrique Laraña, Hank Johnston, and Joseph R. Gusfield, eds., *New Social Movements: From Ideology to Identity* (Philadelphia: Temple University Press, 1994).

McAdam, Doug, John D. McCarthy, and Mayer N. Zald, "Social Movements," in Neil Smelser, ed., *Handbook of Sociology* (Beverly Hills, CA: Sage Publications, 1988).

McCarthy, John D., and Mayer N. Zald, *The Trend of Social Movements in America: Professionalization and Resource Mobilization* (Morristown, NJ: General Learning Press, 1973).

_____ . "Resource Mobilization and Social Movements: A Partial Theory," *American Journal of Sociology*, vol. 82 (1977).

McCarthy, John D., Clark McPhail, and Jackie Smith, "Images of Protest: Dimensions of Selection Bias in Media Coverage of Washington Demonstrations, 1982 and 1991," *American Sociological Review*, vol. 61 (1996).

McNamara, Robert S., "The Military Role of Nuclear Weapons: Perceptions and Misperceptions," *Foreign Affairs*, vol. 62, no. 1 (1983).

Mechtersheimer, Alfred, *Zeitbombe NATO: Auswirkungen der neuen Strategien* (Cologne: Diederichs, 1984).

Mechtersheimer, Alfred, ed., *Nachrüsten? Dokumente und Positionen zum NATO-Doppelbeschluß* (Hamburg: Spiegel, 1981).

Melucci, Alberto, "The New Social Movements: A Theoretical Approach," *Social Science Information*, vol. 19 (1980).

_____ . "The Symbolic Challenge of Contemporary Movements," *Social Research*, vol. 52 (1985).

_____ . *Nomads of the Present: Social Movements and Individual Needs in Contemporary Society* (Philadelphia: Temple University Press, 1989).

_____ . "A Strange Kind of Newness: What's 'New' in New Social Movements?" in Enrique Laraña, Hank Johnston, and Joseph R. Gusfield, eds., *New Social Movements: From Ideology to Identity* (Philadelphia: Temple University Press, 1994).

Merkl, Peter H., *The Origins of the West German Republic* (New York: Oxford University Press, 1965).

_____ . "Mapping the Temporal Universe of Party Governments," *Review of Politics*, vol. 47, no. 4 (1985).

_____ . "How New the Brave New World: New Social Movements in West Germany," *German Studies Review*, vol. 10, no. 1 (1987).

_____ . "The Challengers and the Party Systems," in Kay Lawson and Peter H. Merkl, eds., *When Parties Fail: Emerging Alternative Organizations* (Princeton: Princeton University Press, 1988).

Merkl, Peter H., ed., *West European Party Systems* (New York: The Free Press, 1979).

Mettke, Jörg R., ed., *Die Grünen: Regierungspartner von Morgen?* (Hamburg: Spiegel, 1982).

Miller, Alice, *For Your Own Good* (New York: Farrar, Strauss & Giroux, 1984).

Miller, Susanne, and Heinrich Potthof, *Kleine Geschichte der SPD: Darstellung und Dokumentation, 1848-1983* (Bonn: Verlag Neue Gesellschaft, 1983).

Moe, Terry, *The Organization of Interests* (Chicago: University of Chicago Press, 1980).

Morris, Aldon D., *The Origins of the Civil Rights Movement* (New York: Free Press, 1984).

Morris, Aldon D., and Cedric Herring, "Theory and Research in Social Movements: A Critical Review," *Annual Review of Sociology*, vol. 2 (1985).

Morris, Aldon D., and Carol McClurg Mueller, eds., *Frontiers in Social Movement Theory* (New Haven: Yale University Press, 1992).

Mühleisen, Hans-Otto, "Grundstrukturen der Friedensdiskussion in der Katholischen Kirche," *Politische Studien*, vol. 33 (1982).

Muller, Edward, and Karl-Dieter Opp, "Rational Choice and Rebellious Collective Action," *American Political Science Review*, vol. 80 (1986).

Müller-Rommel, Ferdinand, "Social Movements and the Greens: New Internal Politics in Germany," *European Journal of Political Research*, vol. 13 (1985).

———. "The Social Democrats: The Campaigns and Election Outcomes of 1980 and 1983," in Karl H. Cerny, ed., *Germany at the Polls: The Bundestag Elections of the 1980s* (Durham, NC: Duke University Press, 1990).

Mushaben, Joyce Marie, "Innocence Lost: Environmental Images and Political Experiences Among the West German Greens," *New Political Science*, vol. 14 (1985-86).

———. "The Struggle Within: Conflict, Consensus, and Decision Making Among National Coordinators and Grass-Roots Organizers in the West German Peace Movement," *International Social Movement Research*, vol. 2 (1989).

Niedermayer, Oskar, and Richard Stöss, eds., *Stand und Perspektiven der Parteiforschung in Deutschland* (Opladen: Westdeutscher Velag, 1993).

Noller, Michael, "Neocorporatism and Political Protest in the Western Democracies: A Cross-National Analysis," in J. Craig Jenkins and Bert Klandermans, eds., *The Politics of Social Protest: Comparative Perspectives on States and Social Movements* (Minneapolis: University of Minnesota Press, 1995).

Oberschall, Anthony, *Social Conflict and Social Movements* (Englewood Cliffs, NJ: Prentice-Hall, 1973).

O'Connor, James, *The Fiscal Crisis of the State* (New York: St. Martin's Press, 1973).

Offe, Claus, "Competitive Party Democracy and the Keynesian Welfare State: Factors of Stability and Disorganization," in Thomas Ferguson and Joel Rogers, eds., *The Political Economy* (Armonk, NY: M.E. Sharpe, 1984).

———. "New Social Movements: Changing Boundaries of the Political," *Social Research*, vol. 52 (1985).

———. "Challenging the Boundaries of Institutional Politics: Social Movements since the 1960s," in Charles Maier, ed., *Changing Boundaries of the Political* (New York: Cambridge University Press, 1987).

Olson, Jr., Mancur, *The Logic of Collective Action* (Cambridge: Harvard University Press, 1965).

Otto, Karl A., *Vom Ostermarsch zur APO: Geschichte der außerparlamentarischen Opposition in der Bundesrepublik, 1960-1970* (Frankfurt: Campus Verlag, 1977).

Overby, L. Marvin, and Sarah J. Ritchie, "Mobilized Masses and Strategic Opponents: A Resource Mobilization Analysis of the Clean Air and Nuclear Freeze Movements," *Western Political Quarterly*, vol. 44, no. 2 (June 1991).

Palme Commission, *Common Security—A Programme for Disarmament: Report of the Independent Commission on Disarmament and Security Issues* (New York: Simon & Schuster, 1985).

Paluski, Jan, "Mass Movements and Social Class," *International Sociology*, vol. 8, no. 2 (1993).

Pappi, Franz-Urban, "Neue soziale Bewegungen und Wahlverhalten in der Bundesrepublik," in Max Kaase and Hans-Dieter Klingemann, eds., *Wahlen und Wähler: Analysen aus Anlass der Bundestagswahl 1987* (Opladen: Westdeutscher Verlag, 1990).

Park, Robert, "Human Migration and the Marginal Man," *American Journal of Sociology*, vol. 33 (1928).

Pfaltzgraff, Jr., Robert L., Kim R. Holmes, Clay Clemens, Werner Kaltefleiter, *The Greens of West Germany: Origins, Strategies, and Transatlantic Implications* (Cambridge, MA: Institute for Foreign Policy Analysis, 1983).

Pierre, Andrew J., ed., *Nuclear Weapons in Europe* (New York: Council on Foreign Relations, 1984).

_____. *A Widening Atlantic? Domestic Change & Foreign Policy* (New York: Council on Foreign Relations, 1986).

_____. *The Conventional Defense of Europe: New Technologies and New Strategies* (New York: Council on Foreign Relations, 1986).

Piore, Michael J. and Charles F. Sabel, *The Second Industrial Divide: Possibilities for Prosperity* (New York: Basic Books, 1984).

Piven, Frances Fox, and Richard A. Cloward, *Poor People's Movements: Why They Succeed, How They Fail* (New York: Vintage Books, 1977).

Plotke, David, "What's So New About New Social Movements?" *Socialist Review*, vol. 20, no. 1 (1990).

Plümer, Lutz, *Positionen der Friedensbewegung: die Auseinandersetzung um den US-Mittelstreckenraketenbeschluß—Dokumente, Appelle, Beiträge* (Frankfurt: Sendler, 1981).

Raschke, Joachim, *Soziale Bewegungen: Ein historisch-systematischer Grundriss* (Frankfurt: Campus Verlag, 1985).

Rawlinson, Roger, "Three Nonviolent Campaigns—Larzac, Marckolsheim, Wyhl—A Comparison," in Chadwick Alger and Michael Stohl, eds., *A Just Peace Through Transformation: Cultural, Economic, and Political Foundations for Change* (Boulder, CO: Westview Press, 1988).

Risse-Kappen, Thomas, *The Zero Option: INF, West Germany, and Arms Control* (Boulder, CO: Westview Press, 1988).

Roberts, Adam, "The Critique of Nuclear Deterrence," *Adelphi Paper*, no. 183, part 2, IISS.

Rochon, Thomas R., "Political Change in Ordered Societies—The Rise of Citizens' Movements," *Comparative Politics*, vol. 15, no. 3 (1983).

_____. *Mobilizing for Peace: The Antinuclear Movements in Western Europe* (Princeton: Princeton University Press, 1988).

———— . "The West European Peace Movement and the Theory of New Social Movements," in Russell J. Dalton and Manfred Kuechler, eds., *Challenging the Political Order: New Social and Political Movements in Western Democracies* (Oxford: Oxford University Press, 1990).

Rosenau, James N., "Theorizing Across Systems: Linkage Politics Revisited," in Jonathan Wilkenfeld, ed., *Conflict Behavior and Linkage Politics* (New York: McKay, 1973).

Rosenau, James N., ed., *Linkage Politics* (New York: Free Press, 1969),

Roth, Roland, and Dieter Rucht, eds., *Neue soziale Bewegungen in der Bundesrepublik Deutschland* (Bonn: Bundeszentrale für politische Bildung, 1987).

Rucht, Dieter, "Themes, Logics, and Arenas of Social Movements: A Structural Approach," in Bert Klandermans, Hanspeter Kriesi, and Sidney Tarrow, eds., *From Structure to Action: Comparing Social Movement Research Across Cultures* (Greenwich, CT: JAI, 1988).

Rucht, Dieter, ed., *Research on Social Movements: The State of the Art in Western Europe and the USA* (Frankfurt: Campus, 1991).

Rude, George, *The Crowd in History: A Study of Popular Disturbances in France and England 1730-1848* (New York: Wiley, 1964).

Rupp, Hans Karl, *Ausserparlamentarische Opposition in der Ära Adenauer: Der Kampf gegen die Atombewaffnung in den fünfziger Jahre* (Cologne: Pahl-Rugenstein, 1970).

Scammon, Richard M., and Alice V. McGillivray, Appendix A, in Karl H. Cerny, ed., *Germany at the Polls: The Bundestag Elections of the 1980s* (Durham, NC: Duke University Press, 1990).

Schmid, Gunther, *Sicherheitspolitik und Friedensbewegung. Der Konflikt um die "Nachrüstung"* (Munich: Günter Olzog Verlag, 1982).

———— . "Zur Soziologie der Friedensbewegung und des Jugendprotests," *aus politik und zeitgeschichte*, vol. 24 (1982).

———— . "Die Friedensbewegung in der Bundesrepublik Deutschland," *Europäische Wehrkunde*, vol. 12 (1983).

Schmidt, David S., *Citizen Lawmakers: The Ballot Initiative Revolution* (Philadelphia: Temple University Press, 1989).

Schmitt, Hermann, *Neue Politik in alten Parteien* (Opladen: Westdeutscher Verlag, 1987).

Schmitt, Rüdiger, "Was Bewegt die Friedensbewegung? Analysen zur Unterstützung des sicherheitspolitischen Protests der achtziger Jahre," *Zeitschrift für Parlamentsfragen*, vol. 1 (1987).

Schmitt-Beck, Rüdiger, "A Myth Institutionalized: Theory and Research on New Social Movements in Germany," *European Journal of Political Research*, vol. 21 (1992).

Schmitter, Philippe L., and Gerhard Lehmbruch, eds., *Trends Towards Corporatist Intermediation* (London: Sage Publications, 1980).

Schoonmaker, Donald, "The Challenge of the Greens to the West German Party System," in Kay Lawson and Peter H. Merkl, eds., *When Parties Fail: Emerging Alternative Organizations* (Princeton: Princeton University Press, 1988).

Schwartz, David N., *NATO's Nuclear Dilemmas* (Washington, DC: Brookings Institution, 1983).

Schwartz, William A., and Charles Derber, *The Nuclear Seduction: Why the Arms Race Doesn't Matter—and What Does* (Berkeley: University of California Press, 1990).

Seery, John Evan, *Political Returns: Irony in Politics and Theory from Plato to the Antinuclear Movement* (Boulder, CO: Westview Press, 1990).

Seidelmann, Reimund, ed., *Der Demokratische Sozialismus als Friedensbewegung* (Essen: Print-Service, 1982).

Seiterlich, Thomas, "Basisgemeinden in der Bundesrepublik," *Frankfurter Hefte*, vol. 37, no. 9 (1983).

Sekretariat der Deutschen Bischofskonferenz, ed., *Gerechtigkeit Schafft Frieden: Wort der Deutschen Bischofskonferenz zum Frieden* (Bonn: SDB, 1983).

Sharp, Gene, *The Politics of Nonviolent Action* (Boston: Sargent, 1973).

_____ . *Making Europe Unconquerable: The Potential of Civilian-Based Defense* (London: Taylor & Francis, 1985).

_____ . "The Power of Nonviolence," *Christian Science Monitor*, July 31, 1989.

Sigal, Leon V., *Nuclear Forces in Europe: Enduring Dilemmas, Present Prospects* (Washington, DC: Brookings Institution, 1984).

Skuhra, Anselm and Hannes Wimmer, eds., *Friedensforschung und Friedensbewegung* (Vienna: VWGÖ, 1985).

Smelser, Neil, *Theory of Collective Behavior* (New York: Free Press, 1962).

_____ . *Modern Sociological Explanation* (Englewood Cliffs, NJ: Prentice-Hall, 1968).

Smith, Christian, *The Emergence of Liberation Theology: Radical Religion and Social Movement Theory* (Chicago: University of Chicago Press, 1991).

Snow, David A., and Robert D. Benford, "Master Frames and Cycles of Protest," in Aldon D. Morris and Carol McClurg Mueller, eds., *Frontiers in Social Movement Theory* (New Haven: Yale University Press, 1992).

Snow, David A., E. Burke Rochford, Jr., Steven K. Worden, and Robert D. Benford, "Frame Alignment Processes, Micromobilization, and Movement Participation," *American Sociological Review*, vol. 51 (1986).

Spotts, Frederic, *The Churches and Politics in Germany* (Middletown, CT: Wesleyan University Press, 1973).

Steinbruner, John D., and Leon V. Sigal, eds., *Alliance Security: NATO and the No-First-Use Question* (Washington, DC: Brookings, 1983).

Steinweg, Reiner, "Die Bedeutung der Gewerkschaften für die Friedensbewegung," *Friedensanalysen*, vol. 16 (1982).

Steinweg, Reiner, ed., *Die neue Friedensbewegung: Analysen aus der Friedensforschung* (Frankfurt: Suhrkamp Verlag, 1982).

Stöss, Richard, "Vom Mythos der 'neuen sozialen Bewegungen:' Neun Thesen und ein Exkurs zum Elend der NSB-Forschung," in J.W. Falter, C. Fenner, M.T. Greven, eds, *Politische Willensbildung und Interessenvermittlung* (Opladen: Westdeutscher Verlag, 1984).

Strange, Carolyn, "Mothers on the March: Maternalism in Women's Protest for Peace in North America and Western Europe, 1900-1985," in Guida West and Rhoda Lois Blumberg, eds., *Women and Social Protest* (New York: Oxford University Press, 1990).

Straub, Jürgen, Hans Werbick and Walter Zitterbarth, "Friedensbewegung und Kriegsängste: Über einige Aspekte der Motivationalen Hintergründe Friedenspolitischer Aktivitäten," in Klaus Horn and Volker Ritterberger, eds., *Mit Kriegsgefahren Leben: Bedrohtsein, Bedrohungsgefühle und Friedenspolitisches Engagement* (Opladen: Westdeutscher Verlag, 1987).

Szabo, Stephen F., "Brandt's Children: The West German Successor Generation," *Washington Quarterly*, vol. 7, no. 1 (1984).

Szabo, Stephen F., ed., *The Successor Generation: International Perspectives of Postwar Europeans* (London: Butterworth, 1983).

Tarrow, Sidney, "National Politics and Collective Action: Recent Theory and Research in Western Europe and the United States," *Annual Review of Sociology*, vol. 14 (1988).

_____ . "Struggle, Politics and Reform: Collective Action, Social Movements, and Cycles of Protest," 2nd ed., Cornell Studies in International Affairs, Western Societies Papers No. 21 (1989).

Tatz, Jürgen, ed., *Gewaltfreier Widerstand gegen Massenvernichtungsmittel: Die Friedensbewegung entscheidet sich* (Freiburg: Dreisam, 1984).

Taylor, D. Garth, *Public Opinion and Collective Action* (Chicago: University of Chicago Press, 1986).

Taylor, Richard, *Against the Bomb: The British Peace Movement, 1958-1965* (Oxford: Clarendon Press, 1988).

Taylor, Verta, "The Continuity of the American Women's Movement: An Elite-Sustained Stage," in Guida West and Rhoda Lois Blumberg, eds., *Women and Social Protest* (New York: Oxford University Press, 1990).

Taylor, Verta, and Nancy Whittier, "Collective Identity in Social Movement Communities: Lesbian Feminist Mobilization," in Aldon D. Morris and Carol McClurg Mueller, eds., *Frontiers in Social Movement Theory* (New Haven: Yale University Press, 1992).

"The Talk of the Town," *The New Yorker*, June 18, 1990.

Thompson, E.P., *Exterminism and the Cold War* (London: Verso, 1982).

_____ . *Zero Option* (London: Merlin, 1982).

_____ . *The Heavy Dancers: Writings on War, Past and Future* (New York: Pantheon, 1985).

Thurow, Lester C., *The Zero-Sum Society: Distribution and the Possibilities for Economic Change* (New York: Basic Books, 1980).

Tilly, Charles, *From Mobilization to Revolution* (Reading, MA: Addison-Wesley, 1978).

_____ . "Social Movements and National Politics," in Charles Bright and Susan Harding, eds., *Statemaking and Social Movements* (Ann Arbor: University of Michigan Press, 1984).

Touraine, Alain, *The May Movement: Revolt and Reform* (New York: Random House, 1971).

_____ . *The Post-Industrial Society* (New York: Random House, 1972).

Turner, Ralph H., "The Public Perception of Protest," *American Sociological Review*, vol. 34 (1969).

_____ . "Collective Behavior and Resource Mobilization as Approaches to Social Movements: Issues and Continuities," *Research in Social Movements, Conflict and Change*, vol. 4 (1981).

Turner, Ralph H., and Lewis Killian, *Collective Behavior* 2nd ed. (Englewood Cliffs, NJ: Prentice-Hall, 1972).

Ulmer Ärtzte-Initiative, ed., *Tausend Grad Celsius: Das Ulm-Szenario für einen Atomkrieg* (Darmstadt: Luchterhand, 1983).

van Haaren, Werner, and Almuth Westecker, eds., *Streiten über den Frieden: Strategien-Perspektiven-Alternativen in der Friedensbewegung* (Dortmund: Weltkreis-Verlag, 1982).

Viotti, Peter R., "European Peace Movements and Missile Deployments," *Armed Forces & Society*, vol. 11, no. 4 (1985).

Vogt, Wolfgang R., ed., *Streitfall Frieden: Positionen und Analysen zur Sicherheispolitik und Friedensbewegung* (Heidelberg: C.F. Müller Verlag, 1984).

Voigt, Karsten D., "Erweiterung der Konzeption des militärischen Gleichgewichts," *Neue Gesellschaft* (1980).

_____ . "Nuclear Weapons in Europe: A German Social Democrat's Perspective," in Andrew J. Pierre, ed., *Nuclear Weapons in Europe* (New York: Council on Foreign Relations, 1984).

von Bredow, Wilfried, and Rudolf H. Brocke, "Ost-West Konflikt, Krisenbewusstsein und Protestbewegung in Westeuropa," *aus politik und zeitgeschichte*, no. 5 (1986).

_____ . *Krise und Protest: Ursprünge und Elemente der Friedensbewegung in Westeuropa* (Opladen: Westdeutscher Verlag, 1987).

Wallace, Michael, and J. Craig Jenkins, "The New Class, Postindustrialism, and Neocorporatism: Three Images of Social Protest in the Western Democracies," in J. Craig Jenkins and Bert Klandermans, eds., *The Politics of Social Protest: Comparative Perspectives on States and Social Movements* (Minneapolis: University of Minnesota Press, 1995).

Wallace, Michael D., "Arms Races and Escalation," *Journal of Conflict Resolution*, vol. 23 (1979).

Warneken, Bernd Jürgen, ed., *Massenmedium Straße: Zur Kulturgeschichte der Demonstration* (Frankfurt: Campus Verlag, 1991).

Wasmuht, Ulrike C., "Zur Analyse der Friedensbewegungen in der Bundesrepublik Deutschland," *Wissenschaft und Frieden*, vol. 1, no. 2 (1985).

_____ . *Friedensbewegungen der 80er Jahre—Zur Analyse ihrer strukturellen und aktuellen Entstehungsbedingungen in der Bundesrepublik Deutschland und den Vereinigten Staaten von Amerika nach 1945: Ein Vergleich* (Giessen: Focus Verlag, 1987).

Wasmuht, Ulrike C., ed., *Ist Wissen Macht? Zur Aktuellen Funktion von Friedensforschung* (Baden-Baden: Nomos Verlagsgesellschaft, 1992).

Waterman, Harvey, "Sins of the Children: Social Change, Democratic Politics, and the Successor Generation in Western Europe," *Comparative Politics*, vol. 20, no. 4 (1988).

Weidmann, Bernd, and Herbert Meyer, *500,000 Gegen Reagan & NATO* (Göttingen: Steidl, 1982).

West, Guida and Rhoda Lois Blumberg, eds., *Women and Social Protest* (New York: Oxford University Press, 1990).

Weston, Burns, ed., *Alternative Security: Living Without Nuclear Deterrence* (Boulder: Westview Press, 1990).

Wettig, Gerhard, "Die neue Friedensbewegung in Deutschland," *Aussenpolitik*, no. 3 (1982).

————. *Psychoanalyse, Friedensbewegung und Sicherheitspolitik* (Bonn: Bundesinstituts für ostwissenschaftliche und internationale Studien, 1983).

Wiatr, Jerzy J., "Mobilization of Non-Participants During the Political Crisis in Poland, 1980-1981," *International Political Science Review*, vol. 5, no. 3 (1984).

Wilke, Peter, "Friedensbewegung und grosse Politik—am Beispiel des Konzepts Atomwaffen-freie-Zone," *Jahrbuch für Friedens- und Konfliktforschung*, vol. 10 (1983).

Wilkens, Erwin, ed., *Christliche Ethik und Sicherheitspolitik* (Frankfurt: Evangelisches Verlagswerk, 1982).

Wilson, James Q., *Political Organizations* (New York: Basic Books, 1973).

Zald, Mayer N., and Roberta Ash, "Social Movement Organizations: Growth, Decay and Change," *Social Forces*, vol. 44 (1966).

Zald, Mayer N., and John D. McCarthy, eds., *The Dynamics of Social Movements* (Cambridge: Winthrop, 1979).

Zetkin, Clara, *Der Kampf der kommunistischen parteien gegen Kriegsgefahr und Krieg* (Hamburg: C. Hoym, 1922).

"Zur aktuellen Friedensdiskussion. Eine Stellungnahme des Zentralkomitee der deutschen Katholiken," *Herder Korrespondenz*, vol. 35, no. 12 (1981).

Index